Islam and Democracy in Indonesia

Indonesia's Islamic organizations sustain the country's thriving civil society, democracy, and reputation for tolerance amid diversity. Yet scholars poorly understand how these organizations envision the accommodation of religious difference. What does tolerance mean to the world's largest Islamic organizations? What are the implications for democracy in Indonesia and the broader Muslim world? Jeremy Menchik argues that answering these questions requires decoupling tolerance from liberalism and investigating the historical and political conditions that engender democratic values. Drawing on archival documents, ethnographic observation, comparative political theory, and an original survey, *Islam and Democracy in Indonesia* demonstrates that Indonesia's Muslim leaders favor a democracy in which individual rights and group-differentiated rights converge within a system of legal pluralism, a vision at odds with American-style secular government but common in Africa, Asia, and Eastern Europe.

Jeremy Menchik is an Assistant Professor in the Pardee School of Global Studies at Boston University, and a Faculty Affiliate in Political Science and Religious Studies. He has been Shorenstein Postdoctoral Fellow in Contemporary Asia at Stanford University and Luce Fellow at Columbia University. His research focuses on the politics of religion, with a particular interest in Indonesia and the Muslim world. He has published articles in journals such as *Comparative Studies in Society and History* and *South East Asia Research*. His work has been recognized by several prizes, including the Fulbright award to Indonesia, the Mildred Potter Hovland Journal Article Prize, the Paper Award from the Southeast Asian Politics Group, and honorable mention for the Aaron Wildavsky Dissertation Award.

CAMBRIDGE STUDIES IN SOCIAL THEORY, RELIGION AND POLITICS

Editors

David C. Leege, *University of Notre Dame*
Kenneth D. Wald, *University of Florida, Gainesville*
Richard L. Wood, *University of New Mexico*

The most enduring and illuminating bodies of late nineteenth century social theory – by Marx, Weber, Durkheim and others – emphasized the integration of religion, polity, and economy through time and place. Once a staple of classic social theory, however, religion gradually lost the interest of many social scientists during the twentieth century. The recent emergence of phenomena such as Solidarity in Poland, the dissolution of the Soviet empire, various South American, Southern African, and South Asian liberation movements, the Christian Right in the United States, and Al Qaeda have reawakened scholarly interest in religiously-based political conflict. At the same time, fundamental questions are once again being asked about the role of religion in stable political regimes, public policies, and constitutional orders. The series Cambridge Studies in Social Theory, Religion, and Politics will produce volumes that study religion and politics by drawing upon classic social theory and more recent social scientific research traditions. Books in the series offer theoretically-grounded, comparative, empirical studies that raise "big" questions about a timely subject that has long engaged the best minds in social science.

Titles in the series

Islam and Democracy in Indonesia

Tolerance without Liberalism

JEREMY MENCHIK

Boston University

CAMBRIDGE
UNIVERSITY PRESS

32 Avenue of the Americas, New York, NY 10013-2473, USA

Cambridge University Press is part of the University of Cambridge.

It furthers the University's mission by disseminating knowledge in the pursuit of education, learning, and research at the highest international levels of excellence.

www.cambridge.org
Information on this title: www.cambridge.org/9781107119147

First published 2016

A catalog record for this publication is available from the British Library.

Library of Congress Cataloging in Publication Data
Menchik, Jeremy, 1979–
Islam and democracy in Indonesia : tolerance without liberalism / Jeremy Menchik.
    pages   cm. – (Cambridge studies in social theory, religion and politics)
Includes bibliographical references and index.
ISBN 978-1-107-11914-7 (hardback) – ISBN 978-1-107-54803-9 (pbk.)
1. Islam–Indonesia.   2. Islam and state–Indonesia.   3. Democracy–Indonesia.
I. Title.
BP63.I52M46   2015
297.2'7209598–dc23   2015023015

ISBN 978-1-107-11914-7 Hardback
ISBN 978-1-107-54803-9 Paperback

Contents

Tables and Figures

Tables

Figures

Acknowledgments

This book has been a long time coming. In the summer of 2005 I lived in the Bulak Sumur neighborhood of Yogyakarta, where I divided my time between language study at Gadjah Mada University and weekends traveling around Java in search of an interesting dissertation project and the most delicious fried bananas (*pisang goreng*). I found both and have had the good fortune of accumulating debts to many institutions and people in the ensuing years.

My advisors at the University of Wisconsin-Madison were exceedingly patient even while I spent much of my graduate career away from Madison. Yoshiko Herrera was a supportive advisor from the beginning and taught me how to synthesize the theoretical imperatives of the constructivist tradition with the methodological demands of contemporary political science. Scott Straus was my role model for rigorous field research. Barry Burden demonstrated an impressive ability to translate my work into a language that is broadly accessible to social scientists. Howard Schweber's careful reading of my dissertation exposed several weak arguments in my handling of liberal political theory. I hope that Chapters 6 and 7 of this book address those shortcomings. Tamir Moustafa has continued to generously share his time and insights after we both left Madison.

At the University of Chicago, Dan Slater pushed me to appreciate the strengths of studying Southeast Asia and then export my theories beyond the Indian and Pacific Oceans. Lisa Wedeen's intellectual influence found its way onto every page of this manuscript, and I was grateful to count her as one of my committee members. I learned how to do rigorous qualitative research while engaging political theory at the University of Chicago's Comparative Politics Workshop. At Stanford University, Donald Emmerson and the Edward Shorenstein Asia Pacific Research Center helped me rethink the project's apparatus in transitioning the dissertation into a book and provided me with crucial support during the taxing months on the job market. Lisa Blaydes, Graham

Brown, Elizabeth Shakman Hurd, David Buckley, Jonathan Blake, and Rachel Beatty Riedl deserve special thanks for steering the manuscript in new and fruitful directions. I am grateful to Rochana Bajpai, Karen Barkey, Adrian Blau, Humeira Iqtidar, and Leigh Jenco for their insightful comments on a key chapter presented at the London Comparative Political Theory workshop. Long before I set foot in Java, I had another mentor, Andrei S. Markovits, who was the first professor to recognize my passion for comparative politics and helped me to channel it.

Boston University (BU) has provided an ideal home to transform the dissertation into a book. The university supports a blend of theoretical rigor, methodological pluralism, and attention to addressing contemporary issues. I am also blessed to work next door to some of the country's leading scholars of religion and world politics. I am especially grateful to Nancy Ammerman, Peter Berger, Robert Hefner, Augustus Richard Norton, Cornel Ban, and Adam Seligman for their ongoing feedback. Mary Kate Long and Madelyn Powell provided meticulous editing help in the preparation of the final manuscript. Adria Widyatmoko and Chris Hadisuwarno provided capable research assistance. Adil Najam, Andrew Bacevich, and William Grimes provided vital resources and made clear that my intellectual priorities resonate with those of BU's Pardee School. At a time when primary-source historical research, ethnography, and constructivism are often marginal to political science, there is an extraordinary amount of good work being done at BU.

Sunny Tanuwidjaja, Lina Alexandra, Rizal Sukma, and the late Hadi Soesastro provided me with space to work in Jakarta in the fall of 2008 and helped me navigate the Ministry of Research and Technology. Scholars of Indonesia are lucky to have the Jakarta-based Center for Strategic and International Studies. The only peer library in Jakarta is at the Freedom Institute, where Sugianto Tandra (Aan), Luthfi Assyaukanie, Ulil Abshar-Abdalla, and Ihsan Ali-Fauzi provided me with support in the spring of 2009. That spring I also began making regular treks down to Ciputat in South Jakarta to see Azyumardi Azra, Fuad Jabali, Yusuf Rahman, Windy Triani, and Nur Hidayat Wakhidudin (Iday) at the graduate school of the State Islamic University Syarif Hidayatullah. When I needed help to understand the fatwas of Nahdlatul Ulama, Muhammadiyah, and Persatuan Islam, Windy and Iday became my guides to the Malay, Javanese, and Sundanese texts.

My greatest debts are to the hundreds of members of Nahdlatul Ulama (NU), Persatuan Islam (Persis), and Muhammadiyah who answered my questions with care, and to the leaders who provided me with full access to their archives in Jakarta, Yogyakarta, and Bangil. Before I left for the field, a well-meaning colleague asked whether studying Islamic organizations was feasible at a time of heightened tension between the United States and the Muslim world. "Not everyone can do every project," he noted. Instead, the barriers that I encountered were a product of my own limitations as a scholar or were created by secular government institutions. My requests for a research permit were rejected multiple times by US and Indonesian government agencies that thought my project was 'too sensitive.' NU, Muhammadiyah, and Persis, meanwhile, welcomed me. In particular, I owe Arsul Sani, Nasaruddin Umar, Ulil Abshar-Abdalla, Syahrul Wahidah, Syarul Iskandar, Mifthal Huda, Kahfi Amin, the late Siddiq Amin, Amin Djamaluddin, Maman Abdurrahman, Dody Truna, Untoro Abu Nabilain, Fajar Riza Ul Haq, Zainal Zainuddin, and Hilman Latief a lifetime of gratitude.

Other scholars of Indonesia have provided guidance in the field and throughout the project. Jamie Davidson, Firman Lubis, John Strauss, Mark Cammack, Merle Ricklefs, Michael Buehler, Robin Bush, Greg Fealy, Edward Aspinall, Marcus Mietzner, Michael Feener, Tom Pepinsky, and R. William Liddle have all been generous with their time and advice. A career of conferences is infinitely more appealing when it means getting to see the new cohort of Indonesianists: Joshua Gedacht, Kevin Fogg, Colm Fox, Yosef Djakababa, Sarah Shair-Rosenfield, Shahirah Mahmood, Eunsook Jung, Ehito Kimura, Quinton Temby, Evan Laksmana, and Sunny Tanuwidjaja. I am especially grateful to Kevin Fogg for his meticulous review of the final manuscript. Howard Federspiel provided me with a lengthy bibliography of research on Indonesian Islam. A close reading will reveal that this book would not have been possible without his pathbreaking scholarship. The same is true for the work of Greg Fealy and Saiful Mujani.

The survey would not have been possible without the help of Barry Burden, Kathy Kramer-Walsh, Azmil Tayib, Dodi Ambardi, Mifthal Huda, and Yosef Djakababa. Sarah Shair-Rosenfield deserves special mention for donating too much of her time and wisdom to making the survey a success, and Amnon Cavari for assistance with the analysis. The constitutional court hearing that appears in Chapter 4 would have been less intelligible without the help of Luthfi Widagdo Eddyono who provided me with the transcripts. Mark Cammack helped me make sense of court procedures. Chapter 4 is a revised version of an essay published in *Comparative Studies in Society and History*, April 2014.

Before leaving Indonesia, I had the good fortune of working with the distinguished democratic theorist Alfred Stepan in September 2009, then again for three months at the end of 2010 as a Luce Fellow at Columbia University's Center for the Study of Democracy, Toleration, and Religion. Al and I conducted forty-nine joint interviews in September and October 2009, and I am grateful for his permission to use them here. Besides being a distinguished scholar, Al is a role model for ethically engaged scholarship, and I am thankful for his mentoring. Chapter 7 is dedicated to Al and Daniel Philpott, who together convinced me that taking a normative stance in support of democracy would be an asset, not a liability. Like many scholars, I have reservations about communitarianism and religious modes of government, as well as with liberal imperialism, but I do not think it is necessary to insert those preferences into the book. I am, however, convinced that trying to make democracy work is a common, worthwhile, goal.

I owe the biggest debt to my family. Bettie Landauer-Menchik and Paul Menchik introduced me to the world of ideas in Okemos, and then made real the ideas of the world on family trips around the globe. They and my brother Daniel Menchik have supported me when I needed help the most. I dedicate this book to my parents and brother.

Finally I want to thank Willow Osgood, my best friend and my wife. I am indebted to her for always guiding me toward compassion and honesty, and I am thrilled that we get to spend our lives together. And with our joyful, inspiring son, Nico.

Any errors are my responsibility alone.

Note on Transcription

There are numerous orthographical problems that arise when writing in English about Indonesia and Islamic institutions. These concern the changes in the spelling of the Indonesian language over the past 100 years, the spelling of individuals' and organizations' names, and the transliteration of Arabic terms.

The Indonesian language has undergone tremendous changes in the twentieth century affecting names, places, and concepts. The organization Nahdlatul Ulama, for example, was originally written as Nahdlatoel Oelama or Nahdhatoe'l 'Oelama. I follow the modern convention, which is to render 'dl' as 'd,' 'y' rather than 'j,' and 'u' rather than 'oe' as set out in Echols and Shadily (2002). For personal and organizational names, however, the actor's preferred spelling is used, thus Nahdlatul Ulama rather than Nahdatul Ulama and Soeharto rather than Suharto. Where multiple variants are accepted, I use the one that is most frequent in official documents except for direct quotes.

Arabic terms are spelled in accordance with Indonesian usage and based on Federspiel (1995). Terms that do not appear in either Federspiel or Echols and Shadily are copied verbatim. In cases where the Indonesian or Arabic term is awkward to the ear, such as the plural of fatwa (fatwa-fatwa in Indonesian and fatāwā in Arabic), I follow the common English usage (fatwas).

All translation is by the author unless otherwise noted.

I

After Secularization

The Christians should worship God according to the teachings of Jesus Christ, Moslems according to the teachings of the prophet Mohammed, Buddhists should discharge their religious rites according to their own books. But let us all have Belief in God.... And the state of Indonesia should be a state incorporating Belief in God.

Soekarno, 1945[1]

Rule of law in Indonesia must be understood through the viewpoint of the 1945 Constitution, namely a constitutional state which places the ideal of Belief in God as its foremost principle as well as religious values underlying the movements of national and state life, and not as a country that imposes separation of state and religion or merely holds to the principle of individualism or communalism.

Indonesian Constitutional Court, 2010[2]

Introduction

On March 17, 2010, I was leaving the Indonesian Constitutional Court building with Asrul Sani, the lawyer representing the world's largest Islamic organization, Nahdlatul Ulama (NU), in a hearing on the country's law forbidding religious blasphemy. On the way out we ran into lawyers from some of the country's more conservative Islamic organizations: Abdul Rahman Tardjo from the Indonesian Council for Islamic Propagation (Dewan Dakwah Islamiyah Indonesia) and Lutfi Hakim from the Indonesian Council of Ulamas (Majelis Ulama Indonesia). In the hearings, NU took a similar position as the conservatives and Sani usually chatted amicably with the other lawyers. Sani introduced me, saying, "This is Jeremy, he is an American studying Islam." Sani then paused. "But you will like his research project. It is called 'Tolerance *without* Liberalism.'" When I presented my work at the State Islamic University (UIN)

[1] Soekarno in Yamin (1959, 77–78).
[2] Court verdict, 2010, 140/puu-vii/2009, 3.34.10.

Syarif Hidayatullah in Jakarta, the noted Islamic intellectual Azumardi Azra said, similarly, that in order to understand Indonesian Islamic organizations, it is necessary to differentiate their values of tolerance from their liberal values. "Of course these institutions are tolerant, but they are not liberal, and they do not want liberalism in Indonesia." Likewise, a banner at the 2010 NU congress in Makassar expressed a similar idea by warning leaders of the dangers of fundamentalism, radicalism, and liberalism, even while Christians were publicly welcomed at the meeting.[3] Over and over, the leaders of Indonesia's mass Islamic organizations made the same point: we are tolerant, and we are proud of our country's religious diversity. But our society is not liberal, and we are wary of the influence of liberalism in democratic Indonesia.[4]

In some respects, Sani's and Azra's desire to simultaneously express tolerance but disavow its connection to liberalism is not surprising. Frustration with self-proclaimed liberal Muslim activists is common in the Muslim world. Also common is frustration with the linkage of the liberal conception of religious freedom with other democratic rights such as free speech and political representation. Throughout the twentieth century, the guise of religious freedom has been used as an entry point into Muslim societies by Christian missionaries. It was not a conservative Islamist but rather Indonesia's most outspoken advocate for liberal Islam, Ulil Abshar-Abdalla, who expressed this sentiment most succinctly:

> Even I think that too much liberalism is bad, like with the freedom of religion. That is how the Christians have spread their proselytization, via "freedom of religion." When I was in [Washington] DC, I met with a group of Christians and they had a very sophisticated operation to promote freedom of religion. But I think this is not the same freedom that I am talking about. That is Christianization.[5]

Abshar-Abdalla highlights an important distinction between the right of Indonesians to explore their country's diverse belief systems and the right of foreign churches to build houses of worship in Muslim villages. He supports the first but not the second. His critique of religious freedom dovetails with that of scholars who have shown how the promotion of religious freedom for Christians living in the Muslim lands has served as an entry point for imperialism.[6]

---

[3] Author's observation at the March 2010 NU Muktamar, Makassar. The banner was created by the Riau Islands Province branch of NU.

[4] Liberalism has of course had an influence on Indonesian society through the colonial and missionary encounter as well as through contemporary nongovernmental organizations. Yet, as will become clear, liberalism's influence pales in comparison to the power of historical interactions, ethnic identities, state influence, and Indonesian Islamic political thought in shaping ideas about tolerance.

[5] Ulil Abshar-Abdalla, interview by the author, Jakarta, June 12, 2009.

[6] Mahmood (2006, 327; 2012).

Yet there is something in the sentiment shared by Sani, Azra, and Abshar-Abdalla that goes beyond a wariness of imperialism or Christian proselytizing in the name of religious freedom. Indonesia's mass Islamic organizations value the country's religious diversity but do not want to sanitize the public sphere of religion, see individuals abandon centuries-old religious practices, or destroy institutions that they see as integral to peaceful coexistence in order to promote a volunteerist idea of religious freedom. They see value in diversity and in maintaining practices that have structured social and political life since the Islamicization of insular Southeast Asia.

How do Indonesia's mass Islamic organizations understand tolerance? How do they envision the accommodation of religious difference in state and society? This book is my attempt to explain Indonesian Islamic organizations' vision for tolerance. Putting that vision into practice is exceedingly difficult at a time when secularism is often equated with tolerance and religion is synonymous with intolerance. Although I do not share these organizations' vision uncritically, I believe that their understandings of tolerance are no less worthy of study and debate than the secular-liberal one.

After all, tolerance, defined as the willingness to 'put up with' those things one rejects or opposes, has emerged as the singular solution to the problems of the twenty-first century: how to resolve identity conflicts, how to cope with instability in new democracies, and how to resolve the friction between the dueling projects of liberal secularism and religious revival. Massive education programs are devoted to teaching tolerance of Muslims in France, Jews in the United States, and Christians in Egypt. The institutional framework, however, for religious accommodation is poorly understood in places like Indonesia where religion is central to politics rather than relegated to the private sphere. Although scholars can draw on an extensive body of liberal political theory to explain the system for the accommodation of religious minorities in ostensibly secular states such as the United States, our understanding of the relationship between religion and the state outside of secular-liberal government is limited.

Our understanding of the relationship between religion and the state in such polities is immediately constrained by our vocabulary: the terms 'non-secular' and 'nonliberal' tell us nothing about the civic virtues and institutional structures that underpin democracy in places where religion is central to politics. Likewise, such categories deny agency to actors like NU, which embrace democracy and religious pluralism but not secularism or liberalism; their goal is to see belief in God, religious education, religious values, and religious organizations celebrated and incorporated into social and political life rather than being benevolently tolerated by a secular state.

In explicating Islamic organizations' vision for religious accommodation, then, we must expand our vocabulary for describing the politics of tolerance, democracy, and national identity. As Chakrabarty rightly notes, "European thought is at once both indispensable and inadequate in helping us to think through the experiences of political modernity in non-Western nations, and provincializing Europe becomes the task of exploring how this thought – which is now everyone's heritage and which affects us all – may be renewed from the margins."[7] In other words, we will have to identify the narrowness of the categories of analysis inherited from liberal political thought in order to bypass them. For this project, that means investigating and even embracing political concepts of tolerance, democracy, and nationalism as they are understood in the global periphery.[8]

This need for theoretical renewal is an indicator of a related problem; our explanations for the place of religion in politics have not kept pace with world events. In the twenty years since the field of political science rediscovered religion, scholars have struggled to advance the literature without access to a common paradigm. Both the 'clash of civilizations theory' and secularization theory – the idea that economic and political development would lead to the disappearance of religion – are increasingly doubted if not completely discarded. The task of rebuilding is complicated by events as varied as the attacks of 9/11, Europe's struggle to accommodate public religions, the influence of Christian evangelicals in the United States, and the 'Arab Spring' and its varied aftermaths. How should scholars rebuild the study of religion and politics after the failure of secularization theory?

Rebuilding is especially challenging when it comes to tolerance. Harvey Cox's seminal text *The Sacred City* famously declared that "Pluralism and tolerance are the children of secularization."[9] Yet NU is tolerant, but not secular. Its commitments to religious accommodation come from other sources: historical interactions between Muslim groups, interactions between Muslim groups and Christian missions, Islamic political thought, and the influence of modernizing states. In order to explain both how Islamic organizations understand tolerance and *why*, this book will focus on the historical and causal determinants of social attitudes.

These concerns – the need to understand the meaning of tolerance to Islamic organizations, the limits of our conceptual vocabulary for understanding tolerance in places where religion is central to politics, and the disillusionment with secularization theory's ability to explain the place of religion in modern life – provide the motivation for this book. I examine the origins of tolerance, a core value of modern, plural, democratic life. And I do so by looking for tolerance in one of the most unlikely places: Islamic organizations in the developing world.

The primary goal of *Islam and Democracy in Indonesia: Tolerance without Liberalism* is to explain the meaning of tolerance to Indonesia's mass Islamic organizations in order to understand how their normative values shape politics

---

[7] Chakrabarty (2008 [2000], 16).
[8] My task is inspired by the work of Bajpai (2011), Bhargava (1998), Chakrabarty (2008 [2000]), Euben (1999), and Mahmood (2005).
[9] Cox (1965, 3).

in a Muslim-majority democracy. Each chapter investigates a different aspect of tolerance or intolerance among Muslim democrats.

The second goal of the book is to explain *why* Islamic organizations understand tolerance the way they do. This task demands careful methodology in order to explain the determinants of tolerance, intolerance, and the variation in tolerance across time and toward varied subjects. It entails examining the religious and nonreligious factors that drive Islamic organizations, the local context in which Islamic organizations develop, and the history of relationships between Islamic organizations and other groups.

Finally, explaining the origins of attitudes in Indonesian Islamic organizations means articulating an approach to the study of religion that is minimally beholden to the troubled paradigms of the past. As a result, the third goal is to develop what I call a 'historical constructivist' approach to the study of religion and politics. To do so, I isolate and build on three strategies:

1. Situating religious actors in their local and historical context in order to explain behavior. Religion as an object of study is approached as a discursive and embodied tradition with a past, present, and future embedded in a place with agents and actors, and not as a timeless system of beliefs.
2. Recognizing the coevolution and mutual constitution of states and religion. Rather than developing in isolation, practices of secularism, religious observance, attitudes toward minorities, and policies of the state develop through iterated interactions.
3. Reimagining the meaning of political science concepts such as tolerance and nationalism to travel beyond their secular-liberal and largely European origins.

Together, I hope these strategies effort will help scholars chart a path forward for research on religion, politics, and modernity.

As the largest Muslim-majority country in the world, Indonesia provides an ideal field site for understanding contemporary religion and politics. Indonesia is also home to the world's largest Islamic organizations: Nahdlatul Ulama, Muhammadiyah, and one of the world's oldest Islamist groups, Persatuan Islam (Persis). NU, founded in 1926 in East Java, has more than 60 million members and is the leading traditionalist body in Indonesia.[10] In the Indonesian vernacular, a 'traditionalist' is someone who follows one of the four Sunni schools of jurisprudence. Muhammadiyah, founded in 1912 in Central Java, has between 24 million and 32 million members and is Indonesia's largest reformist organization.[11] Indonesian 'reformers' or 'modernists' are part of the global movement to revitalize Islamic societies through scientific education,

---

[10] NU has between 60 million and 84 million members (interview with NU board member Nasaruddin Umar, Jakarta, July 24, 2009; Mujani and Liddle (2004, 111, 121)).
[11] Mujani and Liddle (2004, 111, 121).

social reform, and reliance on the Qur'an and Hadith for direct interpretation, based on the ideas of Mohammad Abduh and Rasyid Ridha. The third, Persis, founded in 1923 in West Java, is a smaller reformist group with about 500,000 members. All three organizations are crucial cases for understanding politics in the Muslim world.[12] Indonesia is also an ideal place for studying the contribution of Islamic organizations to democratic transition and consolidation. NU and Muhammadiyah's leaders are strong backers of democratic institutions; they are quick to defend the rights of the country's Christian, Confucian, Hindu, and Buddhist minorities. Moreover, their commitment to religious pluralism has proven vital during Indonesia's successful transition from authoritarianism.

Based on twenty-four months of field research, this book intervenes in debates about religion and democracy, Islam and politics, and the future of political theory in a postsecular world. In doing so, it attempts to transcend the narrative of a teleological progression from traditional societies to a modernity organized around secular democracy and the liberal virtue of tolerance.

Contribution of the Book

The pioneers of the modern social sciences – Max Weber, Emile Durkheim, Fredrick Engels, and Karl Marx – believed that religion had a short half-life.[13] Weber said, "The fate of our times is characterized by rationalization and intellectualization and, above all, by the 'disenchantment of the world'."[14] No wonder that political scientists have mostly ignored religion; in almost 100 years, the preeminent journal for political science published only 25 articles with a focus on religion.[15] Even politicians leading religious movements claimed that religious rituals were doomed to disappear in favor of secular endeavors. In the words of David Ben Gurion, "Judaism as religious practice and tradition is Judaism of the ghetto. Judaism in a Jewish state is Judaism of labor and

---

[12] These groups do not fit standard political science terminology. They are organizations in that they have members. But they do more than propagate their faith: they run more than 10,000 schools, as well as banks, hospitals, women's organizations, youth organizations, labor unions, and paramilitary organizations. They are part of civil society in that they are autonomous from the state, but their members *staff* much of the state bureaucracy. Although in the past they have had formal ties to political parties, their associated parties now have autonomy from the central boards. Theoretically, I define them as institutions that "represent socially sanctioned ... expectations with respect to the behavior of specific categories of actors or to the performance of certain activities" (Streeck and Thelen 2005, 9). This definition dovetails with Talal Asad's conception of Islam as a discursive tradition with a history (1986).

[13] Marx and Engels (1999 [1848]); Durkheim (2001 [1915]).

[14] Weber (1918, 155).

[15] Wald and Wilcox (2006). The problem is worse in the *American Political Science Review* than in peer disciplines. From 1906 to 2002, the peer journals for sociologists – the *American Journal of Sociology* and *American Sociological Review* – each printed four times the number of articles with a religious title as their political science counterpart.

creativity in every field of economic and scientific endeavor, for all of man's needs."[16]

Rather than disappearing, however, religious traditions and rituals endure in our modern age. Survey research shows that large percentages of the public continue to express belief in God, belong to religious organizations, and participate in religious rituals. Of Weber's three tenets of secularization – the separation of church and state, the growth of individual disbelief, and the rational extinction of religious organizations – only the first retains support, and even that is bitterly contested.[17] Instead of the world evolving toward a uniform, secular modernity guided by rationality and organized around nation-states, many scholars now contend that the world is composed of 'multiple modernities' where no single trajectory holds true for every society.[18] The influence of religion on politics is marked more by diversity than by convergence to a single, secular-liberal modernity.[19]

These academic debates have been foregrounded by another, more pressing impetus to understand the place of religion in modern life: the declaration of war on the United States by Al Qaeda, the tragedy of September 11, and the ensuing US-led 'war on terror.' The US government highlighted the threat posed by religious organizations in far-flung locations such as Afghanistan and Sudan, even while evidence mounted that these organizations posed less danger than a rational appraisal of their security risk would justify.[20] Part of the miscalculation was theoretical; policy makers were stunned by the relevance of religion to the conflict and miscalibrated their response. Similarly, the war on terror forced international relations (IR) scholars to address the fact that their theories of world politics paid short shrift to the role of nonstate actors, transnational religious movements, and religious ideas in shaping world politics.

Some scholars, however, were prepared for the moment; the war gave prominence to a small group who divided the world into religious 'civilizations.' The wars of the twenty-first century, they argued, would be fought over religion since the values of the West are alien to other civilizations. The 'civilizationalists' devoted their most severe criticism to Islam, which they believed to be incompatible with modernity, tolerance, and democracy.[21] In the years since 9/11, the arguments of the civilizationalists have come to be seen as reflecting the emotional anxieties of a period of economic and global instability rather than rigorous scholarship. Scientific reasoning, rationality, tolerance, and respect for human rights did not originate in the West nor are these values confined to its borders. Wars are not fought on civilizational lines. Rather, differences

---

[16] Ben Gurion Diaries, March 14, 1959. Quoted in Zameret and Tlamim (1999).
[17] Cassanova (1994); Asad (2003); Fox (2006).
[18] Eisenstadt (2000).
[19] Cassanova (1994); Bhargava (1998); Katznelson and Stedman Jones (2010); Calhoun, Juergensmeyer, and van Anteroen (2011).
[20] Brooks (2011); Mueller and Stewart (2012).
[21] Huntington (1993, 1996); Lewis (1990).

between rich and poor states, colonial and postcolonial states, and strong and weak states continue to shape the world's conflicts.[22] Islam is responsible for no more bloodshed than other religions.[23] Democratization can and does thrive in non-Christian states. Democracy even thrives in Muslim-majority states.[24]

To move beyond secularization theory and the civilizational debate, I isolate three strategies for studying religion and politics in an age of 'multiple modernities': situating religious actors in their local and historical context, recognizing the coevolution of states and religion, and reimagining political theory.

Local Genealogies

The first task of reconstruction is building models of religious actors' interests and beliefs that are rooted in local history rather than universal models of rationality or deterministic applications of theology. Religious actors' interests originate in a specific place, time, and set of discourses; their behavior cannot be understood without understanding that context. Indonesia's Islamic organizations develop their understanding of friends and enemies, threats and interests through locally generated social interactions. Drawing on decades of work on religion in anthropology, I suggest that religion as an object of social scientific study should be approached as a discursive tradition with a past, present, and future embedded in a place with agents and actors.[25] In other words, the interests of religious actors cannot be exogenously determined apart from the context that they inhabit.

As a result, the task of understanding the meaning of tolerance for contemporary Islamic organizations must begin with history in order to then explain how Indonesia's Muslim actors came to understand the concept the way they do. This task demands careful causal analysis to explain the determinants of tolerance, intolerance, and the variation in tolerance across time and toward varied subjects. It entails examining the religious and nonreligious factors that drive Islamic organizations. The ethnic makeup of the organization, the interactions during the period of organizational formation, and the relationship between the organization and the state all affect ideas about group identity and interests. Chapter 2 outlines these hypotheses in detail along with the methods to test them. The subsequent three empirical chapters are then devoted to the history of Islamic organizations' relationships with Christians, Communists, Hindus, and Ahmadi Muslims.

The approach of this book stands in contrast to the dominant approaches to religion in political science: rationalism and theological determinism. Rationalist accounts of politics posit that religious actors have fixed preferences that are clearly specified, and that they will select strategies for behavior

---

[22] Fox (2001, 2005); Fearon and Laitin (2003); Fish, Jensenius, and Michel (2010).
[23] Fish, Jensenius, and Michel (2010); De Soysa and Nordås (2007).
[24] Ciftci (2010); Hefner (2000); Stepan (2000).
[25] Asad (1986).

that maximize their utility within given constraints.[26] More than the Islamic revival or even the attacks of 9/11, this approach has helped bring religion and politics out of the shadows and into conversation with the rest of political science. But it has limits. Wildavsky suggests that while a rationalist approach can explain how actors pursue their preferences, the origins of preferences are either assumed or unspecified.[27] In addition, Euben argues that rationalist models of religious actors are poorly positioned to model the preferences of actors whose worldview may be based on nonrational truths, a rejection of individual choice, or conceptual categories that work apart from those that rational choice scholars take for granted, such as the separation of the public and the private.[28]

While these critiques are important, my concerns with rationalist accounts of religion are different. The political economy of religion school defines religion as "a public and collective belief system that structures the relationship of the individual to the divine and the supernatural."[29] This definition is problematic on at least three grounds. First, it ignores religion's communal imperatives. Religious organizations shape individual identities, orient individual values, and mobilize individuals across class, ethnic, regional, and national lines. Ignoring the communal imperatives of religious practice risks misunderstanding a whole range of attitudes and behaviors. Second, this definition of religion as a 'belief system' ignores the fact that 'religion' as a social scientific category is grounded in the political production of knowledge.[30] As Chapters 4 and 5 will make clear, what constitutes 'religion' is an outcome of political struggle. Finally, and this problem may account for the previous two, the political economy of religion school relies on a definition of religion that reveals its parochial genesis; the emphasis on supernatural beliefs and individual choice reflects a *normative* contention that religion should be a private, internal matter sharply differentiated from public comportment. Theirs is the church of John Locke: a 'free and voluntary society' with jurisdiction only over the 'salvation of souls' and nothing in the world. This definition is a mismatch for any religious organization possessing coercive power, institutional rule-making capacity, symbolic power, potential for social movement mobilization, or affiliations with structures that shape individual choice.

My unease with rationalist models does not imply that I endorse a theological approach to the study of religion and politics. Theological accounts place heavy emphasis on the religious ideas held by religious actors in order to explain their behavior.[31] Philpott defines *political theology* as "a set of

---

[26] Gill (1998, 2001); Kalyvas (1996, 2000); Warner (2000).

[27] Wildavsky (1989); see also Philpott (2009, 198).

[28] Euben (1999). See Chapter 2 for further critiques of the 'religious economies' approach.

[29] Gill (2001); Grzymala-Busse (2012).

[30] On the political nature of the category of religion, see Shakman Hurd (2007, 509).

[31] Philpott (2007); Duffy Toft, Philpott, and Shah (2011).

propositions about politics that people hold in their minds, share and develop through language and discourse, and use to persuade and motivate."[32] This approach is laudable for its attention to the role of ideas in constructing an actor's interests, but it is difficult to apply. Within any religious organization there are multiple ideas about political authority, especially within decentralized faiths such as Islam and Judaism.[33] Philpott's second explanatory variable, differentiation – defined as actors' relationship to the state – is similarly ambiguous.[34] As Chapters 2, 3, and 5 will make clear, theological approaches are unable to explain variation across the organizations or change over time, and thus fail also on empirical grounds.

Instead of a rationalist or theological approach, I draw on the growing literature showing that rational interests cannot be determined apart from local ideas, structures, and practices.[35] Meaningful behavior is possible only within a social context. Religious actors develop their relations with others through social interaction and practices. Absent that context, it is not possible for scholars to develop grounded accounts of actors' behavior.[36] The historically grounded approach to religion developed here suggests that actors' interests are generated through social interactions and that these interests, while open to change, shape their subsequent behavior. I demonstrate that ideas about interests, preferences, threats, and strategies emerge from the local context and have long-term effects on behavior.[37] This does not mean that Islamic organizations are not strategic, as we will see. But it means that 'strategy' must be understood within the local and historical context in which interests are generated in order to explain the meaning and practices of tolerance.

The Coevolution of Religion and State

The second strategy for the reconstruction of scholarship on religion and politics is to rethink the relationship between religion and the state. Proponents of secularization argue that with political and economic development, religious organizations and religious life will become irrelevant to state affairs and

---

[32] Philpott (2007).

[33] Rosefsky Wickham (2013).

[34] It is also unclear whether the two variables are distinct. The archetypal example of *social* differentiation is Martin Luther's *theology* of differentiation, specifically his "Doctrine of the Two Kingdoms and the Two Governments," which Philpott argues led directly to the Westphalian system of separation of civil and spiritual authority (2000, 223).

[35] For the clearest applications of this approach to international relations and comparative politics, see Hopf (1998); Kratochwil and Ruggie (1986); Wendt (1987); Herrera (2005). On constructivism and religion, see Laffan (2011); Wedeen (2008, chapter 4); Rosefsky Wickham (2013, 11–12).

[36] Rabinow and Sullivan (1987).

[37] In emphasizing context, I follow the lead of Moaddel: "It is insufficient, if not flatly wrong, to try to explain Islamic society – its concrete political and social institutions and Muslim social behavior – in terms of textual analysis. The analysis of text is important, but it must be complemented by a systematic comparative analysis of historical cases" (2005, 8).

consequently disappear. Scholars of the global religious resurgence, meanwhile, argue that religious actors are increasingly capturing secular state institutions and broadening their base in society, particularly among the lower and middle classes.

The problem with both these arguments is that they ignore the mutual constitution and coevolution of religion and the secular state. As Chapters 4 and 5 demonstrate, religious organizations and secular state authority have coevolved over the course of the twentieth century; one cannot be understood without reference to the actors and organizations that constitute the other. What constitutes religion, and whose religion is tolerated by the state or society, is a consequence of these interactions. What becomes clear from the history of Indonesian Islamic organizations and the Indonesian state is that their interactions are part of a single contested field where the contours of religion and the state are fluid and evolve together over time. To speak of decisions by religious organizations about their political behavior is to assume that the terrain of their decision making is analytically distinct from the act of implementation. Yet their structure, organization, language, identity, and understanding of their interests are as much a consequence of state action as state interests, actions, identity, and organization are a result of the behavior of religious organizations.

Anthropologist Talal Asad provides the clearest articulation of this view in writing about the genealogy of Christianity, Islam, and the secular state. The secular state has been defined in contrast to religion, but it emerged from religious debates and remains in conversation with religion as an object of social control. Likewise, the sovereign state's demand that religion's jurisdiction be private, internal, and depoliticized is a profoundly political act, one that must inevitably engage religion.[38]

Although the state shapes religion, it is also true that religion shapes the state. This is an obvious point in self-proclaimed religious states like Iran and Pakistan. Yet this point has resonance, too, in ostensibly secular republics; Denmark, Finland, Greece, and the United Kingdom all have established churches.[39] This entanglement is further borne out by the literature on Islamic political party moderation. The cases of Indonesia, Egypt, Jordan, and Yemen suggest that when Islamist parties are able to participate in competitive elections, gain political office, and contribute to the formulation of policy, they are likely to moderate their policies from overthrowing the system to reforming it through democratic means. And indeed they do change the state, particularly in areas pertaining to dress, the observance of ritual practices, and public communication. Conversely, when governments attempt to exclude Islamists from political representation, they are more likely to use violence to try and overthrow the system.[40] Recognition of the mutual and inevitable entanglement of state and

---

[38] Asad (2003, chapter 7); Sullivan (1994, 2005).
[39] Stepan (2000, 40–43).
[40] Ashour (2009); Bayat (2007); Browers (2009); Rosefsky Wickham (2004); Tezcür (2010).

religion led democratization theorist Alfred Stepan to argue that secularism is neither necessary nor optimal for democracy to thrive in places with high levels of religious observance.[41] Stepan's argument is borne out empirically. Nearly all the world's states, including the democracies, have some entanglement between religion and the state rather than full separation.[42] Again, the evolving view is one where religion shapes the state, and the state shapes religion.

The centrality of Islamic organizations to Indonesia's successful democratic transition and consolidation has affirmed scholars' view that the inclusion of anti-system parties in the political process fosters their moderation. What this view ignores, however, is that the inclusion of Islamic actors changes the political system as much as it fosters their moderation. What becomes clear from the history of interactions between Indonesian Islamic organizations and the secular state is that their interactions are part of a single contested field where the contours are fluid and evolve together.

In order to understand the role of religion in modern political life, I suggest that scholars need to map the twin projects of our multiple modernities: tracing the influence of religious organizations on modern secular institutions and the influence of secular institutions on religious organizations. This coevolution is one of the underlying assumptions of a historical constructivist approach to the study of religion and politics and stands in contrast to more state- or society-centered explanations. The result is that the contemporary Indonesian state is neither a secular democracy nor an Islamic theocracy, but rather a religious-secular hybrid that makes the promotion of values like belief in God and communal affiliation a major goal for civil society and the state.

Reimagining Political Theory

The third track for reconstruction entails reincorporating religious actors into social science theories that were premised on the eradication of faith from modern life. Bringing religion back into political science requires more than simply 'adding variables' to existing models.[43] It requires at least two moves: developing a theoretical vocabulary that captures the religious-secular hybridity of modern nation-states, and taking seriously the argument that religious actors have ideas about politics different from those derived from secular-liberal political theory. Despite the growing recognition that most of the world's states inhabit a hybrid grey zone between secularism and theocracy, political scientists lack a theoretical vocabulary to map state-religion relations in that grey zone.

---

[41] Stepan (2000).

[42] Fox notes that only one state, the United States, had full separation of religion and state in the period from 1990 to 2002. "Thus in the post–cold war era, full separation of religion and state is far from the norm; rather, it is a rare exception to the more general rule that governments involve themselves in religious issues. In fact it is a unique exception" (2006, 538).

[43] For the adding variables approach to religion and politics research, see Duffy Toft (2007); Ross (2008).

Take, for example, the concept of nationalism. Studies of nationalism in the postcolonial period overwhelmingly rely on Benedict Anderson's definition of the nation as an "imagined political community – and imagined as both inherently limited and sovereign."[44] Anderson argues that beginning with the French Revolution, groups of people in Europe began to see themselves as connected with other people on the basis of their linguistic and cultural practices. Anderson's conception of nationalism is indebted to the predominance of secularism. He argues that the nation originates in secular politics while the mechanisms of its reproduction are language and the institutions of bureaucracy, the military, history, and cartography.

Anderson's conception has been rightly criticized for ignoring the role of religion in producing nationalism. Anthropologist Peter van der Veer suggests that religious discourse may be a core part of national identity rather than epiphenomenal.[45] Similarly, in critiquing the history of nationalism, the political theorist Partha Chatterjee suggests that classical historiographies hide the religious solidarities that underpin national loyalties.[46] And political scientist Anthony Marx productively focuses his critique on the origins of nationalism in Europe. Marx demonstrates that early nationalism in Europe was built precisely on the logic of religious exclusion rather than on the secular grounds proposed by Anderson.[47] By excavating the hidden place of religion in constituting nationalism, van der Veer, Chatterjee, and Marx help scholars to reintegrate religious communities into our theories of the origins of modern nation-states.

In Chapter 4, I build on the work of van der Veer, Chatterjee, and Marx to argue that the truncated pluralism of the Indonesian state constitutes a theoretically neglected form of nationalism that I dub 'godly nationalism.' The term 'religious nationalism' is usually invoked as a conceptual placeholder for particular instances of Jewish, Islamic, Hindu, Christian, or Buddhist nationalism. Yet in demanding that citizens believe in God, while being ambivalent as to which path to God they should choose, Indonesia's brand of nationalism is religious but not particular. I define godly nationalism as an imagined community bound by a shared theism and mobilized through the state in cooperation with religious organizations. As long as citizens believe in one of the state-sanctioned pathways to God, they receive state protection and other benefits of citizenship. Godly nationalism provides one example of how religious commitments are being synthesized with national identity in an age of public and plural religion.

Reimagining political theory also requires taking seriously the argument that Indonesian Islamic organizations have ideas about politics, power, and religious accommodation that may be different from those derived from

---

44 Anderson (2003, 6).
45 van der Veer (1994).
46 Chatterjee (1999).
47 Marx (2003).

European political thought. Whether the categories of analysis most useful to map the attitudes of Indonesian Muslims are the same as those used to map the attitudes of Westerners is a question that must be investigated rather than an assumption that can be taken for granted.

So, what does tolerance mean to Indonesia's Islamic organizations? My goal in Chapters 3, 4, and 5 will be to unearth the conditions that give rise to varying levels of tolerance toward Christians, Hindus, Communists, and Ahmadi Muslims. In Chapter 6, I shift the focus back to ideas, specifically to ideas within Indonesian Islamic political thought, to show that NU and Muhammadiyah are tolerant of religious minorities based on social and state rules that differ from John Locke and John Rawls' model of secular-liberal tolerance. Instead, Indonesian Islamic organizations support tolerance based on group rights, legal pluralism, and the separation of religious and social affairs. Together, I call this set of values 'communal tolerance,' and I use survey data to demonstrate that insights derived from comparative political theory accord with the attitudes of municipal-level leaders of NU and Muhammadiyah. This is both a theoretical and a methodological contribution; by integrating comparative political theory with concept formation and survey research, scholars can explain more attitudes and outcomes than by relying on concepts originating in European political thought.

This approach stands in sharp contrast to that of an important remainder of survey researchers who have sought to revise, rather than discard, the idea that the world is moving toward a single, secular modernity. Pippa Norris and Ronald Inglehart argue that secularization endures in places with high levels of 'existential security' while religious observance is more conspicuous in insecure countries.[48] Norris and Inglehart's argument has received a great deal of attention, not all of it positive. By relying on public opinion data, they neglect the relationship between formal political institutions, social movements, and historical legacies such as colonialism and levels of religious observance.[49] For example, Michael Ross suggests that the lag in support for gender equality between the Muslim world and Western Europe is due to the political economy of oil; in states with oil, women have little role in labor markets and thus little leverage with which to combat patriarchal laws. In states without oil, women have been able to use their economic position to advance gender equality.[50] Instead of using the existential insecurity hypothesis to explain intolerance and secularization theory to explain tolerance, I isolate specific factors that lead to civic virtues. Tolerance is not a consequence of secularization, theology, or rational calculation but is due to interactions between Islamic groups,

---

[48] Norris and Inglehart (2004).

[49] Bellin (2008, 333–334); Gill (2001); Kang (2009); Schwedler (2006).

[50] Ross (2008). A major shortcoming of the study is that it treats Islam – a variable that is heterogeneous across states and over time – as homogenous. This is the essence of Orientalism, although here the fallacy is committed for methodological rather than political reasons.

interactions between Islamic groups and Christian missions, the influence of modernizing states, and Islamic organizations' own ideas about how to accommodate religious difference.

An empirical contribution of the book is focusing on the meaning of tolerance to the leaders of some of the largest and oldest Islamic organizations in the world: NU, Muhammadiyah, and Persis. A total of 75 percent of Indonesia's 200 million Muslims identify with either NU or Muhammadiyah, leading one study to remark that these organizations "constitute the 'steel frame' of Indonesian Muslim civil society."[51] Members of NU and Muhammadiyah can be found in the highest reaches of government and business in Jakarta, as well as the most derelict fringes of Indonesia's vast archipelago. NU and Muhammadiyah are a key reason why Indonesia is a democratic overachiever. A comparatively poor country, Indonesia has avoided the problems of endemic ethnic conflict, political disintegration, or relapse into authoritarianism that have bedeviled other outsized states undergoing political transition, including the former Yugoslavia and the Soviet Union. The organizations' commitment to tolerance has been vital during the transition from authoritarianism, which is why the anthropologist Robert Hefner noted, "Despite thirty years of authoritarian rule, Indonesia today is witness to a remarkable effort to recover and amplify a Muslim and Indonesian culture of tolerance, equality, and civility. The proponents of civil Islam are a key part of this renaissance."[52]

Still, outside of Indonesian studies, NU and Muhammadiyah are poorly understood. Even within Indonesian studies, research on NU and Muhammadiyah pales in comparison to efforts to investigate small, militant Islamic organizations such as Jemaah Islamiyah or equally marginal liberal Islamic groups such as the Liberal Islamic Network (Jaringan Islam Liberal). The former are seen as more perilous to international security, thereby justifying the birth of the field of 'jihadology' after 9/11. The latter are seen as the prospective saviors of the Muslim world through an Islamic reformation, thereby justifying both research and support from the US government and would-be saviors of Islam.

This neglect is consequential. On the substantive side, it distorts our understanding of Islam and politics because NU and Muhammadiyah, alongside the military and electoral institutions, provide the social infrastructure for the largest Muslim-majority democracy in the world. On the theoretical side, the neglect of NU and Muhammadiyah reflects an oversight in grasping the political influence of Islamic organizations that are not liberal, militant, or quietist. Given the anxieties that public religions invoke in democratic theory, particularly for minority rights, addressing this oversight has implications for understanding how public religions impact state policy and notions of civic virtue. In other words, it will have implications for how we understand the future of

[51] Mujani and Liddle (2004, 120).
[52] Hefner (2000, 218).

tolerance in a world where Islam, like other religions, is unapologetically in the public sphere.

A final contribution is to intervene in public debates about tolerance in the Muslim world. Edward Said has challenged scholars to examine how particular types of knowledge worked to serve imperial interests in the Middle East; the idea that Muslims were irrational, intolerant, and oppressive of women aided a project of imperial domination that began with Napoleon and continues into the present.[53] Wendy Brown makes this point in relation to tolerance itself by suggesting that the current prominence of the concept has more to do with sustaining particular power relations than solving social concerns. Brown shows how tolerance is used to depoliticize struggles over material resources, marginalize social claims, and assert civilizational superiority.

Although this book is more empirical than normative, it inevitably addresses a pressing humanitarian concern. By expanding the existing political science conceptualization of tolerance beyond its secular-liberal and European origins, I attempt to destabilize claims of Western cultural supremacy and humanize Islamic organizations at a time when xenophobia plagues the public sphere and informs militarized policies around the globe.

Book Overview

Following the theoretical and methodological analysis, each chapter investigates a different aspect of tolerance, intolerance, or the meaning of tolerance to Indonesia's Muslim democrats while elucidating the historical constructivist approach to the study of religion and politics. The chapters are also roughly in chronological order.

Chapter 2 presents the methodological and theoretical grounds from which to explain varying levels of tolerance in Islamic organizations. I suggest that Islamic organizations develop their understanding of appropriate relations between groups through locally generated social interactions. The ethnic makeup of the organization, the interactions during the period of organizational formation, and the relationship between the religious group and the state all affect ideas about religious accommodation. The remainder of the chapter explains the methodology – a comparative historical analysis of three Islamic groups, a quantitative survey of the organizations' leaders, ethnographic observation, and in-depth interviews – and addresses alternative explanations.

Chapter 3 uses newly collected archival and survey data to argue against the claim that culture, theology, or rational decisions shaped the attitudes of Indonesian Muslims toward non-Muslims. The chapter shows that Muslim organizations fought local battles and responded to context-specific threats by Christian missionaries and rival Islamic groups during the early twentieth century, which saw the development of a national consciousness and

---

[53] Said (2003 [1978]).

the institutions that now organize political life. In areas where missionaries engaged in sharp polemics against Islam, Muslim leaders developed polemical responses. They used pejorative language to describe Christians and Christian theology and urged their followers to avoid interactions with Christians. In areas where Christians and Muslims shared a common ethnicity, however, that identity cleavage diminished the scale of the threat and the ensuing polemics. I draw on two mechanisms of path dependency – the way in which Islamic jurisprudence becomes institutionalized, and patterns of political alliances that cement and reinforce particular types of social polarization – to show how local politics and social cleavages established during the period of organizational formation can explain contemporary attitudes and policies toward Christians. I demonstrate that even in a globalized age, religious organizations base their policies on past interactions more than on global theology or rational calculation.

Chapter 4 explains why Islamic organizations are willing to accommodate some minorities but not others. I make two intertwined arguments to explain intolerance toward Ahmadiyah, a heterodox Muslim sect. I show that both state and society have excluded Ahmadiyah and other heterodox groups since the late 1930s due to an 'overlapping consensus.' Islamic organizations dislike Ahmadiyah for different reasons, but all agree on their distaste for Ahmadiyah. I then show that this exclusion has had surprising effects; it has played a productive role in creating the 'we-feeling' that constitutes contemporary Indonesian nationalism. Indonesian nationalism is modern, plural, and predicated on theological rather than geographic or religious exclusion. This new concept, which I call 'godly nationalism,' provides a template for understanding the relationship between religion and nationalism in societies where religion is part of the public sphere.

Chapter 5 highlights the coevolution of state and religion by focusing on three moments of the shifting practices of tolerance. First, for Persis, the entry of its political party, Masyumi, into government prompted increased expressions of tolerance toward Christians before and after the democratic elections of 1955. Second, from 1953 to 1964, the Ministry of Religious Affairs worked with Balinese elites to mold their religion into a form of monotheism that would be recognized by the state and Islamic organizations. From this point forward, Muslim groups never raised questions about whether Balinese Hindus should be tolerated. Third, in the early part of the twentieth century, the categories of Muslim and Communist were compatible and even overlapping. Yet owing to political polarization in the mid-1960s, Islamic organizations abandoned their allies in favor of confrontation. A focus on NU shows how its alliance with the military prompted an outburst of intolerance toward the Communists, including active support for the mass killings of 1965–1966, structural integration into the armed forces, and a shift in Islamic legal categories to describe Communists. That attitude became a pillar of both state and society and remains salient in the present. These moments highlight the coevolution of religion and state in the twentieth century and the centrality of the state to shaping the views of religious organizations.

Chapter 6 unites the arguments of the book to present a complete portrait of contemporary Islamic organizations' attitudes toward Christians, Hindus, Communists, and Ahmadiyah and the structural factors that shape attitudes toward each group. Then, drawing on comparative political theory and survey research, this chapter explains the meaning of tolerance to NU and Muhammadiyah. I suggest that these organizations are tolerant of religious minorities based on group rights, legal pluralism, and the separation of religious and social affairs – what this book refers to as 'communal tolerance.' I then use survey data to demonstrate that the concept of communal tolerance derived from comparative political theory accords with the attitudes of municipal-level leaders of NU and Muhammadiyah. I end by noting that, for the past twenty years, scholars have been debating how to 'reconcile' Islam and democracy in order to address the democratic underdevelopment of the Muslim-majority countries of the Middle East. They have devoted less attention, however, to the more important question: *what kind of democracy do Muslims want?* NU and Muhammadiyah favor a communal and religious democracy that is comparable to the vision of strong multiculturalists and is marked by a convergence of liberal individual rights and group-differentiated rights within a system of legal pluralism.

Is this preference on the part of NU and Muhammadiyah compatible with democracy? I believe it is, and I demonstrate that communal tolerance and godly nationalism have already been adopted by political institutions elsewhere by showing parallels between Indonesia's policies and those of other consolidated democracies. The book ends by making the case for situating religious organizations and virtues at the center of analysis rather than at the dying periphery in order to open up new ways of understanding social movements, political theory, and the world's multiple modernities.

This claim, however, is built on the back of careful research design including testing of alternative arguments. It is to that task that I turn in the next chapter.

2

Explaining Tolerance and Intolerance

How is tolerance understood by Islamic organizations? Why are some Islamic organizations more tolerant than others? My arguments will develop throughout the book, but here I want to introduce the principal claims to explain the origins of tolerance and intolerance, and the meaning of tolerance to contemporary Islamic organizations. I start with the widely accepted political science definition of tolerance: the "willingness to put up with those things one rejects or opposes."[1] I also begin with the following outcomes: NU is the most tolerant of the three organizations and Persis the least. All three organizations are more tolerant of Christians and Hindus than Ahmadi Muslims and Communists. Also, all three organizations have changed their views over time toward a greater level of tolerance of Christians and Hindus, and less tolerance of Ahmadis and Communists.

Methodologically, my arguments work on two levels: the micro level based on original survey data of 1,000 leaders of NU, Muhammadiyah, and Persis, and the organizational level based on a comparative historical analysis of the behavior of NU, Muhammadiyah, and Persis during the twentieth century alongside key texts in Indonesian Islamic political thought and ethnographic observation. Theoretically, my arguments are causal and conceptual. One set of claims explains why Muhammadiyah, NU, and Persis came to different positions vis-à-vis a common set of minority groups, while the other set of claims is conceptual and explains how elites in the three organizations today understand tolerance and nationalism in comparison to the accepted political science definitions.

Indonesia provides an ideal field site for studying tolerance for at least two reasons. Indonesia is home to approximately 235 million Muslims, the largest population of any state. For this reason alone, Indonesia is a crucial

---

[1] Sullivan, Pierson, and Marcus (1982); Gibson (1992a, 560–577).

empirical case for a theory explaining the meaning and practices of tolerance in Muslim-majority democracies.[2] Furthermore, unlike those in some other predominantly Muslim states, Indonesian organizations are marked by diversity across theoretically relevant independent variables, allowing cases to be selected in order to test hypotheses.

Theory

The first hypothesis is more like an observation. Constructing a binary between authentic/tolerant/quietist Indonesian Muslims and inauthentic/intolerant/politicized ones depends on a shallow dichotomy between good and bad Muslims.[3] NU, Muhammadiyah, and Persis are no more inherently tolerant or intolerant than Germans are inherently racist or Rwandans inherently violent.[4] All have experienced periods of passivity and periods of activism, periods of tolerance and periods of intolerance. All are authentic expressions of Indonesian Islam. Primordialist arguments that posit an essential, unchanging character have long been excised from rigorous social science research even while their residues remain in discussions of religion and politics.

This observation is confirmed by a long-standing empirical regularity in surveys of public attitudes: democratic values such as tolerance are relative to the target and the time period rather than absolute and unchanging. Most individuals are more tolerant of some minority groups than others. This was the case for Americans in the 1950s, who were often unwilling to allow an admitted Communist to teach in public schools or hold public office, but were more willing to allow atheists and socialists these rights. These attitudes are not, however, static; after the Cold War with the Soviet Union ended, those same Americans were more likely to allow an admitted Communist to give a political speech.[5] In order to explain attitudes of tolerance and intolerance, then, we need to separate the actors, targets, time period, and social spheres.

Very few Indonesians (or Americans) are fully tolerant, but they tend to tolerate some minorities more than others. Muslim elites today are more tolerant of Christians and Hindus than they are of heterodox Muslims and Communists. The increases in tolerance toward Christians and Hindus stem in part from state recognition and integration. In most Indonesian's experience, the 1945–1950 revolutionary war against the Dutch was marked by Christian and Muslim unity in defense of the newly proclaimed homeland. As a result of their participation, Indonesian Christians came to be seen as part of the nation instead of foreigners backed by Dutch finances and power.[6] State recognition

---

[2] George and Bennett (2005, 120); Gerring (2007, 108).
[3] Mamdani (2002).
[4] Browning (1998); Straus (2006).
[5] Gibson (2005, 108).
[6] Benda (1958, 176).

of Hindus had similar effects. The opposite is true for Ahmadi Muslims and Communists. Ahmadi Muslims were initially welcomed into society by the leaders of Indonesian Islam in the 1920s, but were then gradually excluded. That exclusionary stance has increasingly been backed by the state. Similarly, in the early twentieth century, the categories of Muslim and Communist were compatible and even overlapping. Yet, during the ensuing years, Communists and Muslims became bitter enemies and this polarization culminated in mass killings of Communists by Islamic organizations, which in some cases functioned as a structurally integrated wing of the military. These shifts in attitudes toward targets of tolerance are useful as they allow us to pinpoint the factors that drive change in Islamic organizations.

A related observation is that tolerance is a continuous variable rather than a dichotomous one. The degree to which an Indonesian Muslim elite is considered tolerant is measured by his or her willingness to allow someone from a group they dislike to run for office, live as their neighbor, worship near their home, give a political speech, or hold a political demonstration. Again, by this definition, very few Indonesians are fully tolerant, but some are more tolerant than others. Most Indonesian Muslim elites are willing to live next door to Christians, have them teach in schools, and hold public demonstrations. But NU leaders are more willing to allow Christians to be mayor and build a church in a heterogeneous area than are Muhammadiyah or Persis leaders. In other words, NU leaders tend to be more tolerant of Christians than Muhammadiyah and Persis leaders. In Chapter 3, I argue that this variation across Islamic organizations reflects the way Muslim organizations fought local battles and responded to context-specific threats by Christian missionaries and rival Islamic groups during the early twentieth century, which saw the development of a national consciousness and the organizations that now shape political life.

Explaining variation in levels of tolerance is the job of comparative historical analysis. I begin with the simple argument that the theological principles to which Islamic organizations subscribe do not determine their behavior. Islamists who seek to establish Islamic government are capable of high levels of tolerance of non-Muslims. Likewise, Sufi moderates (or quietists) are no less likely to undertake acts of extreme intolerance, including genocide, than Islamists. As a result, nontheological variables must be central to explaining the behavior of religious organizations toward non-Muslims. I suggest three primary factors: historical interactions between Islamic organizations and other groups (path dependency), the ethnic composition of the organization, and state support or prohibition of the minority group.

The relationships Islamic organizations had with other groups during their founding period shaped their worldview, as well as their subsequent interactions. In regions where Muslim groups clashed with Communist and Christian groups, they developed beliefs and alliances that reflected those tensions and made subsequent cooperation more difficult. Conversely, in regions where

Muslims clashed with other Muslims it often became easier for the Muslims to work with Christians, and even Communists, against other Muslims. Both cooperative and conflicting alliances crafted in the 1920s and 1930s shaped behavior for decades, even when those alliances undermined the material interests of Islamic organizations.

The ethnic composition of the organization is important as it can make it easier or harder to trust other identity-based groups. Religious groups made up of members with a single religion and single ethnicity are more likely to privilege their religion alone rather than working cooperatively with other religious, ethnic, tribal, or regional groups; these groups also find it difficult to expand beyond their homogenous background and are likely to be small in size but strong in ideology. Conversely, when the ethnic composition stretches across multiple religions, tolerance is more likely. This argument extracts Lipset and Rokkan's contention that crosscutting cleavages are important for understanding conflict and coexistence and applies it to the behavior of religious organizations.[7] I suggest that when the ethnic composition of Islamic organizations is concurrent with a single religion, intolerance toward non-Muslims is more likely than tolerance.

These cleavages persist because of two mechanisms of path dependency. The first mechanism is the 'institutionalization' of attitudes into policies, Islamic law edicts (fatwas), and the discursive tradition into which members of Islamic organizations are initiated. In terms of policies, institutionalization refers to how each organization signals to its membership what should or cannot be done and creates rewards for members of the organization for following the rules about interactions with non-Muslims. In the language of path dependency, these policies shape the incentives and resources of actors.[8] In terms of law, institutionalization refers to the situation where social attitudes are crystalized into Islamic law, which is then used by the organizations to define and promote appropriate behavior for their members. Each organization interprets Islamic law differently and uses those understandings to convey norms, attitudes, and self-regulation to members. Islamic law does not coerce individuals into behavior like state law, but it does shape group norms and is one of the most important mechanisms of transmitting religious values from generation to generation. Education in Islamic law delineates 'us' and 'them,' and helps ensure that attitudes endure over time. Finally, in terms of discourse, institutionalization refers to the development of ideas – collective memories, stories, jokes, and other discursive practices that make up a tradition – to describe non-Muslims, their behavior, and their appropriate relationship to Muslims.[9]

---

[7] Lipset and Rokkan (1967).

[8] Pierson (2004, 35).

[9] See Schmidt (2008); Schatz (2009); Wedeen (1999, 2002) on the power of discursive practices in political science, and Asad on discursive traditions in anthropology: "A tradition consists essentially of discourses that seek to instruct practitioners regarding the correct form and purpose of a given practice that, precisely because it is established, has a history." "For the anthropologist

These ideas developed in the 1930s, but constantly reappear and are reinforced by the professed values of Islamic organizations. In some organizations, these ideas do not develop, and do not appear; such absences or alternatives are just as important for understanding the way that religious actors think about appropriate relations with others.

The second mechanism of path dependency is political alliance, both within formal political institutions and within society, again drawing on Lipset and Rokkan's argument about how social cleavages were sustained through the institutional development of European political parties.[10] Mass Muslim organizations originated in the polarized context of the 1920s and created political vehicles in the 1930s that reflected and exacerbated the social cleavages from which they were born. Ricklefs provides the clearest summary of the long-term implications of the fractious events of the 1920s: "By the 1930s the various categories in Javanese society were widely recognized, less bridgeable, and more politicized than they had been at the start of the century. People in these contending categories had clashed at the village and supra-village level. These groupings were reified in political organisations whose interest it was to maintain social distinctions in order to maintain their constituencies."[11] These mechanisms of path dependency explain how temporally rooted cleavages shape contemporary behavior, and will be illustrated in Chapters 3, 4, and 5.[12]

The third major determinant of religious organizations' attitudes is the state. State protection and promotion of minority groups increases the likelihood that social groups will tolerate those actors rather than face punishment. The converse is also true. State persecution of social groups increases the likelihood that religious organizations will be intolerant toward those actors. As noted earlier, Islamic organizations' attitudes toward Ahmadis, Communists, Hindus, and Christians were significantly influenced by state policy. Of course, Islamic organizations also shape that policy, as Chapters 4 and 5 demonstrate.

The key role of the state in fostering social attitudes raises the question of why the state tolerates some actors but not others, and at some times but not others. Here we find that most often the state will use intolerance or tolerance as part of a broader strategy toward another goal such as winning war, building political institutions, or crafting political coalitions. For example, Chapter 4 argues that social intolerance is a productive part of the process of transforming a latent identity into one that is politically salient by bringing new attitudes to the fore and enabling new political institutions to emerge. Chapter 5 demonstrates that state toleration is granted as a reward

---

of Islam, the proper theoretical beginning is therefore an instituted practice (set in a particular context, and having a particular history) into which Muslims are inducted *as* Muslims" (1986, 14–15).

[10] Lipset and Rokkan (1967, 50).

[11] Ricklefs (2007, 248).

[12] Pierson (2004).

to those groups that manufacture the content of their beliefs and the structure of their organizations in such a way as to facilitate legibility. Chapter 5 further demonstrates the centrality of intolerance to war, with the state and society systematically mobilizing social attitudes in pursuit of their goal of eliminating an enemy; in this case, intolerance does not cause conflict, but it is deliberately harnessed by the state and Islamic organizations for other goals. Taking these points together, we find that understanding the relationship between the state and tolerance calls for a shift in how we think about the role of tolerance in politics. Whether the state celebrates pluralism or persecutes minorities may have more to do with processes of state-building and less to do with values.

After detailing the causal determinants of levels of tolerance, the penultimate chapter shifts to more conceptual theorizing by examining how Islamic organizations think differently about tolerance than we might expect based on categories from liberal political theory. I suggest that NU and Muhammadiyah's visions for religious accommodation are similar in four ways that differentiate them from the liberal model: an emphasis on communal rather than individual rights, support for communal self-governance through legal pluralism, a separation between social and religious affairs, and the primacy of faith over other values. I then test this argument using survey data from municipal-level leaders of NU and Muhammadiyah.

Research Design

Careful research design is essential to assessing the validity of these arguments. The mainstay of this task is triangulation: a comparative historical analysis of three Islamic organizations over a period of one hundred years, ethnographic observation and in-depth interviews, and a quantitative survey of the organizations' leaders. This approach allows me to unearth the origins of Islamic organizations' attitudes, the evolution of their behavior over time, and their contemporary views. This micro-comparative (within country) approach of focusing on three organizations permits greater control over variables than would be possible with a comparison across states. It also permits a fine-grained account of tolerance including the use of primary source texts, interviews in the local vernacular, and attention to regional variation. As a whole, this approach yields both high methodological validity and a substantively meaningful account of Islam in Indonesia.

Political scientists tend not to value primary sources over secondary ones. I believe this devaluation is a mistake, especially at a time when theories of religion and politics are being rebuilt. Primary sources allow scholars to better understand actors' worldviews and the concerns that motivate their behavior. At a time when the paradigms from the past are widely discredited, primary sources allow scholars to bypass the misunderstandings that accompanied modernization theory and infused scholarship on religious organizations.

Take, for example, academic scholarship on NU. In the 1950s and 1960s, American scholars lambasted NU for being opportunist, corrupt, and servile in Soekarno's drive toward authoritarianism.[13] A few decades later in the 1980s and 1990s, Western liberals celebrated NU for its liberalism and tolerance. Did NU undergo a complete ideological revolution between 1960 and 1980? No, though it certainly gained a more charming spokesperson.[14] What changed more fundamentally, however, were NU's political commitments, which ran first against and then alongside those of Western scholars. Instead of relying on secondary sources, then, this book tries as much as possible to use primary sources to give a fuller picture of Islamic organizations' attitudes and behaviors.

Primary source material is from the Indonesian National Archives, the Indonesian National Library, and the archives of Indonesian Islamic organizations. From Muhammadiyah, the magazines *Bintang Islam, Suara Muhammadiyah,* and the *Almanak Muhammadiyah*; notes from the *Muktamar Muhammadiyah* (the organization's national meetings) and local meeting notes from 1922 to 1925 were most useful for tracking its changing policies. NU's writings were more scarce. Although I relied on *Berita Nahdlatul Ulama, Swara NU,* and *Utusan Nahdlatul Ulama* as much as possible, I have also depended on NU's records from the *Muktamar NU,* Ph.D. theses, Indonesian-language writings by NU leaders, and other accounts. Despite Persis's small size, its many periodicals – including *Risalah, Pembela Islam* and *Aliran Islam* – helped to map its behavior in the early period, alongside a key monograph by Federspiel and reprints of works by Mohammed Natsir, M Isa Anshary, and Ahmad Hassan. I also draw on the exciting new scholarship on Islam in Indonesia during the late nineteenth and early twentieth centuries.[15] Previous scholarship on Indonesian Islam has emphasized either the pre-Islamic roots of contemporary religious organizations,[16] the transformative role of the state and key intellectuals in the period 1970–1990,[17] or the period around the Japanese Occupation and Guided Democracy from 1942 to 1965.[18] These periods are important, yet all three overlook the key role of events in the early twentieth century in shaping future conflicts.

This historical material is used to explain the behavior of Islamic organizations, to assess whether their attitudes were consistent over time, and to differentiate levels of tolerance. To demarcate the differences, I created a hierarchical, categorical scale ranging from high tolerance to high intolerance and

---

[13] For a more productive interpretation, see Anderson (1972).

[14] Abdurrahman Wahid's influence on NU was substantial. But the behavior of NU since his passing suggests his influence on the organization has been widely overstated. Moreover, survey data suggests that his attitudes were unrepresentative of NU more broadly.

[15] Hadler (2008); Laffan (2003); Shiraishi (1990); Ricklefs (2007).

[16] Geertz (1976); Hurgronje and Wilkinson (1906).

[17] Barton (1996); Fealy (1998); Hefner (2000).

[18] Slater (2005).

applied to both discourse and behavior. High levels of tolerance are indicated by discourse that publicly recognizes the target group using positive adjectives and calling for its protection and inclusion in social and political matters. Conversely, high levels of intolerance are indicated by actively denouncing the target. Publications urge followers to beware of the target, and the organization actively tries to stigmatize the target. Indicators for behavior are similar; high levels of tolerance mean that the organization actively opposes any restrictions on the behavior of the target and actively supports the target in areas of common interest. The actor seeks out these areas of common interest in order to build interfaith ties. Intolerance, meanwhile, is marked by active persecution of the target in order to eradicate it from society. This may include violence or conflict, and certainly includes organization and mobilization against the target. Table 2.1 summarizes the indicators of tolerance. These indicators are applied in Chapters 3, 4, 5, and 6.

In order to determine whether past interactions shaped contemporary Muslim organizations' expectations for relations with non-Muslims (path dependency), I draw on primary and secondary source material from the 1940s through the present documenting interactions with non-Muslims or discussion of non-Muslims by Islamic organizations. Chapter 3 discusses religious edicts (fatwas) issued from the organizations' foundings until 1936.[19] A fatwa is an answer to an interrogatory and conveys norms, attitudes, and self-regulation. The value of using fatwas from this period is that they demonstrate the emergence, existence, and nonexistence of social cleavages. Comparing fatwas from the three organizations helps assess how their contexts produced different Islamic jurisprudence. Chapters 3, 4, and 5 also demonstrate path dependency by detailing subsequent political alliances, describing the reappearance of polemics, and using key events to show how difficult it is for religious organizations to move offtrack once social attitudes are institutionalized.

The second source of data was in-depth interviews and ethnographic observation. The in-depth interviews were used to obtain basic organizational information such as membership, organizational structure, and contemporary majority-minority relations, and well as more nuanced accounts of social relations than could be obtained through surveys. Interviews were conducted with a wide sample of religious elites, political activists, and political observers. Interviews lasted between forty-five minutes and two hours, and were undertaken in either English or Indonesian, depending on the subject's preferred language.

Ethnographic material is based on personal observation at the 2010 constitutional court hearings; I attended seven of the day-long sessions. Ethnographic observations were supplemented with interviews of lawyers and witnesses at the hearings, as well as court transcripts. Many of my

---

[19] After 1936, interfaith concerns were overshadowed by the Japanese invasion and the revolutionary war.

TABLE 2.1. *Organizational indicators of levels of tolerance*

Level of Tolerance	Behavior Indicators	Discourse Indicators
Full intolerance (*Persecution*)	The actor actively *persecutes* the target in order to eradicate it from society. This may include violence or conflict, and certainly includes organization and mobilization against the target.	The actor is vocal in denouncing the target. Publications urge followers to beware of the target, and the organization actively tries to stigmatize the target.
Semi-intolerance (*Discrimination*)	The actor works to maintain strict, hierarchical boundaries between groups but does not mobilize violence. The actor polices boundaries and restricts the autonomy of the target.	The actor denounces the target but does not urge action against it. Difference is noted in order to police hierarchical boundaries and to subordinate the target through discrimination.
Neutrality	The actor does not interact with the target.	The actor does not discuss the target.
Semitolerance (*Support*)	The actor supports the target in having its distinct religious identity. Boundaries are maintained but with geographic and ideological space allotted to the target. The actor may support the target on some issues of common interest.	The actor speaks of the target in terms of difference and separation but not pejoratively. Sometimes the actors addresses the ideas and behavior of the target in positive terms.
Full tolerance (*Recognition, cooperation, alliance*)	The actor actively opposes any restrictions on the behavior of the target and actively supports the target in areas of common interest. The actor seeks out these areas of common interest in order to build interfaith ties.	The target is actively supported, with the actor calling for its protection and inclusion in both social and political matters.

insights came from the kind of interactions that occur when living in the field for two years and attending the conferences of NU, Muhammadiyah, and Persis. Jokes, reactions to questions, and everyday behavior helped me to understand the meaning and practices of tolerance. In 2009, I taught a course at the State Islamic University (UIN) Syarif Hidayatullah, which enabled me to bounce ideas off a group of thoughtful MA and Ph.D. students. I presented parts of the text to critical audiences at UIN Syarif Hidayatullah, Gadjah Mada University, and the Paramadina Islamic University, who helped expose holes in my thinking that my audiences in the United States may not have detected. Rather than contract my survey to a local firm, I wrote the questions myself, translated them (going through seventeen drafts), and pilot tested the survey with a group of NU youth who pinpointed issues that otherwise would not have been apparent. Tolerance is a concept fraught with ambiguity and sensitivity. The instrument demanded equal sensitivity in its construction and could not have been completed without first living for a year among my informants.

The third method is original quantitative survey research. After completing a year of archival research and interviews, I collected survey data from a random sample of municipal (*cabang*) leaders from Persis, NU, and Muhammadiyah. These are the leaders of the institutions on the ground: they choose the central board, they implement all the organization's programs, raise funds, shape relations with political parties, and govern interfaith/intrafaith relations at the local and national level. The survey data is based on a newly collected stratified random sample of municipal-level leaders and is the first and only representative survey of the leaders who shape interfaith and intrafaith relations throughout Indonesia. I surveyed them at their national meetings (*muktamar*), which take place every five years and are attended by elites from all over the country. I randomly selected respondents by approaching every third person who was walking in a central area. The subsequent sample consisted of 1,000 leaders (379 NU, 387 Muhammadiyah, and 234 Persis), representing a total population (*N*) of 6,550 leaders (3,500 NU, 2,300 Muhammadiyah, and 750 Persis). The surveys were undertaken at the 2010 meeting for each organization.

Details of the protocol and the instrument (in both Indonesian and English) can be found in the appendix and are discussed at length in Chapter 6. Here, I want to briefly discuss the survey questions. Indicators of tolerance in other studies focus on education, worship, speech, political representation, and recognition. That said, the existing indicators used by the World Values Survey and General Social Survey, the most important survey instruments measuring tolerance, are problematic in that they rely on indicators implicitly rooted in liberal political theory. The first major survey on tolerance was a 1955 study by Samuel Stouffer on Americans' tolerance toward groups that were known to be disliked: communists, accused communists, socialists, and atheists. Stouffer's work was path breaking in that it set the stage for decades of subsequent research but also path dependent in that it prevented the development of alternative conceptions of tolerance. As a rule, survey researchers repeat past questions in order to track longitudinal change. The downside of replication is that the limitations of past measures go unresolved and the existing indicators can develop a taken-for-granted quality. While this was not problematic in the

US context, it became so after the indicators were exported to countries with different social and political traditions.[20]

Indicators of tolerance developed in the United States, a liberal democracy, are now used to assess levels of tolerance in countries with a wide range of political systems and ideas about how politics should be organized. While the definition of tolerance adopted by most researchers, "willingness to put up with those things one rejects," is globally useful, the specific indicators are narrowly rooted in liberal political theory, particularly Locke's distinction between the public and private, and his vision of a public sphere undifferentiated by geography or demographics. Though I entered the field with a set of indicators rooted in the accepted indicators, it quickly became apparent that those indicators failed to capture the worldview of Islamic organizations. Indonesian Islamic organizations are willing to 'put up with' groups that they reject based on communal rather than individual rights, support for communal self-governance through legal pluralism rather than a unitary legal system, a separation between social and religious affairs rather than the separation of public and private, and the primacy of faith over other values such as individual freedom. For that reason, I developed new indicators that would shed light on how politics works in Indonesia.

There are some limits to the generalizations that can be made from the survey sample. The sample is not completely random in that only leaders who attended the 2010 meetings of their respective institutions were surveyed; inactive elites may have different attitudes. The mass membership of the organizations was also not included in the sample, so it is not possible to say with certainty that their opinions match those of the elites. That said, a 2010 survey of mass members by Robin Bush shows remarkable similarity between the two populations.[21] On the question of non-Muslims building a house of worship in their community, Bush finds that 76 percent of Muhammadiyah's mass members object and 63 percent of NU members object. Comparably, I find that 78 percent of Muhammadiyah members and 71 percent of NU members do not think a Christian church should be allowed to be built in their community. Bush finds that 30 percent of Muhammadiyah and 29 percent of NU members object to a non-Muslim living in their community. Similarly, I find that 29 percent of Muhammadiyah leaders and 30 percent of NU leaders object to living in the same village as a Christian. Like Bush, I find that education is a good predictor of increased tolerance, and I find differences in levels of tolerance toward minority groups in urban and rural areas. The most noticeable difference between our samples is regarding education, with Bush finding that 20 percent of Muhammadiyah members and 30 percent of NU members object to non-Muslims becoming a teacher at a national school; I find less

---

[20] For a more detailed discussion of the problems of path dependency in the evolution of survey research questions see Menchik (2011, chapter 2).
[21] Bush (2014). Bush does not include Persis members in her sample.

intolerance, with only 12 percent of Muhammadiyah and 11 percent of NU members objecting to a Christian teaching in a national school. Compared to Bush's survey of the masses, then, my survey finds somewhat higher levels of tolerance among the elites on one question, but overall the differences are minor, suggesting that my sample of Muslim elites is illustrative of the attitudes of the mass membership of NU and Muhammadiyah.

There is some evidence to suggest that my sample of Muslim elites is also representative of the opinions of the broader Indonesian Muslim population. In Saiful Mujani's 2001 and 2002 surveys of Indonesian Muslims, he found that 15–16 percent object to living next door to a Christian, while I found that 16 percent object. He found that 82–84 percent object to a Christian president, while I find that 67 percent object. And he found that 63–64 percent object to building a church in a predominantly Muslim community, while I found 73 percent object to the building of a new church in the predominantly Muslim city of Banda Aceh.[22] So my sample of Muslim elites appears to be similar to the broader Indonesian population in social relations, more tolerant in political affairs, and less tolerant in religious affairs.

Alternative Explanations

There are four salient alternative explanations that merit attention in the case selection: theology, culture, regime type, and rational decision making. The most important alternative explanation for tolerance is theology, which remains the most commonly invoked explanation for the behavior of religious organizations. Theology refers to a set of religious ideas held and practiced by an actor.[23] In this instance the relevant theologies are ideas about the proper relationship between Muslims and non-Muslims as well as ideas about the proper role of religion in the state.[24] Recent work on religious organizations emphasizes the central role of political theology in explaining behavior ranging from political violence to democratization.[25]

Since all three organizations are Sunni, a strict theological determinist account cannot explain the variation in tolerance among them. A more nuanced theological account fares equally poorly. NU places emphasis on the Syafii *mazhab*, one of the four main Sunni schools and the dominant one in Southeast Asia, while Muhammadiyah and Persis hew closely to individual interpretations of the Qur'an and Sunnah, supplemented by the traditions of the Prophet (*hadith*). According to this theological explanation, Muhammadiyah and Persis should behave similarly. Yet both quantitative and qualitative indicators show that Muhammadiyah is more tolerant than Persis. An even more

[22] Mujani (2003, 174, 177).
[23] Philpott (2007).
[24] Arat (1998); Brumberg (2001); Hall (1993).
[25] Philpott (2007); Duffy Toft, Philpott, and Shah (2011).

nuanced theological explanation recognizes that Muhammadiyah and Persis make individual interpretations based on Quranic exegesis (*ijtihad*). Here we reach another limit of theological determinism; if interpretations vary based on individual reasoning, then other variables are needed to explain variation at the organizational level.

To go beyond theological determinism, I chose three organizations with different founding theologies. This deviates from the most common strategy for testing the effects of theology: choosing separate countries with the same religion but with different outcome variables.[26] The problem with this approach is that religious organizations in separate states are likely to exhibit significant theological differences, despite falling under the same moniker. For example, Islam entered Morocco and Indonesia in different ways despite both being predominantly Muslim societies, with important implications for Islamic organizations in each state.[27] A second common strategy is to choose a large number of cases and statistically control for some variables while testing the impact of having a majority population with a single religion.[28] The problem with this technique is temporal: using population as a proxy for theology treats as a constant something that changes over time.[29]

Rather than trying to control theology as a static variable, I chose organizations with three distinct frameworks within Sunni Islam and follow their ideas over time. Muhammadiyah is modernist, NU is traditionalist, and Persis is Islamist. This strategy mimics both Lijphart's and Mill's most-different methods, by maximizing variation on a key independent variable.[30] If the theological explanations for organizational behavior were correct, Persis would be uniformly intolerant, while Muhammadiyah would be semitolerant and NU more consistently tolerant.[31]

Yet each organization varies in its levels of tolerance toward different minority groups and changes its views over time, suggesting the limits of theological explanations for the behavior of religious actors. For the first years after its founding in 1912, Muhammadiyah actively promoted tolerance toward Christians. Muhammadiyah leaders spoke highly of Christian pedagogy, maintained close relations with religious and ethnic minorities, and joined forces with other religious groups to combat defamation and hate speech against any group regardless of religion. Yet in 1927, Muhammadiyah engaged in regular polemics against Christianity. These polemics continued throughout the 1930s then subsided during the revolutionary war from 1945 to 1950 when the collective struggle of Indonesian Christians and Muslims against Dutch imperialism

---

[26] Gill (1998); Kalyvas (1996).
[27] Geertz (1968).
[28] Fish (2002); Ross (2008).
[29] Asad (1986, 1993).
[30] George and Bennett (2005, 156); Gerring (2007, 139–144); Mill (1843).
[31] Alfian (1989); Barton (1996); Federspiel (1970).

improved interfaith relations. Yet again in the 1990s, Muhammadiyah's chair, Amien Rais, lambasted the influence of 'Christianization' in Indonesia and called for jihad against Christians in the country's outer islands.

In contrast to Muhammadiyah, NU has maintained its tolerant policies toward Christians. A common joke in NU circles is that they are closer to the Protestants than to the modernist Muhammadiyah, and even closer still to the Catholics. This is more than pure jest. Since the early 1980s, the Indonesian Catholic Church has mandated that young Jesuit priests live in an NU boarding school for at least two weeks. Furthermore, in private conversations with Catholics, NU leaders often ask whether they would fight alongside NU in the event of a war with Muhammadiyah.[32] Despite NU's continued tolerance of Christians, it has had a more tumultuous relationship with Indonesian Communists. In the 1950s NU joined the nationalist Ali Sastroamidjojo cabinet, which was backed by the Indonesian Communist Party (PKI) alongside the center-left Progressive Faction. Yet, though NU spent a decade working alongside the Communist Party in coalition with Soekarno, his rapid marginalization at the hands of the military provided an opportunity for NU leaders to support military action against the Communists. NU backed the slaughter of the Communists during the mass killings of 1965–1966 and provided both physical and rhetorical support to the military by declaring the Communists to be hypocrites (*munafik*), unbelievers who are belligerent toward Islam (*kafir harbi*), and rebels against a legitimate government (*bughat*).

Placed in historical context, then, NU's and Muhammadiyah's behavior appears to follow a pattern of oscillation between conflict and coexistence: tolerance toward some religious minorities but not others and tolerance at some times but not others. Given this variation, theology is a poor predictor of either the discourse or the behavior of Islamic organizations.

Culture is also of limited utility in explaining the behavior of Islamic organizations. Clifford Geertz developed the most common cultural explanation for political behavior in his studies of Muslims in Java. Geertz divides Javanese society into three groups: *priyayi*, *abangan*, and *santri*.[33] The priyayi are the administrative upper classes who practice a form of 'Javanese religion' that combines Islam with mystical and Hindu practices. Their class status differentiates them from the abangan. The abangan are then contrasted with the santri, who are outwardly orthodox Muslims in their dress, living arrangements, and religious rituals. Owing to the abangan's syncretic beliefs, a Geertzian explanation stresses the relative intolerance of the santri compared to abangan Muslims.

Geertz's work has been criticized for overlooking the influence of secularism, conflating class and religious categories, and overstating the influence of Hinduism on Java.[34] A further critique charges that Geertz treats Javanese

---

[32] Interview with Franz Magnis Suseno SJ, Jakarta, September 2009.
[33] Geertz (1976, 5–6).
[34] Anderson (1977); Bachtiar (1973); Hodgson (1974); Woodward (1989).

culture as coherent and fixed rather than fractured and historically situated.[35] Indeed, there is no evidence that the abangan-santri split existed before the mid-nineteenth century.[36] This critique explains why Geertz's framework cannot account for variation between NU, Muhammadiyah, and Persis; the emphasis on coherence among the santri glosses over differences between NU and Muhammadiyah, who he presented as having a similar relationships with non-Muslims: "The relation between the two groups being only somewhat hostile, the sense of difference only rarely gets intense enough to blot out the sense of commonality of religious belief throughout the whole *ummat* [community]."[37] Because of its emphasis on coherence, Geertz's framework cannot explain variation.

A third alternative explanation is regime type, specifically democracy or authoritarianism. Modernization theory suggests that newly open political institutions should increase tolerance by channeling discontent into formal politics and promoting postmaterialist values.[38] Similarly, insofar as tolerance is an inherent democratic norm, Islamic organizations' policies should become more tolerant as democracy is consolidated.[39] Although democratic societies may have high levels of disagreement concerning religious and political issues, Islamic organizations' commitment to the procedural rules of democratic contestation should propel them to tolerate minority groups as long as those groups do not threaten them in a meaningful way. Consolidated democracy, meanwhile, should increase tolerance by creating mechanisms for the resolution of grievances among religious groups and creating the opportunity for otherwise intolerant groups to gain voice.[40] Democracy may, therefore, lead to greater tolerance. Meanwhile, authoritarianism is often blamed for the outbreaks of intolerance, or uncivil Islam, in Indonesia.[41] Periods of authoritarianism should therefore correlate with intolerance.

Diachronic case studies allow me to test the effect of regime type on the behavior of Islamic organizations. Since 1900, Indonesia has experienced colonial rule, two periods of democratization, two periods of relatively consolidated democracy, and two periods of authoritarian rule. By showing that levels of tolerance do not increase during periods of democracy and do not necessarily decrease during periods of authoritarianism, I demonstrate the limits of regime-centered explanations for tolerance and intolerance.

A fourth alternative is rational choice. Existing rationalist explanations for religion and politics have limited value here for many reasons. First, as discussed in Chapter 1, religious actors' worldviews may be based on Islamic

[35] Wedeen (2002, 716).
[36] Ricklefs (2006); Ricklefs (2007, 6, 263).
[37] Geertz (1976, 176).
[38] Inglehart (1990, 1997).
[39] Rawls (1996).
[40] Schwedler (2006).
[41] Hefner (2000, chapters 4–6).

political thought, nonrational truths, and the rejection of the very discourse of individual choice, public, and private that rational choice models take for granted.[42] Second, rationalist models produce predictions that accord poorly with the behavior of Islamic organizations. As Chapter 3 makes clear, it would have been rational for Persis to be tolerant of Christians, who had greater access to education in the early twentieth century and would have been more capable than Muslims of teaching math and science in Persis schools. It would have been rational for Muhammadiyah to promote intolerance since its economic interests were in trade and its sister organization, Sarekat Islam, advocated boycotting non-Muslim businesses. NU expressed frequent concern with the 'Christianization' of the Muslim world including its membership; it should have promoted intolerance. Yet the opposite is true: NU is the most tolerant of Christians, followed by Muhammadiyah and Persis. An alternative rationalist approach might incorporate these conflicting incentives by predicting a combination of intolerance and tolerance at a single point in time and recurrent change over the course of the twentieth century. Yet, empirically, Indonesian Muslim organizations have been marked by mostly consistent behavior. The third and most important reason that the rational choice (or religious economies) approach to religion is unhelpful is definitional, as discussed in Chapter 1; the definition of religion in the religious economies approach as a 'belief system' rather than a set of practices, organizations, or a discursive tradition is a mismatch for any religious group possessing coercive power, institutional rule-making capacity, symbolic power, the potential for social movement mobilization, or an affiliation with structures that shape individual choice.

One final point on case selection: 'Islamic organizations' is a broad category that includes civil society organizations such as mosques, universities, and health organizations, as well as overtly political bodies such as political parties and government commissions. In a predominantly Muslim country such as Indonesia, almost any organization could be considered 'Islamic.' As a result, it is important to recognize the underlying basis of support for an institution and the relationship between the elites and the constituency.[43]

Here, I want to distinguish between mass organizations, political parties, and elite coalitions. Mass organizations are groups that have a formal, mass membership based in civil society[44] and an elected or appointed leadership. Political parties are Islamic organizations that seek to gain formal political power through elections. Elite coalitions are made up of elites that represent organizations or mass movements, but have power based on other mechanisms, most likely by state appointment. Rather than testing the influence of these differences on Islamic organizations' behavior, I sought to control for it by

[42] Euben (1999); Philpott (2009).

[43] Braungart and Braungart (1986).

[44] While all three organizations loosely fit Putnam's notion of horizontally structured social organizations that form the backbone of society (2000), they engage in formal and informal forms of politics.

choosing three membership-based groups. I excluded elite-only organizations since there are *a priori* reasons to believe their behavior will be driven by the state more than by members' preferences or organizational structures. I also excluded purely political organizations since electoral incentives are likely to shape their interests.[45] All three civil society organizations share similar structures based on membership, although they are organized in slightly different ways, as will become clear in subsequent chapters.

Conclusion

How do Islamic organizations envision the accommodation of religious difference in social and state practices? Chapters 3, 4, and 5 demonstrate that understanding the levels of tolerance in Islamic organizations requires separating the targets, actors, and time period in order to explain the push and pull factors that underpin social attitudes. Chapter 6 then shows how Islamic organizations think about tolerance in comparison to the secular-liberal conception of it. Chapter 7 concludes by helping scholars envision a world of peaceful democracies that are not organized around a secular-liberal modernity but a plural, religious modernity. This observation is prescriptive and predictive; other Muslim-majority democracies are likely to face many of the same challenges that Indonesia faces in balancing individual rights of minorities and the democratic demands of the majority-Muslim population.

---

[45] All organizations have had either formal or strong informal ties with political parties: NU with *Partai Kebangkitan Nasional Ulama, Partai Kebangkitan Bangsa, Partai Persatuan Pembangunan* (PPP), and Masyumi; Muhammadiyah with *Partai Amanat Nasional*, PPP, and Masyumi; and Persis with Masyumi, *Partai Bulan Bintang* and PPP. The salience of these ties and their relevance to tolerance is explained in Chapters 4 and 5.

3

Local Genealogies

Why are some Muslim organizations more tolerant than others? This chapter uses archival and survey data to argue against the claim that theology, transnational influence, or strategic decisions shaped the attitudes of Indonesian Muslims toward non-Muslims. Merging constructivist and historical institutionalist arguments, the chapter demonstrates that locally specific ideas about friends, enemies, allies, and threats had important causal influence during the period of organizational creation. Islamic organizations fought local battles and responded to context-specific threats by Christian missionaries, Dutch colonial rulers, and other religious organizations. These ideas also have long-term, path-dependent effects on behavior. While there is a growing literature in comparative politics on the conditions under which Islamic movements and political parties change their policies, this chapter offers a cautious reminder that legacies of the past often shape the politics of the present. Even in a globalized age, religious organizations form their policies more on the basis of local politics and past interactions than in response to international forces.

Explanations for Intolerance by Islamic Organizations

Before the period 1880–1930, Islamic society in the three regions of West, Central, and East Java was homogenous in religious practices and intergroup relations; European and Javanese travelogues suggest that Islamic practices were standardized and uniformly followed.[1] Between 1880 and 1930, however, social relations became polarized by missionary activity and Islamic reform. In areas where Christian missionaries engaged in sharp polemics against Islam, Muslim leaders developed polemical responses and a Christian-Muslim cleavage developed. They urged their followers to avoid unnecessary interactions

[1] Ricklefs (2007, 6).

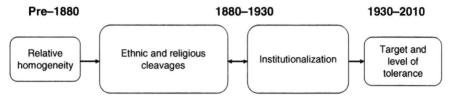

FIGURE 3.1. Causal logic of social cleavages, institutions, and intolerance.

with Christians. They used pejorative language to describe Christians and Christian theology. This pejorative language was reflected in fatwas issued during the period of organizational formation and delineating the leaders' expectations for members' interaction with Christians. This language encouraged intolerant behavior and attitudes toward Christians, propelled Islamic organizations toward political alliances designed to repel the Christian threat, and resulted in the creation of a discursive tradition of polemics toward Christians. Meanwhile, in areas where Christian missionaries did not engage in sharp polemics but Muslim reformers attacked existing practices, an intra-Muslim cleavage developed instead of a Christian-Muslim one. There, reformist Muslims launched polemical attacks on traditional ritual practices while other Islamic elites developed defenses of those practices, used pejorative language to describe other Muslims, and began to see Christians as potential allies rather than threats. In sum, this situation encouraged members of the organization to see Christians as allies rather than enemies, thereby shaping subsequent political alliances and creating very different discursive structures.

This polarization was exacerbated or alleviated by the ethnic composition of the organizations. When the ethnic composition stretched across multiple religions, tolerance across religious lines was more likely. Conversely, Islamic organizations made up of members of a single ethnicity were less likely to work cooperatively with other ethnic or religious groups. During the founding period, Muslim organizations developed ideas about friends, enemies, allies, and threats. These ideas were not a product of theology or rational calculation; they were a product of local politics and history.[2] Figure 3.1 details the logic of the argument.

Within Indonesia, the three regions of West, Central, and East Java where the Islamic organizations were founded witnessed different kinds of polarization. In West Java, the threats were from Christians and the traditionalists who wanted to preserve religious practices that reformists considered deviant. In Central Java, the threats were similar but were alleviated by a crosscutting cleavage of Javanese ethnicity. In East Java, only reformist Muslims were

---

[2] One other alternative explanation deserves mention; the Christian population in 1930, when the organizations' divergent attitudes became apparent, was 0.31 percent in West Java, 0.27 percent in Central Java, and 0.20 percent in East Java. The presence of such a small population cannot explain the variation.

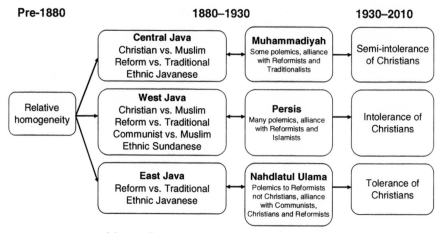

FIGURE 3.2. Causal logic of social cleavages, institutions, and intolerance applied to West, Central, and East Java.

salient threats, while Christians were increasingly seen as allies. The cleavages that were established in the regions then became embedded in organizations, institutionalized in Islamic law, discursive traditions, and political alliances, and translated into social attitudes. Figure 3.2 applies the causal logic to the three Islamic organizations.

In describing the conditions that gave rise to three distinct institutions, I follow Asad and Wedeen by focusing on the micro practices that created and sustained group difference. These practices help shape political relations in the sense in which Arendt defines the political: being based on the activities of ordinary citizens who, through the exercise of agency and within the context of interaction, shape their collective existence.[3] These practices include discussions about the orientation of prayer houses, funeral rituals, the classification and hierarchical ranking of sacred texts, and the appropriate behavior for interactions with non-Muslims.

After completing the historical research to build the argument, I undertook a survey of municipal-level leaders of the three organizations in order to assess levels of tolerance in the present; the leaders of NU were consistently the most tolerant of Christians and those of Persis the least tolerant. After presenting the qualitative material, I will return to the quantitative data at the end of the chapter.

Muhammadiyah

Muhammadiyah was founded on November 12, 1912, by Ahmad Dahlan and a group of friends in Kauman, Yogyakarta, Central Java. The village where

[3] Arendt (1958).

Dahlan grew up was located next to the palace (*kraton*) of the Sultan, along-side the Sultan's Mosque and surrounded by homes of other santri. Dahlan's parents belonged to an elite circle; his father was appointed religious scholar of the Sultan Mosque while his mother was the daughter of a high-level civil servant for Islamic affairs. The initial membership of Muhammadiyah reflected both Dahlan's religious ideals and this class component; the initial leaders were religious elites from the upper middle class.[4]

The motivation to establish Muhammadiyah stemmed from Dahlan's frus-tration with the religious practices at the Sultan Mosque and his support for Islamic reform movements. After his elementary school education in Yogyakarta, he went to Mecca in 1890 for one year, then again for two years around 1902. There he was exposed to Sjech Ahmad Chatib, the famous scholar of the Syafii school who taught many elites including the founder of NU, Hasjim Asj'ari.[5] By 1912, it was thought that he was well acquainted with and sympathetic to the ideas of the reformist Muhammed Abduh through the magazine *Tafsir Al-Manar*.[6] In 1896, Dahlan discovered the Sultan Mosque was not facing Mecca, the correct direction for prayer, so he painted lines on the floor to redi-rect people. When the chief civil servant for Islamic affairs, Muhammed Chalil, discovered this, he ordered the lines erased. Dahlan responded by building his own prayer house facing Mecca, which Chalil then burned down in retaliation. Dahlan threatened to leave Yogyakarta and relented only when his brother-in-law promised to rebuild the prayer house. The prayer house was rebuilt, but not to face Mecca, so Dahlan again painted lines on the floor.[7]

Muhammadiyah's leaders encountered opposition to their efforts to promote Islamic reform from the very beginning. During these years Muhammadiyah developed a coherent mission and set of organizational practices including religious propagation (*dakwah*), publicly discussing religious questions, circu-lating reformist publications from Singapore and the Middle East, and distrib-uting alms (*zakat*). During these years Muhammadiyah was highly tolerant of the fledgling Christian community. "Dahlan himself took an uncommon, and very probably unprecedented, attitude toward the Christians by successfully establishing close friendships with many of their clergymen such as Fathers van Dress and van Lies, Reverend Baker, as well as with their foremost strategists in Indonesia such as Dr. Zwemer, Dr. Laberton, and Dr. Hendrik Kraemer."[8] Historians of both Muhammadiyah and the Christian missions report that Dahlan, Baker, and Kraemer had regular meetings. Kraemer even regarded Dahlan as a friend.[9]

---

[4] Alfian (1989, 166).
[5] This overlap provides a nice reminder that even while boundaries between social identity groups are being constructed, the flow of personnel across those boundaries continues (Barth 1969, 10).
[6] Noer (1978, 76 fn. 132).
[7] Noer (1978, 74); Alfian (1989, 146–147).
[8] Alfian (1989, 160).
[9] Hallencreutz (1966, 159–162); Alfian (1989, 161 n. 42 and 43).

Friendly relations were maintained as the Christians' presence grew. In 1918, Christian missionaries began building a Bible school in Yogyakarta with support from the government. Dahlan's protégé, Hadji Fachruddin, wrote in *Sri Diponegoro* that Muslims were falling behind Christian efforts to educate their children: "If the Muslims failed to act as fast as the Christians in this field, there was a very good possibility that their future grandchildren would eventually become Christians as could easily be seen from the rapid growth of their educational system which would soon penetrate the entire society."[10] Unlike in later writings, however, at this point Muhammadiyah leaders exhibited no sign of animus toward the Christians.

That said, there is reason to be skeptical of some of this research. The writings of Muhammadiyah historians tend to glorify Dahlan's tolerance. It is not surprising that Christian missionaries would claim to have an amicable relationship with Muhammadiyah. Moreover, Dahlan copied the curriculum of missionary schools to build Muhammadiyah's educational system.[11] A skeptic might argue that Dahlan's behavior reflected intelligence gathering more than tolerance toward Christianity as an idea or Christians as a minority. Missing from the existing record are primary source documents that discuss Muhammadiyah's attitudes toward the nascent Christian community.

With that goal in mind, I obtained Muhammadiyah's bimonthly meeting notes from August 11, 1922, to November 22, 1924, from the Indonesian National Archives (INA). To my knowledge, no other scholars have utilized these materials. I will describe relevant content of these meetings in order to illustrate Muhammadiyah's tolerance toward Christians from 1912 to 1923.

According to the notes, the most significant interaction between Muhammadiyah and the Christian community occurred in 1922 in reaction to a speech by a controversial missionary, Samuel Zwemer, at a Protestant church. Zwemer is well known among historians of missions for his outspoken criticism of Islam.[12] Zwemer claimed that Islam contained both strengths and weaknesses. The strengths were the number of its followers, its system of propagation, Sufism, and equality among Muslims. The weaknesses he described were familiar to polemical literature on Islam: Muslim women were mistreated, equality in Islam was only for Muslims, and Islam permitted no freedom of thought.[13]

---

[10] Alfian (1989, 162) citing *Sri Diponegoro*, no. 17, October 28, 1918.

[11] Alfian (1989, 161).

[12] Beck (2005, 210, 218); Steenbrink (1993, 154).

[13] Sekretariat Muhammadiyah, "Minutes, August 11–12, 1922," Muhammadiyah folder 28, INA; Wilson (1952, 121). Zwemer spoke in Yogyakarta on July 24 and 26, 1922. Zwemer's biographer reports that despite the polemical character of his speech, the audience was respectful. "In a public meeting at a large church in Djokjakarta, Zwemer spoke for a full sixty minutes on *The Strength and Weaknesses of Islam*. The attention was very good and at the close a Moslem leader who had been on the pilgrimage to Mecca arose and stated that he wished to thank the speaker for pointing out the weakness of Islam and stated that he would like to have a similar meeting to point out the weakness of Christianity! On many occasions the friendly spirit of

In his conclusion, Zwemer called on Muslims to come to the truth and to follow Jesus.[14]

Muhammadiyah's response was consistent with descriptions in the previous literature. It responded by inviting Muslim leaders, Jesuit leaders, a Chinese organization, the Dutch regent, and other elites to a debate. According to notes from the following week, the debate proceeded as planned, although other sources suggested that Zwemer lacked "the courage to enter into a discussion with Dahlan."[15] Regardless, there was no evidence of a reciprocal polemic toward Christians.[16]

When Zwemer visited Yogyakarta, Muhammadiyah was acutely aware of the Christians' growing presence. In an article in the March 5/6, 1922, issue of *Suara Muhammadiyah*, the author asked rhetorically, "are there really no Muslims on Java?" because while there were eighteen schools for Christian teachers in Yogyakarta, there were none for Muslims.[17] The increase stemmed from changes in colonial government policy in 1901 when the head of the Christian Revolutionary Party, the Calvinist Abraham Kuyper, became prime minister in Holland. Thereafter, and through the administration of Colonial Minister Alexander Willem Frederik Idenburg, churches and missionaries were exempt from duties and taxes, had their salaries and travel to Indonesia paid by the state, and were provided subsidies for schools, hospitals, and orphanages. While the effects were felt in the 1920s, the roots of the change in relations between the colonial government and missionaries were in 1909 when Idenburg became a Dutch representative in Indonesia. Idenburg supported the missions with both funding and political cover.[18]

Articles in the July 1922 issue of *Suara Muhammadiyah* illustrated the pressure on Muhammadiyah. One article by Colonial Minister Idenburg stated that the Netherlands must convert the East Indies to Christianity: "If the Netherlands gives only the cultural fruits to the East Indies, it won't be enough … Christian missionaries should be deeply inserted into the world of the Eastern people, the people of Muhammad."[19] In a commentary, Fachruddin of Muhammadiyah reminded the readers of Idenburg's influence as the Minister of the Colonies and said the collaboration of Christian missionaries and the government threatened Indonesian Muslims. He called on

Moslems in the East Indies was quite in contrast to conditions in Arabia, Egypt and other predominantly Moslem areas" (Wilson 1952, 121).

[14] Muhammadiyah meeting notes, August 11–12, 1922, Muhammadiyah folder 28, INA.

[15] Boland (1982, 213 n. 102).

[16] Muhammadiyah's patience was especially remarkable because Zwemer's speech was in Javanese rather than Dutch. Zwemer's mission marked the beginning of an increase in missionary work targeting the Javanese (Beck 2005, 12).

[17] *Suara Muhammadiyah* vol. 3, 5, 11–14. See Muhammadiyah Sekretariat, "Vergadering jang kedoewa, pada hari minggoe sore," March 5/6, 1922, Muhammadiyah folder 28, INA.

[18] Noer (1978, 168–173); Steenbrink (1993, 109); van Niel (1960, 83).

[19] Alexander Willem Frederik Idenburg, "Christen dan Mohammedanen," *Suara Muhammadiyah*, Trans. Hadji Fachruddin, 3:8, August 1, 1922.

all Muslim people to fight against this threat: "In truth, the destruction and the endurance of the independence of Islam in the East Indies will depend on the power of the Muslim people.... Brothers! Remember that the Islamism of Muslim people, particularly in the East Indies, has been very long disturbed. [It will] not [be] easy for us to make it right if we don't work together to fight against the threat to Islam."[20]

Yet this pressure did not yet manifest itself with any polemic toward non-Muslims. In the same issue, Nilie Poetri (a pseudonym) wrote that Muslims offered their condolences to Catholics for the passing of Pope Benedictus XV. The pope was recognized as a spiritual guide for all mankind, and his passing as a great loss.[21]

That said, as Christian missionary activity increased, Muhammadiyah's attitudes began to sour. In 1902, there were fifty-two Christians in Yogyakarta and no schools. Between 1913 and 1933, church membership in Yogyakarta grew from 587 to 2,498. By 1931, the surrounding region of South Central Java had 131 missionary schools with 15,284 students.[22] And while Protestant and Catholic mission schools received extensive subsidies, Islamic schools either were denied support or received substantially less funding than their Christian counterparts.[23] Bias against Muslims was also manifest within the colonial administration; civil servants were overwhelmingly chosen from the Christian communities. Ropi notes, "The unfair manner in which civil servants were recruited, and the differing salaries paid to Europeans and Indonesians for the same profession, further raised the ire of the Muslim community. Of one thousand prospective employees accepted, not a single Muslim was among them. Moreover, the salary of a European clergyman was ten times higher than that of a Muslim *penghulu* [judge]."[24]

The first sign of polarization between modernist Muslims and Christians came in March 1925 at the 14th Congress of Muhammadiyah. Muhammadiyah had discovered that the Dutch governor of Yogyakarta had cut subsidies to Muhammadiyah hospitals while increasing those for Christians. Fachruddin's brother delivered a scathing criticism of the governor and the sultan of Yogyakarta, who administered the subsidy.[25] In a letter to the governor, Muhammadiyah noted:"This matter is considered by Muhammadijah as an obstacle which might hamper Muhammadijah activities, while assisting in the works of the Christians.... We as Muslims who live in a Muslim country feel disheartened to observe this situation."[26] A similar speech by the

[20] H. Fachruddin, "Christen dan Mohammedanen," *Suara Muhammadiyah*, 3:8, 1922, 9–10.
[21] Nilie Poetri, "Sampoen halit manah," *Suara Muhammadiyah*, 3:8, August 1, 1922.
[22] Sumartana (1993, 103–113).
[23] Centraal Kantoor voor de Statistiek (1931, 109, 131).
[24] Ropi (1999, 84).
[25] Alfian (1989, 209–210); Beck (2005, 17–18).
[26] Alfian (1989, 210), citing Mailrapport 569x/25, "Brief van H.B. Moehammadijah, Jogjakarta, 1925" in the Department van Kolonien, Ministerie van Binnenlandse Zaken (afschrift)

Muhammadiyah secretary claimed that the Christian missions constituted an imminent danger.[27]

In a more polemical speech, Hadji Hadjid said that Islam was the best religion and Christianity was the worst. He claimed that Christians used a Bible that had been tampered with and spread their corrupted religion all over the world. Hadjid said that Christian books were poisoning Muslim children. Beck notes, "Hadjid's argumentation can be seen as one answer to the Christian activities among the people which had been stepped up at Zwemer's advice."[28]

Soon after, the pages of *Suara Muhammadiyah* were littered with polemical tracts about Christians and Christianity. A July 1927 article stated that huge resources were being spent by missionaries trying to convert people but with little success because of Christianity's inherent shortcomings.[29] A 1928 article stated that teachers in missionary schools in East Java would go to hell.[30] There were also frequent references to 'descent' into Christianity. A 1928 article lamented how Christian missionaries manipulated Muslims into conversion.

> Many of our dearest brothers in the East Indies have fallen into Christianity. And a lot have been deceived. Christian missionaries propagate Christianity not by delving into a discussion at home or in churches, like the Muslim leaders, but with propaganda.[31]

The report from the 1929 Muhammadiyah congress echoed the idea that Christians were manipulative and Christianity inferior to Islam.

> In Manado there is an Islamic group that is attempting to spread Islam to the left and the right: [they have] already progressed to request becoming a branch of Muhammadiyah.... If God wills it they will succeed in spreading Muhammadiyah in Manado to the left and right so that it will be known by those groups who are now Christian, since [Christianity] is very much worse than Islam.[32]

The key to these passages is not that Islam is considered superior to Christianity; that is not necessarily evidence of a social cleavage. The key is the denigration of Christianity as a religion, the denigration of Christians, and the declaration of the inherent inferiority of Christianity.

After 1925, polemics appeared with increased frequency in the pages of *Bintang Islam*, a publication of Sarekat Islam by two leaders of Muhammadiyah. Themes included the denigration of Christianity as a "pagan" religion; the claim

---

["Letter from the Headquarters of Moehammadijah, Yogyakarta, 1925" in the archives of the Netherlands Department of Colonies, Ministry of Interior (transcript)].

[27] Beck (2005, 17).

[28] Beck (2005, 18).

[29] J. Drijowongso, "Masoek Islam," *Suara Muhammadiyah*, 9:1 July 30, 1927.

[30] *Suara Muhammadiyah*, "Zendings Modjowarno," 9:8, December 31, 1928.

[31] Kendal Moenawar, "Betapakah Keadaan Igama Kita Islam di Hindia Timoer," *Suara Muhammadiyah*, 9:7, December 31, 1928.

[32] Muhammadiyah (1929).

that science and Christianity were incompatible; that while early Christianity possessed truth the faith had since been corrupted; that Christianity was not a religion but a political tool for governments; that Christianity was an exclusionary religion based on hierarchical racial differences; and that churches in Europe were empty.[33] The intensity of the periodical's rhetoric is instructive for understanding the depth of the Christian/Muslim cleavage in Yogyakarta.

That cleavage was then made manifest and institutionalized in Muhammadiyah's fatwas. From 1926 to 1936, Muhammadiyah issued thirty edicts in total, including five differentiating traditional and reformist practices and seven differentiating Muslims from non-Muslims. One edict specifically differentiated Muslims from Jews and Christians; Muhammadiyah stated that while it was obligatory for Muslims to recognize the other books revealed by God and brought by the prophets Jesus and Moses, as well as the psalms of David, the final book was brought by the Prophet Muhammad. The effect here was to differentiate the Muslim community from the followers of Moses (Jews) and Jesus (Christians).[34]

Other edicts differentiated reformist and traditionalist practices. Before reformist practices gained influence, Muslims in Java adhered to legal decisions by previous jurists (*taklid*). Muhammadiyah said that although trusted past decisions were to be followed, individuals should also use their own judgment (*ijtihad*).[35] By emphasizing judgment rather than adherence to tradition, Muhammadiyah differentiated its followers from the broader Muslim community. Muhammadiyah further differentiated reformist Muslims on the question of determining the beginning and end of fasting. Before then, the dominant method used to mark the start of fasting was sighting the new crescent moon (*ru'yah*). Muhammadiyah, meanwhile, advocated the use of astronomical calculations (*hisab*).[36]

Muhammadiyah's fatwas to other Muslims were not pejorative but sought to differentiate reformist Muslims from traditionalists and Christians. They raised concerns about traditional practices but did not use pejorative language. They recognized that Christians followed other religious texts than Muslims, but did not call those texts inconsistent or polluted. Although these distinctions may seem banal on their own, their significance for understanding Muhammadiyah will become clear in comparative perspective; the differences articulated by Persis were more extensive and polemical, while NU focused on establishing differences with other Muslims and turned a blind eye to non-Muslims.

---

[33] *Bintang Islam*, "Perasaan Paham Baroe Dalam Agama Geredja," 3:6 1925; "Sepongang dari Mecca," 3:1 1925; "Perasaan Paham Baroe Dalam Agama Geredja II," 3:3 1925; "Agama Kekasihan," 3:20 1925; "Tjara-Kata Indjil dan Filosofinya," 3:16 1925; "Perasaan Paham Baroe Dalam Agama Geredja III," 3:4 1925.

[34] Muhammadiyah (1929, 10–14).

[35] Muhammadiyah (1929, 5).

[36] Muhammadiyah (1974, 291–292).

Persatuan Islam

Persis was founded in Bandung, West Java, in 1923, which was relatively late to establish an Islamic organization. By that time the nationalist party Sarekat Islam and Muhammadiyah were both well established and Sarekat Islam leader Abdoel Moeis was already making waves in Bandung by opposing Communism and warning Muslims of the threat of Christians. As with Muhammadiyah, the reformist publications *Tafsir al-Manār* and *al-Munir* provided the background for Persis' creation. In contrast to Muhammadiyah, Persis was founded in an atmosphere of polemics and polarization, which was reflected in its policies toward Islamic reformists and traditionalists, Christians, and Communists.

The first social cleavage that shaped Persis policies was the division between Communism and Islam. Abdoel Moeis was one of the early leaders of Sarekat Islam, which in 1921 split between the Communist and Islam branches with Moeis being one of the most prominent leaders in favor of expelling the Communists. Moeis continued rallying against the Communists throughout the 1920s and shaped the thinking of other Persis leaders on the incompatibility of Islam and Communism.[37] In subsequent decades, Persis would play a pivotal role in developing pointed critiques of Communist ideas, shaping collective memories of injustices committed by Communists against Muslims, and trying to develop political alliances to combat the Communist threat (see Chapter 5).

Persis was similarly influenced by the debates between traditionalists and reformists. In its early years, Persis membership included both reformists and traditionalists. Given the polarizing debates in Java, however, the organization inevitably divided with one of its most prominent leaders, Ahmad Hassan, already having been exposed to the work of Muhammadiyah and dedicated to reforming traditional Islamic practices. The organization thus split into two camps: the traditionalists in the Islamic Association (*Permoefakatan Islam*) and Persis, which declared itself officially reformist. Hassan opposed the practice of kissing the hand of another person as a sign of respect (*takbil*), and the practice of adherence to the previous jurists (*taklid*) – positions that became the policies of Persis.[38]

The final cleavage shaping Persis policies was between Christians and Muslims. This division mapped onto an ethnic division in Bandung between Sundanese and non-Sundanese. Unlike the initial members of Muhammadiyah and NU, who were ethnic Javanese, most of the early members of Persis were ethnic Sundanese. Historians of Indonesia and Christian missions have argued that the link between the Sundanese identity and Islamic identity was much closer than that between Javanese identity and Islamic identity. And unlike the

[37] Federspiel (1970, 12–13); Shiraishi (1990, 231); Wildan (1995, 28–29).
[38] Federspiel (1970, 13–14); Noer (1978, 87).

Javanese, almost no Sundanese converted to Christianity.[39] That the Sundanese were uniformly Muslim cannot explain Persis' contemporary intolerance toward Christians, but it may help to explain why the missionary activity in the Sundanese area of Bandung was unsuccessful and unwelcome. It also helps to explain why West Java became more deeply polarized than Central Java despite similar polemics; in Central Java, an overarching Javanese identity helped ameliorate the cleavages that emerged from 1923 to 1925.

Missionary activity in the Sunda region began in 1863 when the Dutch missionary organization Nederlandsche Zendingsvereening established missions in Bandung, Cianjur, Bogor, Indramau, and Cirebon. The missions had no success in the direct conversion of Sundanese and turned instead to education, health care, and the conversion of ethnic Chinese. A Sundanese-language version of the New Testament was finished in 1879 and a Christian Bible in 1891; in 1926, a new missionary, Bernard Arps, established new churches in Bandung in order to try again to convert Sundanese.[40]

Persis' principal interlocutor with the Christian missions was Mohammad Natsir, who joined Persis in 1931 but had been previously been active in the Young Muslims Union (*Jong Islamieten Bond*, JIB), a splinter group from a nationalist organization of both Christian and Muslim students that had broken apart because of the influence of Christian missionaries. Not surprisingly, JIB and Persis became home to the most anti-Christian polemics of the period.

The most polemical articles in the Persis magazine *Pembela Islam* were published in response to a 1931 article written by the priest J. J. ten Berge. Ten Berge's article called the Prophet Muhammad a 'stupid Arab' and an 'aspirant self-murderer' who abused women.

> One can see that according to Muhammad, Christians conceive of a father and a mother and a son in a sexual sense. How would it have been possible for him, the anthropomorphist, the ignorant Arab, the gross sensualist who was in the habit of sleeping with women, to conceive of a different and more elevated conception of Fatherhood?[41]

The Persis response was immediate. Along with Muhammadiyah and Sarekat Islam, Persis held demonstrations in Bandung and Surabaya. In his article "Islam, Catholicism and the Colonial Government," Natsir called for Muslims to unite to defend their religion and criticized the colonial government for prosecuting Muslims for 'hate speech' while ignoring ten Berge's screed.[42]

Elsewhere Natsir attacked Christian teaching as distorted.[43] His prompt here was not ten Berge's article, but a book by Hendrik Kraemer, *The Religion of Islam*, a controversial Christian textbook that claimed Muhammad was

---

[39] Aritonang and Steenbrink (2008).
[40] Aritonang and Steenbrink (2008, 656–657).
[41] Ropi (1999, 42); Steenbrink (1993, 118–119).
[42] Mohammad Natsir, "Islam, Katholiek, Pemerintah," *Pembela Islam* 33, 1931, 2–7.
[43] Natsir, "Ruh Suci," *Pembela Islam* 13, 1930, 5–10; Natsir (1969).

only a minor religious figure with 'human weakness' and that political alliances were behind Muhammad's choice to pray toward Mecca rather than toward Jerusalem. Kraemer equated Islam with fascism, which was similarly backward, fundamentalist, and lacking the spiritual dimension of Christianity. Without a trace of irony, Kraemer portrayed Islam as lacking respect for other faiths, in contrast to Christianity.[44]

All three social cleavages – Communist/Muslim, traditionalist/reformist, Christian/Muslim – became embedded in the early writings of Persis leaders. In contrast to those of Muhammadiyah, Persis' fatwas were more voluminous and combative. Major themes included the inconsistency of the New Testament[45] and the danger of traditional practices.[46]

While five of Muhammadiyah's fatwas differentiated reformist and traditionalist practices, twenty-one Persis fatwas addressed such differences. Three deplored the traditional practice of *tahlil*, the recitation of the phrase "La ilaaha illa 'llah" ("There is no god but God") over a dead body.[47] Other practices that Hassan condemned included performing the call to prayer to announce new births, following an previous jurist's teachings instead of those of the Qur'an and the Sunnah, raising hands when praying, and the Javanese practice of praying to saints as intermediaries. In sum, Hassan's edicts both reflected and exacerbated a cleavage between reformists and traditional Muslims.

Hassan criticized other practices besides those of traditionalists. Shia Muslims and some Hadrami Arabs, including those in Indonesia, claimed special status among Muslims due to a genealogical connection to the Prophet. Hassan argued that any group that claimed to be elevated because of their genealogy should be told that Jews, too, descended from Arabs, but were certainly not a group to emulate. Hassan also criticized the Javanese royal families; he said those who claimed to be from a royal family should be told that there is only one king, Allah.

The divisions between Persis followers and non-Muslims were equally deep. While Muhammadiyah issued seven fatwas differentiating Muslims and non-Muslims, Hassan issued seventeen such fatwas, and with far more pejorative language. Most notably, Hassan referred to polytheists as "filth"[48] while other Persis writers referred to the Christian holy books as inconsistent and distorted.

In sum, while Muhammadiyah had concerns about differentiating Christians and Muslims and appropriate practices within Islam, Persis' concerns were

[44] Ropi (1999, 86).
[45] *Al-Lisaan*, "Ruangan Kristen," 1:27, December 1935, 17; "Ruangan Kristen," 3:24 February 1936, 22–24; "Ruangan Kristen," 5:27 April 1936, 24–26.
[46] *Pembela Islam*, "I'tiqad Al-Ba 'Alawi tentang Ziarah Qoeboer," 44, March 1932, 13–16; "Itu Pertemuan 'Ulama' di Tegal," 49, 1932, 24–28; *Al-Lisaan*, "Verslag Debat Taqlied," 1:27, December 1935, 28; "Berita Nahdlatoel-'Oelama' Tentang Taqlied," 4, 1936, 28–30; "Pengarang Berita Nahdlatoel-Oelama Marah," 5, 1936, 35–36.
[47] Hassan, Ma'sum, and Aziz (2007, 215–219).
[48] Hassan, Ma'sum, and Aziz (2007, 31–32, 339–340).

more exacting, and their fatwas were more pejorative of non-Muslims. Persis'
fatwas suggest that it translated the high level of polarization in Bandung into
its interpretation of Islamic law. As we will see, this polarization had future
implications well beyond interpretations of sacred texts.

Nahdlatul Ulama

The differences between East Java and Central/West Java during the national
awakening could not have been starker. While Muhammadiyah and Persis bat-
tled Christian missionaries, a hostile colonial state, and Indonesian Communists,
the ulama of East Java faced a different challenge: Islamic reformers in Java
and the Arabian Peninsula. Noer provides an instructive summary of the forces
of polarization leading to NU's creation: "The traditionalists in Java thus felt
as if they had been attacked from two directions: in the cradle of Islam by
a new regime that had come to power, imbued with ideas which they could
not tolerate; at home by reformist ideas, which they considered to be similar
to Wahhabism and which had gained substantial ground."[49] As a result, East
Javanese Muslims were split along traditionalist/reformist lines rather than
Muslim/Christian or Communist/Muslim lines. This division shaped NU's
emphasis within the sacred texts, as will be shown in its jurisprudence, and in
its future relations with other groups.

The earliest conflict occurred when Dahlan tried to orient prayer in
Yogyakarta toward Mecca. In later years Muhammadiyah advocated other
controversial reforms including rejecting both sacrificial meals and visits to the
graves of saints. Traditionalists mounted numerous objections; Muhammadiyah
meeting notes state that Kyai Hadji Asnawi, who later formed NU, accused
Dahlan of creating his own scripture: "Dahlan considers himself God, when
after the *hijrah* [the flight of Muhammad from Mecca to Medina] there are no
more *mujtahid*."[50] Asnawi forbade the use of the name 'Muhammadiyah' by
any Islamic school.[51]

The first public confrontation took place at the 1922 meeting of the Indies
All Islam Congress (Kongres Al-Islam Hindia).[52] Asnawi and Kyai Abdul
Wahhab charged the leaders of Muhammadiyah with being non-Muslims
and polytheists. They attacked Muhammadiyah's teaching methodology,
teaching materials, and choice of religious texts.[53] The divisions deepened
in December 1924 at the Central Caliphate Committee (Centraal Comité
Chilafat) meeting. In the opening speech, the Muhammadiyah reformist Agus

---

[49] Noer (1978, 228).

[50] A *mujtahid* is a scholar who defines Islamic law for new situations.

[51] Sekretariat Muhammadiyah, "Minutes, August 28, 1922," Muhammadiyah folder 28,
Indonesian National Archives (INA).

[52] *Suara Muhammadiyah*, "Verslag oetoesan ke Cheribon perloe mengoendjoengi Al Islam congres," 3:12, November 30, 1922, 1–29.

[53] Noer (1978, 227).

Salim hailed the conquest of Mecca by Ibn Saud, a Salafi. This speech "sowed the seeds of discord in the Congress, for traditionalist Muslims saw many of their religious beliefs and practices under threat from Wahhabis ruling in Mecca."[54]

At the meeting, it was decided that a delegation of reformist and traditionalist leaders would attend a conference in Cairo that would attempt to resolve the future of the caliphate. Before their departure, however, the division between reformists and traditionalists climaxed at the August 1925 All Islam Congress. Salim again trumpeted support for Ibn Saud despite reports that the latter had destroyed tombs of traditionalists and prohibited the reading of prayers by the traditional mystic, al-Ghazali. Wahhab proposed that the delegation visit Ibn Saud after the Cairo conference to request that he tolerate traditional practices, yet his appeals fell on deaf ears.[55]

By January 1926, the traditionalist/reformist cleavage was institutionalized. Reformists sent their leaders to Mecca while traditionalists convened an alternative committee, the Committee for the Consultation about Hijaz Questions (Comite Merembuk Hidjaz), which was transformed into the Community of Nahdlatul Ulama (Jami'ah Nahdlatul Ulama) in 1926. NU's goals at the founding reflected its station: counteracting the rise of reformists in Java and remedying traditionalists' exclusion from the mission.

While conflict with reformists led to the creation of NU, its interactions with Christians were respectful. The Christians of Central/West Java were colonialists in that they worked with the Dutch government to promote their faith, their funding came from abroad, and their agenda was designed to help pacify the Islamic movements. The Christians of East Java, however, were not colonialists: their policies were often in opposition to the colonial government, their communities were built apart from Muslim ones, and their practices were coterminous with local beliefs:

> In the beginning the formation of a Christian congregation in East Java did not involve the role of a mission body, as happened in Central Java. The rather conspicuous difference was that the growth of the Christian community in East Java came at the same time as the establishment of villages that were led by Javanese Christians. They built the Christian villages on their own initiative.[56]

These villages were built by followers of Coenraad Laurens Coolen, an Indo-European preacher and dissenter from the colonial cultivation system. On multiple occasions he denied the assistant district commissioner's requests that his tenants work for the state.[57] In his services Coolen mixed local culture with Christianity and Islam. Afterward, villagers gathered for Javanese music and theater performances based on Christian themes. He even created a

---

[54] van Bruinessen (1995, 115–140).
[55] van Bruinessen (1995, 11–12); Noer (1978, 223–224).
[56] Sumartana (1993, 117).
[57] van Akkeren (1969, 57).

Christian version of the Muslim confession of faith.[58] And although this community was established apart from Muslim communities, it was not exclusive; Coolen brought in an imam to support Muslim residents.

Coolen's template for a harmonious community spread to another community, Mojowarno, which split off in 1840 and received government funding. In another illustration of the difference between East and West/Central Java, the Dutch advisor for Islamic affairs protested the funding of the Mojowarno hospital because "the European administration abused its authority by supporting the Christian missionary activities though contributions that were taken from specific Muslim sources."[59]

Another reason NU was not threatened by Christians is that they arrived late to East Java. From 1808 to 1927, there were only a few priests in Surabaya, and they engaged in little missionary work. By 1926, there were only one hundred Catholics. Not surprisingly, once the national awakening began, the Christians of East Java were marginal figures.[60] In sum, the Christian missionaries in East Java were inconsequential in their conversion efforts and respectful of the Muslims as demonstrated by patterns of community development and recognition. This respect stemmed in part from the development of the Christian community of East Java, which was distinctly Javanese and autonomous from the foreign missionaries.

NU embedded its conflicts in its Islamic jurisprudence. NU's magazine *Suara Nahdlatul Ulama* began publishing in 1927 and among its most frequent topics was the defense of practices critiqued by reformers.[61] Issue 1, number 5 defended the practice of organizing ritual meals. Issue 1, number 6 defended the schools of jurisprudence.[62] Issue 1, number 9 contained an extended polemic against Mustafa Kemal of Turkey, charging that he neglected Islam by repudiating Islamic law and replacing it with laws from Switzerland and by allowing Muslim women to act as though they were Europeans.[63] In issue 2, number 4, NU issued a polemic in response to Muhammadiyah's contention that Muslims who treated graves as sacred were apostates:

> NU believes that Muslims receive religious wisdom from the Qur'an, the Sunna and from ulama in the period of the Companions until the period of the four Imams of the *fiqh* schools. Today Muslims obey their fatwas. As a result, any knowledge that is not based on the fatwas of the four Imams is considered a new model of knowledge; *bidah* [unwarranted innovation]. This is the knowledge of Muhammad ibn Abd al-Wahhab together with his "two thumbs," Muhammad Abduh and Rasyid Ridha as well as their colleagues who consider *ziyaratu al-qobr* [visiting graveyards]

---

[58] van Akkeren (1969, 66).

[59] Aritonang and Steenbrink (2008, 715), citing Hurgronje (1959, 806–807).

[60] Sumartana (1993, 130).

[61] The magazine was published in Javanese written in Arabic script. Translations by Nur Hidayat Wakhidudin.

[62] *Suara Nahdlatul Ulama*, "Min al-Faqir Tirtorejo," 1:6, 1927 [1346], 10.

[63] *Suara Nahdlatul Ulama*, "Musthafa Kamal Kaliyan Agami Islam," 1:9, 1927 [1346], 17–18.

haram [prohibited]. However, the Prophet Muhammad made a devotional visit to Baqi'. In addition, other religious people such as Christians, Jews, and Majusi also conducted such deeds. There is only one group that hates visiting graveyards. The group is called the religion of Samin Ibn Sura Surantika. Therefore, NU regards that any people who consider visiting graveyard haram as the people who stray from the right path, and they adhere to Samin's religion.[64]

Surantika was the leader of a syncretic, pre-Islamic sect. NU's linking of Ridha, Abduh, and Wahhab to Surantika was highly pejorative.

Although the bulk of its early writing focused on reformers, NU was also aware of a growing non-Muslim population. NU was clearly wary of non-Muslims in Java and urged its followers not to become Christians or idol worshippers.[65] Yet, unlike Muhammadiyah and Persis, NU marked these differences by delineating boundaries rather than issuing polemics; NU instructed followers on wearing perfume mixed with alcohol,[66] interacting with non-Muslims,[67] and using the Dutch language.[68] One of the most difficult tests for tolerance is in matters of conversion and political power. Here, too, NU drew more on patience than polemic: "Whenever a Muslim converts into Christianity he then becomes an apostate and he should not take care of Muslims' affairs. In addition, the Muslim people have the right to ask the Dutch Governor to replace such person with another person who is Muslim."[69] NU made no calls for the convert to be punished, killed, or exiled. NU did not deride the convert as 'below' Muslims, like Muhammadiyah, or refer to Christians as filth or polytheists, like Persis.

To conclude, the social polarization behind NU's creation lay in Muslim reform in the Middle East and its echoes on Java. Ibn Saud's limitation on traditionalist practices, the growth of reformists, and the exclusion of traditionalists from the 1925 mission to the Hijaz sparked the creation of NU, while its relations with Christians were collegial. NU fatwas from the founding period focused on defending religious practices under attack by reformists. Those addressing interfaith relations were marked by the delineation of boundaries rather than polemics.

Path Dependency

The twentieth century was a tumultuous time for Indonesian Islamic organizations. Yet the cleavages that were established in West, Central, and East Java and embedded in corresponding organizations endure due to Islamic

---

[64] *Suara Nahdlatul Ulama,* "Akhbar Mutanawwi'a," 2:4 1928 [1347], 80. In response to *Suara Muhammadiyah,* "Fatsal Berhoeboengan Hidoep Dengan Jang Mati," 8:7, 1927, 198–201.

[65] *Utusan Nahdlatul Ulama,* "Penerang Bagai Hati yang Cengkal dan Bebel dengan Beberapa Ayat Qur'an yang Diakui Benar oleh Bibel," no. 1, December 1929, 9–16.

[66] *Suara Nahdlatul Ulama,* "Surat Soal Saking Banyuwangi," 2:4, 1928 [1347], 70.

[67] *Suara Nahdlatul Ulama,* "Masalah Tanah Tilas Masjid Lan Awlad al-Kuffar," 2:10, 1928 [1347], 400–401.

[68] *Suara Nahdlatul Ulama,* "Al-I'lan – Wara wara," 3:9, 1929 [1348], 186.

[69] *Suara Nahdlatul Ulama,* "Khilqa al-As'ila wa Khilqa al-Ajwiba," 3:11 1929 [1348], 218.

legal edicts discussed earlier, political alliances, and broader discursive practices. These mechanisms of path dependency have had the effect of ensuring that in the years following their founding, the attitudes of Muhammadiyah, Persis, and NU and their respective relations to Christians persisted. The result of these divergent interactions in the 1920s was that in subsequent years, Muhammadiyah, Persis, and NU would often have different reactions to the same events. They saw the same events through different eyes. Their experiences with Christian missionaries meant that Muhammadiyah and Persis would see conspiracies behind Christian activities, while NU, though wary of the same actions, saw them as part of the larger problem of proselytizing and missionizing, of which Muhammadiyah was no less guilty.

Muhammadiyah has long been hasty to accuse Christians of plotting to convert Muslims. For example, Article 177 of the Constitution of the Indies (Indische Staatsregeling [IS]) stipulated that all Christian missionary workers required special permission to work in any area of the East Indies. Until 1928, this regulation was used to forbid missionary work in certain areas such as Aceh, West Java, and Bali because the government felt these were areas with strong faiths that would react negatively to missionary activity. Catholics were particularly opposed to this article, while Protestants and Muslims were opposed to Article 178, which stated that supervision of non-Christian religions was to be carried out by regents. Muslims felt that this subjected them to restrictions from which Christians were exempt.[70] In 1928, however, Article 177 was abrogated and all of the East Indies opened to missionary activity.[71] Secular and Islamic leaders alike protested the removal of Article 177. Soekarno wrote an article against the abrogation of 177 and the admission of missionaries to Bali: "In that way we might in the future come to witness a Roman Catholic Bali, which would form a wedge between Java and the islands to the East. There is already such a Christian wedge between Aceh and Minangkabau, christened Batakland."[72] Likewise, at its congress in May 1939, the High Islamic Council of Indonesia (Madjelis Islam A'la Indonesia [MIAI]) presented a motion to reinstate Article 177 while canceling Article 178. Muhammadiyah responded to the repeal of 177 with polemics, accusing Christians of another effort at mass conversion, quoting verse 2:120 of the Qu'ran: "Never will the Jews or the Christians be satisfied with you until you follow their religion." Muhammadiyah went on: "According to God's commandment, the Christians and the Jews in each of their tactics will always go against Islam and try to convert Muslims to their religions, out of Islam. Therefore we must be careful and always be ready to stand against them, through strengthening and spreading Islam all over Indonesia."[73]

---

[70] Steenbrink (2007, 426–427).
[71] Furnivall (1944, 279).
[72] Muskens (1979, 165).
[73] *Suara Muhammadiyah*, no. 1, April 1939, 11.

NU also protested the repeal of Article 177. NU criticized the Christians for being insensitive to Muslim concerns and lamented the political weakness of Muslims. Some branch representatives of NU voted to remove both IS 177 and 178, others voted to only remove IS 178, and the rest voted for no removal at all.[74] At the same conference, NU criticized the unequal subsidies given to Christians and Muslims, which had caused such furor in Muhammadiyah. Yet NU simply asked for either equalization or a removal of the subsidies.[75] Similarly, the Wonosobo branch of NU reported an incident where a Christian was buried in a Muslim cemetery, and recommended that the congress forward a motion to the government making clear that "Muslim cemeteries are not for burying Christians."[76] Unlike Muhammadiyah and Persis, NU did not resort to polemics against Christians or Christianity.

In addition to establishing a discursive legacy in that period, Islamic organizations made political alliances that ensured continuity between the past and the present. Founded amid polemics between Christians and Muslims as well as traditionalists and reformists, Muhammadiyah allied with other reformists, including Islamists, and formed uneasy alliances with traditional Muslims. In the 1930s and 1940s, this entailed working through coalitions of traditionalist and modernist Muslims, such as the MIAI and the Consultative Council of Indonesian Muslims (Madjelis Sjuro Muslimin Indonesia, or Masyumi) in opposition to the nationalists and Christians. In the liberal democratic period of the 1950s, Muhammadiyah worked through Masyumi but found relations with traditionalists and Christians increasingly fraught, with tensions culminating in the 1952 split between traditionalists and modernist Muslims.[77] Persis, founded amid polemics between Christians and Muslims, Communists and Muslims, and traditionalists and reformists, continued promoting high levels of intolerance of both Christians and traditional Muslims in subsequent years. Although it was able to overcome its animosity to Christians in the 1950s and promoted tolerance of Christians, it reverted to hostility after its gestures to the Christians were rejected and its members banned from government (see Chapter 5).[78] And, in subsequent years, NU, founded as a response to the growth of reformists, went on to ally with Muslim reformists as well as with Christians and Communists. In the 1950s, it worked alongside the

---

[74] Nahdlatul Ulama, "Majlis ke II: Tentang Hal yang Bersangkutan dengan Pemerintah," *Verslag-Congres Nahdlatul Ulama Yang ke 14 di Kota Magelang* July 3, 1939, 48–49.

[75] NU, "Majlis ke II," 55.

[76] NU, "Majlis ke II," 57.

[77] Feith (1978 [1962]).

[78] Federspiel (1970, 179–181). In Chapter 5, I demonstrate that from 1951 to 1960, prominent Persis leaders made repeated promises to protect the religious and political rights of Christians, even by use of force if necessary. To explain the shift, it is necessary to look at the political alignments of the 1950s; the Indonesian Communist Party was growing in power, and often aligning with the secular-nationalists. In response, Natsir and Anshary appealed to the Christians to join with Muslims and form a common anti-Communist front.

Christian and Communist parties and in opposition to the Muslim reformists of Masyumi after the 1952 split.

In the 1960s, Muhammadiyah's concern with Christianization reemerged and was bolstered by its close relationship with Persis' sister movement, the Indonesian Council for Islamic Propagation (DDII). DDII was created after Mohammad Natsir was banned from public life, at which point many Persis members fled to Pakistan. Persis teachers continue to follow a similar migratory route today; they consider the Indonesian state Islamic universities too liberal and send their students to Egypt, Libya, Saudi Arabia, and Pakistan for college, taking refuge in the global Islamist movement fighting against 'Christianization.'[79] In 1963, Muhammadiyah warned its members of a conference in East Java planning to Christianize the entire country within fifty years through interfaith marriage: "Word has spread in the community regarding the result of the Christian Conference in East Java to Christianize the country, with a 20-year plan for Java and 50-year plan for the whole country. Such a decision truly is a challenge to Islam, which is now embraced by the majority of Indonesians."[80]

Relations between Muhammadiyah and Christians reached a low point in the mid-1960s when, by Alwi Shihab's estimate, 2 million Javanese abangan Muslims converted to Christianity to escape the mass killings of Communists. "For the Muslims, the church's protection of the former communists who turned Christian was an act of taking advantage of the political situation – fishing in troubled waters."[81] The recruitment strategies used by Christian missionaries allegedly included building churches in historically abangan villages and offering financial aid, educational scholarships, and protection for accused communists. A 'foster parent' system was even introduced to ease the conversion to Christianity. In response, Muhammadiyah renewed its tradition of polemics. Haji Djarnawi Hadikusomo wrote two books in 1965, *On Christology: For Internal Use of Muhammadiyah's Missionaries* (Sekitar Kristologi: Chusus untuk Muballighin Muhammadijah) and *The Old and New Testament* (Perdjandjian Lama dan Perjandjian Baru). Both books argue that Christian doctrines lack authenticity and reliability.[82] A 1964 pamphlet by Bisjron A. Wardy, *To Be Aware of Christian Activities* (Memahami Kegiatan Nasrani) alleged that Roman Catholic and Protestant churches held a conference in 1962 in order to develop a plan to convert all of Java within fifty years.[83] Lukman Harun of Muhammadiyah pointed to the Meulaboh incident

---

[79] Mustain (teacher at a Pesantren school in Bangil and vice secretary for the local chapter of Persis), interview by the author, Bangil, July 26, 2010.

[80] *Suara Muhammadiyah*, "Mempertajam Kewaspadaan Islam Tentang Berita Hasil Konferensi Katolik / Protestan Jawa Timur akan Mengkristenkan Seluruh Indonesia," no. 25, 1963, 5.

[81] Shihab (1995, 306).

[82] Shihab (1995, 308). Burhani suggests that these books were strongly influenced by Ahmadi writings (Burhani 2014, 146).

[83] Shihab (1995, 309).

of 1967 in West Aceh, where a church was erected in a community in which there were no Christians. This was also alleged to have occurred in Ujung Padang, Jakarta, Bukit Tinggi, and elsewhere.[84] In response, Harun, a member of the House of Representatives, proposed a parliamentary interpellation on July 10, 1967, urging the government to regulate the building of places of worship, methods of religious propagation, and channeling of foreign aid. "As it is evident, the whole purpose of the interpellation was specifically aimed at curbing the activities of the Christian mission in Indonesia."[85] The result was government decrees 70 and 78 of 1978.[86]

Relations between Persis, Muhammadiyah, and Christians did not improve in the 1970s. To the contrary, Persis' sister movement, DDII, sent pamphlets and intelligence about 'Christianization' to Muhammadiyah. In a 1970 letter from DDII to Muhammadiyah, accompanied by an organizational chart mapping Catholic missionary work in Central Java, Sahlan Rosjidi explained that Catholics' missionary tactics were similar to those of DDII, and included helping villagers with financial and material needs. The letter also mentioned an intelligence-gathering program whereby Muhammadiyah college students investigated a monastery in Rowoseneng, Central Java, that sold coffee and milk for low prices in an attempt to attract converts from Islam.[87]

Fear of Christianization continued in the 1970s and was made manifest through repeated polemics and reinforced with reference to news abroad. A September 1971 article in Suara Muhammadiyah criticized the Catholic practice of celibacy as unsustainable,[88] while another claimed that Christian marriages were designed to prevent adultery, rather than to build strong, loving families.[89] An October 1971 article reported that Catholics were eradicating Muslim minorities in the Southern Philippines: "And the fates of Muslim minorities in countries with a Christian majority in Asia-Africa are roughly the same. Isolated, made stupid and retarded, then suppressed and eliminated. This is what is happening in the Philippines." The author went on to draw parallels between the Phillippines, Africa, and Java: "The Christian mission is persistent and eager to undertake proselytization. They build hospitals, schools, and religious organizations and provide other forms of social services. Thus the poor Muslims become entangled in their webs. They receive education, health care, food and clothes, even sometimes money.... They

---

[84] Shihab (1995, 312, fn. 67) citing Harun (1991).
[85] Shihab (1995, 314).
[86] Keputusan Meteri Agama no 70 dan 78 tahun 1978.
[87] Sahlan Rosjidi, Surat Kepada Ketua Dewan Dakwah Islamiyah Indonesia Pusat dari Dewan Da'wah Islamijah Indonesia Perwakilan Djawa Tengah Tentang Kegiantan Kristenisasi, October 17, 1970. Muhammadiyah folder 2467, INA.
[88] Masbuchin, "Masalah Selibat Dalam Geredja Roma Katolik," *Suara Muhammadiyah*, no.18, September 11, 1971, 21.
[89] Immawan Sudidbjo Markoes, "Broken Home," *Suara Muhammadiyah*, no. 21-22, November 1-11, 1971, 9.

(Christians) have succeeded in pushing Muslims to neglect their religion."[90]
While converts from Islam to Christianity were disparaged, converts moving
in the other direction were celebrated and lauded as role models.[91] Even while
authors in *Suara Muhammadiyah* took pride in having interfaith harmony in
Indonesia, they warned the Muslim community to be vigilant against attempts
at Christianization.[92]

In the middle of the 1970s, the lens of Christianization colored nearly every
interaction between Muhammadiyah, Persis, and non-Muslims. A June 1974
article on Bali celebrated friendships and common values between Hindus
and Muslims there, while accusing Christians of offending Hindu sensibilities due to aggressive proselytization.[93] Djarnawi Hadikusama wrote a series
of articles from July through September of 1974, titled "Christianization in
Indonesia," detailing the strategies used by Christians to convert non-Muslims
and Muslims including politics, state policies, economic incentives, and social
outreach.[94] A 1973 bill in the parliament that would permit interfaith marriage
was lambasted as a veiled attempt at Christianization.[95] And, of course, a proposed 1975 conference in Jakarta of the World Council of Churches (WCC)
was decried as yet another attempt by international evangelicals to use the
guise of religious freedom and human rights to convert Muslims: "Having the
WCC conference in the capital of the Indonesian Republic, whose Muslims
represent the largest Islamic community in the whole world, can only be understood as a provocation to the Islamic world."[96]

By the mid-1970s, Muhammadiyah, Persis, and DDII had built up an elabo-
rate discursive and social infrastructure to combat the threat of Christianization.
They had also built connections with international organizations with similar
goals including the Council of Foreign Ministers of the Organisation of Islamic
Cooperation (OIC) and the Saudi Muslim World League (Rabit'at al-Alam
al-Islami), which in return channeled resources and information back to Java.
For example, Muhammadiyah forwarded its 1974 letter to Soeharto about the

---

[90] Fuad Mohammad Lathif, "Ummat Islam Philipina," *Suara Muhammadiyah*, no. 20, October 11,
1971, 10.
[91] Muhammadiyah, "Gerak Islam Indonesia: Masuk Islam," *Suara Muhammadiyah*, no. 7–8, April
1–11, 1972, 24.
[92] Natsir, H. Mohd, "Kerukunan Hidup Antar-Agama," *Suara Muhammadiyah*, no. 11, June 1,
1973, 4.
[93] Margono Puspo, "Obyek Turis Dan Da'wah," *Suara Muhammadiyah*, no. 11, June 1, 1974, 18.
[94] Djarnawi Hadikusuma, "Kristenisasi di Indonesia," *Suara Muhammadiyah*, no. 13, July 1, 1974;
Djarnawi Hadikusuma, "Kristenisasi di Indonesia", *Suara Muhammadiyah*, no. 15–16, August
1–2, 1974, 14; Djarnawi Hadikusuma, "Kristenisasi di Indonesia," *Suara Muhammadiyah*,
no. 17, September 1, 1974, 14.
[95] H. M. Rasyidi, "RUU Perkawinan," *Suara Muhammadiyah*, no. 17, September 1, 1973, 6.
[96] Muhammadiyah, "Umat Islam Indonesia Menolak Diadakannya Sidang Raya Dewan Gereja
Sedunia di Jakarta Thn. 1975. Sidang Tak Lain Hanya Manifestasi Kristenisasi," June 20, 1974,
1–18, Muhammadiyah folder 4368, INA; see also Muhammadiyah, "SR Dewan Gereja Sedunia
Mungkin Tak Jadi Di Jakarta," *Suara Muhammadiyah*, no. 15–16, August 1, 1974, 7.

WCC conference to the OIC for backing.[97] And, in 1981, the secretary general of the Muslim World League sent Muhammadiyah a list of forty-one books being published and circulated by missionaries that specifically targeted Muslims for conversion: "Keeping in mind how dangerous the Christians' methods are, the Secretary General of the Rabitha hopes that you will ask those with authority in your country to prevent the distribution of the Christianization pamphlets and books for the safety of Islamic faith. The Secretary General of the Rabitha also asks of you to send the Christianization books that have arrived in your country here, for investigation."[98] A few years later DDII forwarded to Muhammadiyah a missionary newsletter, *Focus on Christian-Muslim Relations*, published by the London-based Islamic Foundation, which was dedicated to Muslim evangelism.[99] These connections strengthened the discourse of Christianization and made sure that polemics against Christians continued long after the 1920s.

While NU was equally opposed to Christian missionary work, and especially to secular marriage, its opposition never took the form of polemics against Christians in Indonesia, polemics against the inherent flaws of Christianity in comparison to Islam, or mobilization against Christianization. In the 1990s both NU and Muhammadiyah launched banking programs for their members in cooperation with ethnic Chinese and Christian-owned banks. Kato Hisanori points to these programs, as well as the leadership of Abdurrahman Wahid of NU and Amien Rais of Muhammadiyah, as evidence of the organizations' religious tolerance.[100] Other scholars have similarly credited Wahid and Rais for pioneering a break from past policies and moving the organizations toward a more liberal future. Such claims, however, discount the power of the past in shaping the contemporary behavior of both organizations. While Rais has promoted religious pluralism, he has just as frequently demonized Chinese Indonesians and railed against Christianization.[101] And even if Rais were more consistently tolerant of Christians, it is unclear whether Muhammadiyah members would follow suit. Asyari notes that Rais' political vehicle, PAN, has been more open to non-Muslims than Muhammadiyah leaders. The chairman of South Kalimantan Muhammadiyah, Muhammad Ramli, said, "We have 100%

---

[97] Muhammadiyah, "Umat Islam Indonesia Menolak Diadakannya Sidang Raya Dewan Gereja Sedunia di Jakarta Thn. 1975. Sidang Tak Lain Hanya Manifestasi Kristenisasi," June 20, 1974, 1–18, Muhammadiyah folder 4368, INA.

[98] H. R. Soemihartono, "Foto copy surat berikut terjemahannya dari Rabithah Alam Islami – Mecca," July 9, 1981. AN Muhammadiyah folder 3351, INA.

[99] Muh Mansur, Surat bersama foto copy majalah *FOCUS on Christian-Muslim Relations*. February 23, 1984. Muhammadiyah folder 3351, INA.

[100] Hisanori (2002, 113–114, 174).

[101] Compare Stepan and Kunkler (2007) to Hefner (2000, 179, 200). Similarly, in the run-up to the 2014 presidential election Rais gave speeches about the "Jewish-Christian" threat (Persatuan Islam Facebook Page, "Umat Islam Indonesia Harus Bersiap Menghadang Kepentingan Yahudi-Nasrani di Indonesia." https://www.facebook.com/infopersis/photos/a.10150562450665 213.376342.135086215212/10152086298600213/?type=1&theater (accessed June 15, 2014)).

support for Amien Rais, but for PAN there is a slogan 'Amien Rais Yes, PAN NO' ... because PAN is an open political party in which every segment of society can join, even infidels; there are Chinese and Christians."[102]

My account of the organizations' history would not be surprising to their leaders. A 2010 book published by Muhammadiyah to mark the 100-year anniversary of its founding was titled *100 Years of Muhammadiyah: Its Mission to Prevent Christianization and Liberalization.*[103] The book is inspired by and directly builds on Alwi Shihab's 1995 doctoral dissertation, which argues that combating Christian missionary activity is central to its mission:

> We would argue that the Muhammadiyah throughout its career, from its inception to the present time, no matter what may have been the dictates or personalities of the time, has always trodden the same path. Although Dahlan used conciliation and a friendly spirit to permit him to gain his ends, and did not have a zealot's personality, he was no less firmly committed to the goals of opposing Christian penetration and building Islamic consciousness in Indonesia.[104]

In the book, articles by prominent leaders critique the introduction of liberal ideas to Muhammadiyah youth, the excessive pluralism of the democratic period, and the continued missionary work of Catholics and Protestants.[105]

The social cleavages that developed in the 1920s continue to shape Muhammadiyah's attitudes toward and relations with other groups. This outcome is neither theologically determined nor rationally calculated but is a result of local politics and path dependency from the late colonial period. Muhammadiyah today is moderately tolerant of Christians. It has organized joint political movements, has supported their rights, has employed Christian teachers in its schools and universities, and has even operated schools in which Christians are the majority.[106] Muhammadiyah leaders have also, however, engaged in polemics against Christianity and Christianization that are reminiscent of the late 1920s. While the sharp polarization of the 1920s introduced significant intolerance toward Christians within Muhammadiyah, these tensions have been partly ameliorated by a crosscutting ethnic cleavage of Javanese identity and periodic political alliance.

Similarly, Persis' policies are not a result of theology or rational calculation. Rather, they are the result of social cleavages originating in the 1920s and translated into political alliances and Islamic law. Persis today is intolerant of Christians. It publishes polemics against Christians, partners with organizations that endorse and engage in violence against Christians, opposes

---

[102] Asyari (2009, 358).

[103] Muhammadiyah (2010).

[104] Shihab (1995, 287).

[105] See chapters by M. Syukriyanto A. R. Adian Huseini, Fathurrahman Kamal, and the interview with Amien Rais, in Muhammadiyah (2010).

[106] Mu'ti and Riza Ul Haq (2009).

having Christian teachers in its schools, and criticizes Muslims who promote religious pluralism. Most recently, Persis partnered with Muhammadiyah to protest Christianization, and Persis Chair Maman Abdurrahman made clear that Muslims should not allow a non-Muslim to become the governor of Jakarta.[107] This outcome is not a product of rational decisions or global theology; rather, it reflects the sharp polarization of West Java during the period of Persis' founding and the ethnic Sundanese identity of its members, which has limited the group's appeal and made it more difficult to cooperate with other groups, even when such cooperation would advance Persis' interests.

NU still views Christians as allies against the dominance of reformist Muslims. NU's goals at its founding reflected its station: to counteract the rise of the modernists in Java and Mecca, and remedy the exclusion of the traditionalists from the mission of the Hijaz. NU's most salient concern continues to be counteracting reformists, and that means working with Christians and other groups. This goal – to counteract the Muslim reformists – is as clear from its behavior in 1926 as it is today. One of the most recent analyses of NU, Robin Bush's 2009 book, *Nahdlatul Ulama and the Struggle for Power in Indonesia*, is centered on the notion that NU's behavior during the 1980s and 1990s was driven largely by its fraught relationship with the modernists.[108] Not surprisingly, then, NU today is highly tolerant of Christians. It has good day-to-day relations with Christian elites, has organized joint movements to advance their common interests, has publicly supported Christians' rights when they have been attacked, and has not engaged in polemics against Christians. The combination of its history, crosscutting identity, and the pattern of alliance with Christians against the threat of modernist Muslims explains NU's high levels of tolerance today.

Contemporary Attitudes toward Christians

This section now returns to the survey data to show that region, ethnicity, and organizational membership continue to shape elites' attitudes toward Christians. I expect elites from East Java to be the most tolerant, followed by those from Central Java and West Java. I expect respondents with a Javanese ethnicity to be more tolerant than respondents from other ethnic groups. I expect that when other variables are controlled for, organizational membership will correlate with levels of tolerance.

---

[107] Islampos, "Persis: Jangan Sampai Jakarta Dipimpin Non-Muslim," May 25, 2014, from http://www.islampos.com/persis-jangan-sampai-jakarta-dipimpin-non-muslim-111986/ (accessed May 29, 2014).

[108] Bush (2009, 17). NU's distaste for reformism has proven useful more recently; in tours of Europe, NU leaders have recycled polemics from the 1920s against the Muslim reformist Ibn Wahab.

TABLE 3.1. *Leaders' tolerance toward Christians*

Survey Question	NU	Muhammadiyah	Persis	Sig.
Should Christians be permitted to ...				
... become the mayor in Jakarta?	52% (354)	43% (384)	17% (232)	***
... build a new church in Jakarta?	48% (357)	42% (380)	19% (230)	**
... teach in public schools?	85% (366)	85% (379)	63% (230)	**
... hold public demonstrations?	76% (364)	73% (379)	61% (231)	n/s
I would not want to live next door to a Christian.[a]	84% (366)	79% (383)	68% (231)	*

Significance (Sig.): $***p < 0.01$; $**p < 0.05$; $*p < 0.1$; n/s – not significant. The significance of the difference between group means is measured using Pearson's χ^2 tests. Percentage refers to tolerant (positive) response. Sample size is in parentheses.
[a] Percentage refers to tolerant (negative) response.

Table 3.1 describes the variation in the dependent variable. NU is the most tolerant of Christians, followed by Muhammadiyah and Persis. These quantitative indicators are consistent with the qualitative indicators mentioned.

Table 3.2 presents responses to the survey questions broken down by region and demonstrates that elites from East Java are the most tolerant of Christians, those from Central Java the second most, and those from West Java the least. The survey responses depart from this pattern only when elites consider Christians living next door. Elites from West Java are the most intolerant but the levels of tolerance in East and Central Java are similar. This result is consistent with interviews with East Java respondents, who stated that tolerance there is aided by village autonomy: "It is no problem to live in the same city as them [Christians] because that is an area that is mixed. But the village is homogenous and so more difficult."[109]

Given that Jakarta is located in West Java, does the difference between regions on questions related to Jakarta stem from the respondents' not wanting Christians in their backyard? If so, then questions about Christians in other areas should not produce the same gap. Yet this pattern is also present when elites consider Christian mayors in Banda Aceh (Sumatra) and Manado (Sulawesi).

To assess the relationship between ethnicity and levels of tolerance toward Christians, I used the results from a question in which respondents self-identified their ethnicity. I expect that Javanese will be more tolerant than Sundanese. This relationship should hold when I examine other ethnic groups

[109] Author interview with Syamsul Maarif, Bangil, East Java, July 19, 2010.

TABLE 3.2. *Leaders' tolerance toward Christians, by region*

Survey Question	East Java (n = 182) (%)	Central Java (n = 131) (%)	West Java (n = 293) (%)	Sig.
Should Christians be permitted to ...				
... hold public demonstrations?	81	77	68	***
... build a new church in Jakarta?	49	40	24	***
... teach in public schools?	90	83	72	***
... become the mayor in Jakarta?	48	45	25	***
... become the mayor in Manado?	77	74	60	n/s
... become the mayor in Banda Aceh?	23	16	9	**
I would not want to live next door to a Christian.[a]	84	84	74	**

Significance (Sig.): $***p < 0.01$; $**p < 0.05$; $*p < 0.1$; n/s – not significant. The significance of the difference between group means is measured using Pearson's χ^2 tests. Percentage refers to tolerant response.
[a] Percentage refers to tolerant (negative) response.

that are uniformly Muslim: Malays, Minagkabau, Madurese, Bugis, Banjar, and Acehnese. The results confirm my expectations. Table 3.3 describes attitudes of Javanese, Sundanese, and other uniformly Muslim ethnic groups.

To control for other factors that might explain the varying levels of tolerance, I created three ordered logit regression models with an aggregate of three questions as the outcome variable: respondent's willingness to allow Christians to demonstrate, become president, and live next door. This dependent variable is similar to those used in other survey research studies of tolerance.[110] For each question, a tolerant response was coded as 1 and an intolerant one as −1, and the combined scale ranged from −3 to 3.

Key independent variables include ethnicity and organizational membership. I expect Javanese ethnicity to be associated with tolerance and Sundanese ethnicity to be associated with intolerance or not significant. The reference group is respondents who did not specify Sundanese or Javanese as their ethnicity ($n = 552$). For organizations, I expect Persis members to be consistently the most intolerant, followed by Muhammadiyah members, with NU members as the reference group.

Control variables include threat, contact with non-Muslims, age, and income. Threat is among the most reliable predictors of intolerance. From South Africa to Russia to the United States, respondents who feel that their lives or welfare are threatened are unlikely to be tolerant.[111] The same should

---

[110] Marquart-Pyatt and Paxton (2007, 89–113); Weldon (2006, 331–349).
[111] Anderson and Fetner (2008, 942–958); Gibson and Gouws (2001, 1067–1090).

TABLE 3.3. *Leaders' tolerance toward Christians, by ethnicity*

Survey Question	Javanese (n = 263) (%)	Sundanese (n = 185) (%)	Other Uniformly Muslim Ethnicities (n = 80) (%)	Sig.
Should Christians be permitted to ...				
... demonstrate in Jakarta?	83	66	68	***
... build a church in Jakarta?	51	22	35	***
... teach in public schools?	88	71	79	*
... become the mayor in Jakarta?	51	20	40	***
I would not want to live next door to a Christian.[a]	84	77	76	**

Significance (Sig.): ***p < 0.01; **p < 0.05; *p < 0.1; n/s – not significant. The significance of the difference between group means is measured using Pearson's χ^2 tests. Percentage refers to tolerant response.

[a] Percentage refers to tolerant (negative) response.

be true in Indonesia, where those who report that Christians threaten their way of life are more likely to be intolerant.

Conversely, contact is a good predictor of tolerance.[112] Contact with non-Muslims forces individuals to acknowledge religious diversity and increases the likelihood of intergroup cooperation. I expect that those who have frequent contact with non-Muslims are more likely to be tolerant, and those who never or rarely have contact with non-Muslims are more likely to be intolerant. The reference group is those with some contact with non-Muslims. Existing scholarship has not agreed on a clear relationship between wealth and tolerance.[113] I expect the influence of age on tolerance to be a function of cohort experience.[114] Younger elites are likely to be more influenced by the democratization movement that crossed religious lines. Respondents under age forty are more likely to be tolerant, while respondents over fifty are more likely to be intolerant relative to the reference group (those over sixty years old). Results are reported in Table 3.4.

The results confirm my expectations. Controlling for other factors, membership in Persis is correlated with the most intolerance, followed by Muhammadiyah, in comparison to NU. Javanese ethnicity is strongly related to tolerance while Sundanese ethnicity is associated with neither tolerance nor

[112] LeVine and Campbell (1972); Tessler (1978, 359–373).
[113] Gibson (1992b, 346).
[114] Wilson (1996, 253–274).

TABLE 3.4. *Three ordered logit models of tolerance toward Christians with organizational and ethnic variables*

Variable	Model 1	Model 2	Model 3
Membership: Persis	−0.964***	−0.993***	−0.991***
	(0.213)	(0.203)	(0.201)
Membership: Muhammadiyah	−0.575**	−0.555**	−0.453**
	(0.191)	(0.172)	(0.170)
Ethnicity: Javanese	0.574***	0.567***	0.671***
	(0.152)	(0.149)	(0.146)
Ethnicity: Sundanese	0.0265	0.130	0.255
	(0.184)	(0.180)	(0.176)
Threatened by Christians	−1.461***	−1.480***	−1.455***
	(0.166)	(0.160)	(0.159)
Frequent Contact with Non-Muslims	0.473**	0.333**	0.433**
	(0.171)	(0.166)	(0.163)
No/Rare Contact with Non-Muslims	−0.316	−0.383	−0.328
	(0.244)	(0.238)	(0.236)
Income: <$44 per month	−0.493	0.139	
	(0.408)	(0.361)	
Income: $44–$110	−0.0150	0.220	
	(0.290)	(0.236)	
Income: $110–$330	0.391	0.605**	
	(0.258)	(0.198)	
Income: $330+	0.472*	0.649**	
	(0.265)	(0.203)	
Age: <40	1.220***		
	(0.228)		
Age: 40–50	0.923***		
	(0.182)		
Age: 50–60	0.484**		
	(0.195)		
N	907	1,000	1,000

Note: Standard errors in parentheses.
***$p < 0.001$; **$p < 0.05$; *$p < 0.10$.

intolerance. As the historical material suggests, Persis, born in West Java, is strongly intolerant, whereas Muhammadiyah's intolerance is somewhat ameliorated by its predominantly Javanese membership. As the literature on tolerance suggests, I find that threat is a strong and consistent predictor of intolerance, frequent contact with non-Muslims is associated with tolerance, and never or rarely having contact with non-Muslims is associated with intolerance. Higher income appears to be related to increased tolerance although the relationship is inconsistent, and younger elites tend to be more tolerant than older elites.

Conclusion

This chapter traced the origins of three Muslim organizations' relations with Christians to social cleavages that developed in the early twentieth century. Differing kinds of colonial, missionary, and reformist Muslim activity led to social cleavages that were translated into organizational policies and have endured in contemporary attitudes. Beyond Indonesia, an unexplained puzzle in studies of religious movements is why Islamists vary in their relations with other groups: even across similar theologies, some fight other religious groups while others work cooperatively. This chapter suggests that the local origins and historical interactions of religious organizations are crucial for understanding their subsequent behavior.

This argument also provides a framework for understanding the causal role that ideas play in the behavior of religious actors. Contemporary scholars of religion are divided between those who think that ideas are always salient[115] and those who argue that ideas are largely epiphenomenal to behavior.[116] I demonstrate that ideas do matter, but not always and not only religious ones. Regardless of the actor, I suggest that a religious organization's local and historical origins are central to explaining its behavior.

[115] Philpott (2007).
[116] Kalyvas (1996, 2000).

4

Godly Nationalism

In Islamic jurisprudence it is said that one of the duties of the state is *hirasatud-din wa siyasatud-dunya*: guarding religion and managing the world. Guarding religion from the people who would tarnish, damage, and destroy it. In Indonesia, there is religious freedom but there cannot be freedom to blasphemy religions that are followed by other citizens, either by harassment, damaging the existing teachings, or by activities that give rise to social conflict as was done by the deviant sects.

Maman Abdurrahman, Chair of Persatuan Islam (Persis)[1]

Since the fall of President Soeharto in 1998, Indonesia has played host to a curious form of internecine conflict: Islamist vigilante groups have been attacking members of a small, socially marginal Muslim sect called Ahmadiyah. Ahmadiyah is a controversial sect with followers around the globe. Many Sunni Muslims charge that Ahmadis are not true Muslims due to their belief that their founder, Mirza Ghulam Ahmad, was a prophet. The vigilantes claim that Ahmadiyah is damaging Islam by propagating the belief that another prophet came after Muhammad and have dubbed Ahmadiyah a 'deviant sect,' invoking a 1965 presidential decree that demands all Indonesians adhere to one of the six religions sanctioned by the state: Islam, Protestantism, Catholicism, Hinduism, Buddhism, and Confucianism. For over ten years, the pillars of Indonesian democracy – the state, the police, and Muslim civil society – have been either unwilling or unable to stop the attacks.

---

[1] Mahkamah Konstitusi Republik Indonesia, 2010. *Risalah Sidang Perkara Nomor 140/ PUU-VII/2009: Perihal Pengujian Ungang-Undang Nomor 1 Tahun 1965 Tentang Penyalahgunaan dan/atau Penodaan Agama Terhadap Dasar Negara Republic Indonesia Tahun 1945* [Constitutional Court for the Republic of Indonesia, Transcript no. 140/puu-vii/2009 Concerning the Examination of Act No. 1 of 1965 Presidential Decree on the Abuse and/or Blasphemy against Religion based on the 1945 Constitution of the Republic of Indonesia (hereafter "Court transcript")], no. 140/puu-vii/2009, VI, 70–73.

What explains the prolonged violence toward Ahmadiyah?[2] What, if anything, is significant about the targeting of Ahmadis? The leading explanation treats the attacks as a product of democratization, decentralization, and the influence of small but vocal vigilante groups such as the Islamic Defender's Front (FPI) and Hizb ut-Tahrir Indonesia, which use the issue to gain public support. As the International Crisis Group (ICG) explained, "With the advent in 2005 of direct local elections including at the district level, hardline groups have found it expedient to lobby locally for policy changes, from banning alcohol to closing Ahmadiyah mosques."[3] Human rights advocates have lambasted the state for bowing to pressure from these hardline groups. Against US secretary of state Hillary Clinton's lauding of Indonesia for its democratic transition, longtime human rights advocate Andreas Harsono branded Indonesia 'no model for Muslim democracy' due to the state's unwillingness to protect religious minorities.[4]

This explanation for intolerance toward Ahmadiyah is consistent with assumptions about the moderate character of Islam in Indonesia and the secular state; scholars have long argued that in contrast to Middle Eastern states, in the world's largest Muslim-majority country Islamist movements have failed to find a foothold.[5] For example, the historian Robert Elson asserts that Islam exerted little influence on Indonesian politics before independence in 1945 and thereafter remained "marginalized and relatively unimportant in a political sense" and "greatly overshadowed by a form of political thinking usually called 'secular nationalism.' "[6] Yet this assumption is not supported by empirical data. Contemporary surveys with leaders of Muslim civil society suggest that rather than being tolerant toward Ahmadis, an overwhelming majority believes Ahmadis should not be allowed to hold public office, build houses of worship, or teach Islamic studies.[7] Those same leaders, however, believe

---

[2] While there were similar instances of violence toward minority Christians and Shi'ites during this period, the attacks on Ahmadiyah members were more enduring and departed from the trend of decreasing ethnic conflict since 2003. My tabulation of acts of physical violence against Ahmadiyah members from 2002 to 2006 shows a peak in 2005, with nineteen incidents, and a low of two incidents each in 2003 and 2004. The Setara Institute's list of 'acts of intolerance' for 2007–2012 extends beyond violence to include polemics, municipal regulations restricting religious freedom, and 'state inaction' in preventing violence. Setara's data show a rise in such acts in 2008 and 2011, with a low in 2007. My data are compiled from *Koran Tempo, Bisnis Indonesia, Republika, Gatra.com, Jakarta Post, Suara Karya, Media Indonesia, Suara Pembaruan, Kompas, Detik.com*, and *Riaupos.com*. See also Varshney, Panggabean, and Tadjoeddin (2004).

[3] ICG (2012, 10; 2008); Human Rights Watch (2013).

[4] Harsono (2012).

[5] Hefner (2000); Mietzner (2009); Pringle (2010); Mujani and Liddle (2009). The 'greening' period of the state, from 1988 to 1992, and a current campaign of 'stealth Islamization' are considered exceptions. Liddle (1996); Pepinsky, Liddle, and Mujani (2010). For an alternative account, see Laffan (2011).

[6] Elson (2009b, 106).

[7] Seventy-five percent of Muhammadiyah leaders and 59 percent of NU leaders said that no Ahmadiyah member should be allowed to become the mayor in Jakarta. Eighty percent of Muhammadiyah leaders and 67 percent of NU leaders said that Ahmadiyah members should

that Christians and Hindus should be permitted greater religious and political freedom (see Chapter 6). Ahmadiyah, it would seem, marks the boundary of Indonesia's much-lauded "generally tolerant brand of Islam."[8]

Nor is intolerance toward Ahmadis a recent by-product of democratization; it preceded the establishment of the state in 1945 and continues to reflect its policies. The first closing of an Ahmadiyah mosque in Indonesia was by order of the Regent of Batavia in 1936.[9] Leading Muslim organizations deemed Ahmadiyah heretical in the 1920s and 1930s, and in 1980 and 2005 the quasi-governmental Indonesian Council of Ulamas (MUI) and its regional bodies issued fatwas against the sect.[10] Municipal and provincial government bans on Ahmadiyah occurred throughout the 1970s, 1980s, and 1990s.[11] According to the Ministry of Religion (MORA), religion is a privileged category, and mystical movements such as the Javanese *kepercayaan* and heterodox movements such as Ahmadiyah have long been refused recognition.[12] Despite claims to being a 'secular democracy,' the state is fully involved in the firm demarcation of religious orthodoxy.

In this chapter, I suggest an alternative reading of intolerance of Ahmadiyah by excavating overlooked aspects of the tangled relationship between religion and nationalism. I suggest that the privileging of religious orthodoxy and the truncated pluralism of the Indonesian state constitute a theoretically neglected form of religious nationalism that I dub 'godly nationalism.' The term 'religious nationalism' is usually invoked as a conceptual placeholder for particular instances of Jewish, Islamic, Hindu, Christian, or Buddhist nationalism. Yet in demanding that citizens believe in God, while being ambivalent as to which path to God they should choose, Indonesia's brand of nationalism is exclusively religious though not particular.

I theorize godly nationalism as an imagined community bound by a common, orthodox theism and mobilized through the state in cooperation with religious organizations in society.[13] As long as citizens believe in one of the state-sanctioned pathways to God, they become full members of civil society and receive state protection and other benefits of citizenship. Conversely, the advocacy of disbelief is actively discouraged; not only are disbelievers thought incapable of ethical behavior, they are thought to make belief in God more difficult for the rest of society by confusing true beliefs with false ones, propagating falsehoods, and undermining religious education. For a godly nation to endure, it must privilege some beliefs and prosecute acts of deviance as blasphemy.

---

not be allowed to build a house of worship in Jakarta. Eighty-eight percent of Muhammadiyah leaders and 82 percent of NU leaders said that Ahmadiyah members should not be permitted to teach Islamic studies in public schools.

[8] Rogers (2012).
[9] *Al-Lisaan* 5, 1 (April 27, 1936): 38.
[10] Crouch (2009); Menchik (2007).
[11] Crouch (2009, 10–12).
[12] Abalahin (2005, 127); Mulder (1978, 5–6, 109).
[13] Orthodoxy is locally and temporally defined. Asad (1986).

Like other forms of nationalism, Indonesia's godly nationalism is a product of specific practices; I demonstrate that the persecution of heterodox and liminal faiths brings together groups that are otherwise at odds due to differences in religious doctrine, political interests, or economic class. In that respect, the answer to my question, 'What, if anything, is significant about the targeting of Ahmadis?' is that intolerance and nation building are part of a mutually constitutive process. The campaign against Ahmadiyah is part of a broader effort by civil society and the state to constitute the nation through belief in God. In that respect, contemporary intolerance to Ahmadiyah is merely the most recent manifestation of a long-standing effort to promote godly nationalism while dislodging secular or Islamic alternatives.

Indonesia is not the only country to host debates over belief in God, religious freedom, and blasphemy. In one prominent case, the High Court of Egypt convicted a professor of Arabic language and literature, Nasr Hamid Abu Zayd, of apostasy on the grounds that he was no longer a Muslim because he supported liberal ideas. The international human rights community decried the verdict against Abu Zayd as an affront to freedom of religion, and labeled his accusers "intellectual terrorists."[14] Such accusations of ideological intolerance are often read backward into debates over blasphemy. Yet focusing on the ideological origins of intolerance overlooks the productive, community-forming practices that acts of exclusion make possible. I suggest that the debates over blasphemy are an attempt to affirm (by Muslim civil society) or disrupt (by liberals) norms and laws that help constitute the nation through belief in God. While highlighting the productive effects of intolerance may be normatively discomforting to scholars, ignoring the results of intolerance means misunderstanding a long-standing and perhaps increasingly common form of nationalism.

In the next section I describe the trajectory of scholarship on religion and nationalism to highlight overlooked areas. Two empirical sections on 'Productive Intolerance' that follow focus on the key events in twentieth-century Indonesia to illuminate the coming together that the exclusion of heterodoxy enables: the first explores primary-source archival material on the history of Ahmadiyah and its relation to early state formation. The second section shows how godly nationalism was institutionalized in 1965, and then draws upon ethnographic observations from the most important court hearing on religion and politics during Indonesia's post-1998 democratic period. I conclude the chapter by drawing parallels to other cases.

Nationalism and Religion

Studies of nationalism in the postcolonial period overwhelmingly rely on Benedict Anderson's definition of an "imagined political community – and

---

[14] Johansen (2003).

imagined as both inherently limited and sovereign."[15] Anderson argues that beginning with the French Revolution and print capitalism, groups of people began to see themselves as connected with other people through their linguistic and cultural practices. Nationalism developed slightly differently in postcolonial states: secular schools created an educated indigenous upper class; the census created categories of racial groups with which to organize formal political institutions; maps defined the nation's political boundaries, along which narratives of conquest and control were woven; and museums manufactured the archaeological truths of the nation.[16]

Anderson's conception of modern nationalism has been criticized for ignoring religion. In an influential early critique, Peter van der Veer suggested religious practice and discourse may be a constitutive part of national identity rather than epiphenomenal or a smokescreen for hoary political interests. He focused on everyday practices, including conversion, pilgrimages, and the deployment of religious symbols, to argue that the activities that underpin nationalism are dynamic rather than a relic of colonialism.[17]

Since the late 1990s, accounts of religion and nationalism that emphasize hybridity and fluidity have become dominant and, in doing so, have challenged the secularity of core concepts in political theory.[18] Drawing on a comparison of Asian and European nationalism, van der Veer and Hartmut Lehmann suggest that hybridity is not the exception but the norm.[19] Van der Veer moreover suggests that the modern subject is produced alongside the modern public, and both are infused with religion. Likewise, in critiquing the history of nationalism, Partha Chatterjee suggests that classical nationalist historiographies often hide the religious solidarities that underpin national loyalties.[20]

While the first generation to rethink religion and nationalism crossed religious lines, the second generation has drawn its inspiration more from the Muslim world. Talal Asad built on his earlier work on the anthropology of Islam by arguing that the social solidarities of the Muslim *umma* (community) neither mimic nor compete with nationalism, since the modern community is theologically rather than territorially defined, self-governing rather than unified by an overarching political unit, and produced through embodied ritual rather than the formal institutions of the modern state.[21] Asad's student, Charles Hirschkind, echoed van der Veer in suggesting that the ethical

---

[15] Anderson (2003, 6).

[16] Anderson (2003, 163–185).

[17] van der Veer (1994).

[18] There are important exceptions. Juergensmeyer relies on a Geertzian conception of religion and a Weberian approach to politics to suggest that these two totalizing aspects of culture are in perpetual competition. See Gellner and Smith for parallel accounts of how religion constitutes nationalism. Juergensmeyer (1995); Gellner (1983); Smith (2003, 2008).

[19] van der Veer and Lehmann (1999).

[20] Chatterjee (1999); Marx (2003).

[21] Asad (2003).

sensibilities cultivated by modern religious movements redefine the boundaries between public and private, religious and secular. In doing so, religious movements return religious authority to the public sphere but do not undermine nationalism.[22]

Like Hirschkind and van der Veer, Lisa Wedeen focused on everyday practices rather than formal doctrine or nationalist historiography. She argued that nationalism is no more static than any other aspect of culture. Drawing on the synthesis of theological and nationalist imagining in the Yemenese newspaper *al-Īmān*, Wedeen persuasively argued against teleological conceptions of secularism as either following religious nationalism or competing with it.[23]

In parallel to these advances on Anderson's conception of nationalism, scholars of Indonesia have developed sophisticated alternative visions. Among the more underappreciated theoretical critiques of Anderson is Michael Laffan's 2003 book *Islamic Nationhood and Colonial Indonesia*, which maps the writings of Muslims from Southeast Asia who studied in the Hijaz and Cairo during the late nineteenth century. Once abroad, Laffan found that members of the emergent Indonesian Muslim *ecumene* felt a heightened sense of belonging to Muslim Southeast Asia, and upon their return their periodicals *al-Imam* and *al-Munir* were instrumental in forming a sense of community.[24] The subtitle of *al-Imam*, "The Voice of Indies Muslims Who Love Their Religion and Their Homeland," captures the reformers' overlapping commitments.[25] Rather than working against nationalism, Laffan suggests, Islamic reform played a key role in the imagining of the *Indonesian* umma.

More recently, Chiara Formichi and Kevin Fogg, though they emphasize the repeated failures of Islamists in national politics since the 1950s, have shown how religious and national commitments can be coterminous. While Elson claims, "Islamist ideas were late in emerging in modern Indonesia, and long remained marginal to Indonesians' ideas of what their nation should be and do,"[26] Formichi shows how, in fact, pan-Islamic and then Indonesian Islamic nationalist ideals endured beyond the late colonial period in the writings of the influential leader of *Darul Islam*, Kartosuwiryo.[27] On the grassroots level, Fogg reveals how pious Muslims experienced the 1945 revolution as an explicitly Islamist struggle, even while their leaders in Jakarta were hopelessly fractured by theology, political practice, and an inability to pass their legislative agenda.[28] Fogg, Formichi, and Laffan demonstrate that Islamism was crucial to the coming together of the Indonesian nation, and thus provide a vital historical corrective to Anderson's vision of the triumph of secular nationalism.

---

[22] Hirschkind (2001).
[23] Wedeen (2008, 9–14); Brubaker (2004).
[24] Laffan (2003, 176).
[25] Laffan (2003, 18).
[26] Elson (2010, 328).
[27] Formichi (2010, 2012).
[28] Fogg (2012).

That said, insofar as Fogg, Formichi, and Laffan delegate religious nationalism to the dustbin of history or the geographic and intellectual periphery of national politics, these advances are incomplete. As I will show, Indonesian nationalism continues to be rooted in religious solidarities even while it is not an Islamic state. My argument challenges scholarly conceptions of the triumph of the 'secular' state and the failure of its counterpart, the Islamic state, by mapping the genealogy of the godly state and its concurrent practices.[29]

As Indonesian politicians often point out, the Pancasila state is not secular. Pancasila is the basis of Indonesian national ideology; its five principles are belief in God, humanitarianism, national unity, social justice, and democracy as expressed through representatives of the people. In the 1950s, both secular nationalists and Islamists saw Pancasila as an alternative to Islamic nationalism. In the 1970s, Soeharto made it the ideological pillar of the regime and forced civil society organizations to pledge their allegiance to it. In the 1980s, opponents of the regime articulated a diverse set of goals employing the language of Pancasila. In a thoughtful text, Douglas Ramage described this hybridity and embraced Pancasila as supportive of nation building and democratization, and a bulwark against an Islamic state.[30] Yet Ramage ignores the place of heterodox faiths and the inherent limits of tolerance in a state that makes belief in God obligatory while defining religion narrowly. He celebrates the non-Islamic aspect of Pancasila but ignores the nonsecular element. Similarly, Saiful Mujani and R. William Liddle tweak the definition of secular actors so as to include those who identify with Pancasila and its demand that adherents possess "belief in the one high God."[31] Like Ramage's view, this surprising redefinition is made possible by the endurance of a false binary between Islamic and secular nationalism. Since Pancasila is not Islamic, the reasoning goes, it must be secular.

Luthfi Assyaukanie, however, provides a hint of a middle category by delineating three 'models' of state-Islam relations. The first is an Islamic democratic state governed by Islamic law. The second is a secular liberal democratic state. The third model is a religious democratic state. Importantly, in differentiating the religious democratic state from the liberal democratic state, Assyaukanie notes that followers of heterodox faiths are not recognized in the former.[32] Yet Assyaukanie's sympathies are with the liberals and, as a result, he does not discuss the limits of his third model. This is likely deliberate, since making the state secular and liberal would demand a radical restructuring of Indonesian nationalism.

[29] See, for example, Mujani and Liddle (2009); Salim (2008). Similarly, Anderson's most recent statement on Indonesian nationalism celebrates the unifying, productive power of secular nationalism against regional and ethnic particularism. His only mention of religion pejoratively links it to the mass killings of Indonesian Communist Party members in 1965–1966 (Anderson 1999, 10).

[30] Ramage (1995).

[31] Mujani and Liddle (2009, 577–578).

[32] Assyaukanie (2009, 155–158).

In what follows, I build on the work of van der Veer, Asad, Wedeen, Laffan, and Assyaukanie to argue that Indonesia contains a form of nationalism that is neither Islamic nor secular, but rather exclusively and assertively religious. Active state support for religion did not die in 1945 with the failure of the Jakarta Charter and the state's embrace of Pancasila, or in 1952 with the rejection of Islamic law, or in 2002 when the parliament again rejected the incorporation of Islamic law into state law, or with the repeated failures of Islamists in electoral competition despite moderation of their demands. Rather, the privileging of religion is made manifest through state support for religious orthodoxy over liminal and heterodox faiths.

I define godly nationalism as an imagined community bound by a common, orthodox theism and mobilized through the state in cooperation with religious organizations in society. Godly nationalists feel that belief in God is a civic virtue that accrues both individual and social benefits. For individuals, belief in God brings an enlightened understanding of the world that is preferable to premodern beliefs such as animism, heterodox beliefs, or secular worldviews. Individuals who believe in God are seen to be wiser, more compassionate, generous, and tolerant. The archetype of a good citizen is one who believes in God and uses that belief to motivate his or her behavior. Likewise, social and political institutions are thought to perform better if individuals working within them believe in God.

Although belief in God is a goal for good citizens, it is not necessarily based on coercion. Godly nationalism may be formally established by the state and coercively enforced by the police, bureaucracy, and courts, such as through personal status laws based on religious principles and limits on individual freedom. Alternatively, godly nationalism may be informally policed though social norms, religious organizations, media, and the family. Regardless of the degree to which godly nationalism is enforced, belief in God is seen as a virtue that should be promoted through education, ethical guidance, and social norms. A godly nation limits individual freedoms so as to ensure that disbelievers do not tarnish, damage, or destroy the world's religions.

Godly nationalism should not be construed with being compatible with but contrary to secular nationalism, as Hirschkind and Asad contend is the case with religious nationalism. Rather, godly nationalism occupies one middle position between religious and secular nationalism. Nor does this make Indonesia an example of the ambiguity that accompanies modern secularism. In contrast to religious nationalism, godly nationalism is plural; the state promotes belief in God through multiple religions. In contrast to secular nationalism, godly nationalism is predicated on theological rather than geographic or ethnic exclusion; liminal groups, heterodox groups, and nonbelievers are denied the full benefits of citizenship. While Hussein Agrama's astute reading of Egypt suggests that the blurring of the religious and the secular serves the expanding regulatory capacity of the modern state, I detail an alternative that does not necessarily move toward either liberal secularism or theocracy.[33] Godly nationalism is also distinct from Robert Bellah's "civil religion."[34] The state is not the focus of worship in godly nationalism; it is rather the conduit for religious belief, guiding its citizens toward proper faith and behavior.

In the next section, I delve into key events in the history of religion and politics in Indonesia to flesh out the argument that godly nationalism is an overlooked form of nationalism, in which intolerance toward heterodoxy constitutes the nation. I show that the earliest contacts between Ahmadiyah representatives and Muslim organizations were respectful but soured quickly, culminating in Ahmadiyah's exclusion from membership in the country's first important Muslim political coalition. This act of exclusion helped to congeal the fractious Muslim groups and contributed to the institutional foundation for the postcolonial state, thereby demonstrating the productive power of exclusion for generating solidarity in the emergent nation.

Productive Intolerance, Part I

Ahmadiyah is a small Muslim sect that originated in Qadian, South Asia, in the late nineteenth century and spread to Sumatra and Java in the 1920s. The movement's founder, Mirza Ghulam Ahmad, was a controversial figure who made two claims that ran counter to mainstream Sunni doctrine. First, against the Sunni Muslim belief that the prophet Jesus had not died a natural death but had been taken from the earth by God and would return to earth on Judgment Day, Mirza Ghulam Ahmad held that Jesus had died a natural death and could not return. His second, related claim was that he was the Mahdi, the prophesied messiah of Islam heralding Judgment Day.[35]

From 1923 to 1929, Ahmadiyah and the leading Islamic reform movement, Muhammadiyah, were able to work together based on a shared commitment to Islamic modernism.[36] After 1925, however, Muhammadiyah leaders began to ask whether these two Ahmadiyah beliefs – that Jesus died a natural death and that Ghulam Ahmad was a prophet or 'renewer' – were sufficiently deviant to be considered non-Muslim.[37] In 1928, Muhammadiyah's central board

---

[33] Agrama (2010b).

[34] Bellah (1975).

[35] The two factions of Ahmadiyah Indonesia – Qadiani and Lahore – are seen as differing on the question of the finality of the prophethood of Muhammad. Qadiani Ahmadis believe that Ghulam Ahmad was a prophet who came after Muhammad. Lahoris believe that Ghulam Ahmad was a renewer (*mujaddid*) of Islam (Beck 2005; Pijper 1992).

[36] Ali (1925); Beck (2005); "Noeroellah dan Peradaban Moeslimin Oleh S.J. Hasan," *Suara Muhammadiyah* 8 (1927): 349–350; "Ma'loemat dari Hoofdbestuur Moehammadijah," *Suara Muhammadiyah* 10 (1928): 33; and "Poeteosan Congres 1928," *Suara Muhammadiyah* 10 (1928): 34.

[37] Ichwan notes that a translation and exegesis of the Qur'an by Ahmadi leader Maulvi Muhammad Ali was condemned by Rasyid Ridha for distorting verses to claim revelation for Ghulam Ahmad and for being a literal translation of a text that should be read in the original Arabic. While the

declared that, because Ahmadis believed in a prophet after Muhammad, it would be forbidden to teach the views of Ahmadiyah, and the next year the religious council proclaimed that members of any group that believed in a prophet after Muhammad were unbelievers.[38] After the split, Ahmadis became objects of ridicule and were removed from their positions in Muhammadiyah.[39]

Similarly, Persis underwent an evolution from embracing to repudiating Ahmadiyah. From 1930 into 1931, Persis extolled Ahmadis as leaders of Islamic reform, promoted their founding principles, circulated speeches from the Ahmadiyah Lahore congress,[40] and published letters from Muslims who had been tempted to convert to Christianity but were 'reclaimed to Islam' by Ghulam Ahmad.[41] In June 1931, however, Persis leader Ahmad Hassan published a critical study of Ahmadis, which examined whether they believed that Muhammad was the final prophet.[42] Ghulam Ahmad's claim to prophethood rested on the notion that other prophets could be sent by God to reform religion.[43] Ahmad Hassan followed up by challenging the Ahmadiyah Qadian to three nights of public debate in which he interrogated Ahmadiyah representatives on whether the prophet Jesus had died, and thus whether he could return to earth on Judgment Day.[44] A second round of debates was held in November 1934. Between these two debates, Persis published an open letter to Ahmadiyah leaders, describing its disputes with Ahmadi belief and practice.[45] Persis invited the Ahmadiyah members to read foundational Ahmadiyah texts and see the teachings and offered to visit Ahmadis' homes. The March 1934 edition of *Pembela Islam* featured articles in which the beliefs of Ahmadiyah were

---

condemnation influenced Muhammadiyah's break from Ahmadiyah, the translation continues to be used by Indonesian Muslims, and was even approved and certified by the MORA (Ichwan 2001); see also Amrullah (1982).

[38] Pimpinan Besar Muhammadiyah, *Pemandangan: Agama Islam dan Kaum Moeslimin* (Yogayakarta: P. B. Moehammadijah Almanak Moehammadijah, 1929), 63–64.

[39] Beck (2005, 24).

[40] "T. M. Ng. M. Djojosoegito," *Pembela Islam* 1, 8 (May 1930): 17; "Ahmadijah dan India (Dari madjallah Al-Fat-h)," *Pembela Islam* 1, 12 (September 1930): 14; "Comite Pendirian: N. V. Drukkerij Moeslim Indonesia, Mataram," *Pembela Islam* 1, 14 (November 1930): 31–33; and "Soera Islam di Lahore-Congress: Choeth-bah Beiga Maulana Moehammad Ali," *Pembela Islam* 2, 19 (February 1931): 32–35.

[41] "Soerat terboeka," *Pembela Islam* 2, 22 (March 1931): 23–25; "Kiaji masoek Kristen," *Pembela Islam* 2, 29 (July 1931): 10; and "Doenia Islam," *Pembela Islam* 2, 34 (September 1931): 27–30.

[42] Ahmad Hassan, "Ahmadijah: Keterangan tentang Nabi 'Isa tidak berbapa," *Pembela Islam* 2, 28 (June 1931): 37–39.

[43] Federspiel (2001, 151–154).

[44] "Mendjawab tantangar Ahmadijah," *Pembela Islam* 2, 56 (December 1932): 48; "Perdebatan Antara Pembela Islam dan Ahmadijah," *Pembela Islam* 3, 57 (January 1932): 37–42; and "Perslag Opisil dari Perdebatan: Pembela Islam – Ahmadijah Qadian," *Pembela Islam* 3, 61 (May 1933): 37–42; and continued in 3, 62 (June 1933): 25–30; 3, 63 (July 1933): 27–32; and 3, 64 (August 1933): 20–25.

[45] "Soerat Terbuka Kepada Saudara-Saudara jang termasoek Ahmadijah," *Pembela Islam* 66, 4 (January 1934): 6–7.

derided, not merely categorized as outside mainstream belief.[46] An article on the opposite page described why Ahmadiyah doctrine betrays the pillars of Islam and declared its fundamental beliefs erroneous.[47] This marked the first instance when Ahmadiyah was designated deviant (*aliran sesat*) by an Islamic organization. In later years the Indonesian state would echo this designation.

Designating Ahmadiyah as a deviant sect was the first step toward excluding its members from Muslim civil society. In various articles in 1936, the Persis magazine *Al-Lisaan* labeled Ahmadiyah followers apostates, non-Muslims, and crazy, and repeatedly called Ghulam Ahmad a false prophet, liar, and deceiver. Seventeen Ahmadis who had left Ahmadiyah and joined Persis were celebrated.[48] The back cover of the April issue featured the photograph of an Ahmadiyah Qadiani mosque in Batavia that had been closed by decree of the regent, and in June the magazine announced formation of the Anti-Ahmadiyah Committee, aimed at calling the issue of Ahmadiyah to the attention of Muslims.[49] Similarly, the Committee for the Elimination of Ahmadiyah in Medan was formed in November 1935 to issue a fatwa against Ahmadiyah.[50] The staff at the office of marriage in Medan subsequently refused to marry Ahmadis and prohibited them from entering prayer houses, mosques, or other Islamic sites.[51] In 1936, the Sultan of Deli in East Sumatra, the region's religious leader, determined that Ahmadis could not be buried in Muslim cemeteries, and in 1937 in Bukittinggi, 180 ulama declared that Ahmadiyah Qadiani were non-Muslims.[52] On multiple occasions, *Al-Lisaan* stated that Ahmadiyah was a "British tool" for destroying Muslims.[53] In short, by the end of 1936, Ahmadiyah had been pushed outside of the theological and social boundaries of the *umma*. In the coming years, as shared opposition to Ahmadiyah provided the glue for Muslim organizations to work together politically, the policies of the nascent Indonesian state would formalize Ahmadiyah's marginalization.

Like Muhammadiyah, the traditionalist[54] Islamic organization NU warned its followers that Ahmadiyah denied the articles of faith.[55] In a debate between NU and Persis on the practices of *taklid* (adherence to legal precepts set by the

---

[46] "Si Goblok," *Pembela Islam* 4, 69 (January 1935): 17–18.

[47] "Satoe i'tiqad jang sesat," *Pembela Islam* 4, 69 (January 1935): 19–20.

[48] "Qoerban di Soekawarna," *Al-Lisaan* 1, 3 (February 24, 1936): 38–39.

[49] *Al-Lisaan* 1, 5 (April 27, 1936): 38; and "Comité Anti Ahmadijah," *Al-Lisaan* 1, 7 (June 25, 1936): 31.

[50] "Comite Pembanteras Ahmadijah Medan," *Al-Lisaan* 1, 1 (December 27, 1935): 24–25.

[51] Pijper (1992, 39).

[52] Pijper (1992, 39–40).

[53] "Roeangan Dadjdjal," *Al-Lisaan* 7, 1 (June 25, 1936): 15–17; and "Ahmadijah Lahore mendjawab," *Al-Lisaan* 7, 1 (June 25, 1936): 26.

[54] In the Indonesian vernacular, a 'traditionalist' is someone who identifies with practices of Islam laid down in the Syafii school of jurisprudence.

[55] *Swara Nahdlatul Ulama* 2, 5 (1928 [1347]): 102–103; and 2, 6 (1928 [1347]): 122–123. Opposition to Ahmadiyah was one of very few causes that NU and Muhammadiyah shared in the late 1920s (Benda 1958, 54). Another was the dissolution of the caliphate.

early schools of jurisprudence) and *ijtihad* (setting aside precedent in favor of
a new interpretation), Ahmadiyah was cited as a problem that resulted from
independent reasoning by individuals untrained in Islamic law.[56] Persis, meanwhile, used the question of Ahmadiyah to attack the NU practice of *talkin*
(giving instructions to the deceased).[57] As with NU and Muhammadiyah in
the late 1920s, Ahmadiyah's deviance was one of the few issues on which NU
and Persis took a similar stance.[58] And when Soekarno was accused of being
an Ahmadi, he too used the Ahmadi question as an opportunity to denounce
his enemies. He wrote that although he admired Ahmadiyah for its rationalism
and modernism, it was also "devoted to British imperialism."[59]

This opposition to Ahmadiyah enabled a coalition that other pressing
issues facing the Muslim community did not: Dutch colonialism, the dissolution of the caliphate, the restrictions on religious propagation, and opposition
to Christian missionaries. Throughout the 1920s and early 1930s, events in
which the major Muslim organizations came together were marked by clashes
rather than cooperation.[60] In 1935, however, NU leader Kiai Wahid Hasjim
called for traditionalists and reformists to set aside their differences concerning
minor questions: "Do not make the differences [in *fur'iyah*] a reason for disunity, discord, treachery ... while our religion is one and the same, Islam! Our
mazhab is one and the same, *Sjafi'i*! Our region is one and the same, Djawa!
All belong to Ahlu Sunnah wal-Djama'ah."[61] Hasjim's use of the term Ahlu
Sunnah wal-Djama'ah is instructive, since Sunni Muslims used it to describe
themselves, usually in distinction to the Shi'ite and other sects.[62]

Despite the growing cooperation of modernist and traditionalist Muslims,
NU maintained its distance when the modernists created the High Islamic
Council of Indonesia (MIAI) in 1937. Two issues kept NU from joining. First,
the meeting was framed as a continuation of previous congresses, in which
modernists had derided traditional practices. NU's response was to propose
that the previous congresses be treated as merely 'provisional' regarding future
policies. The MIAI leadership agreed, and NU joined the 1939 meeting.[63]

---

[56] "Al-Lisaan Contra B.N.O," *Berita Nahdlatoel-'Oelama* 5, 7 (February 1, 1936): 6–10.

[57] "Roengan Dadjdjal: Ahmadijah dan N.O.," *Al-Lisaan* 1, 13 (December 23, 1936): 16; and
"Ahmadijah dan Talqien," *Al-Lisaan* 1, 13 (December 23, 1936): 16.

[58] For example, the NU magazine *Berita Nahdlatoel-'Oelama* reprinted wholesale a Persis denun-
ciation of Ahmadiyah, while other pages of the magazine were used to dispute Persis doctrine.
"Achmadijah: Dari Pembela Islam Lahat kita terima soerat sebaran berikoet ini; Sifat Propaganda
Achmadijah, Perloe Awas!" *Berita Nahdlatoel-'Oelama* 5, 11 (April 1, 1936): 14–16.

[59] "Soerat dari Ir Soekarno dari Endeh," *Al-Lisaan* 1, 13 (December 23, 1936): 17–20.

[60] Bruinessen (1995, 12).

[61] Noer (1978, 241). *Fur'iyah* is a term in Islamic jurisprudence that describes matters of difference among Muslims that do not affect basic belief and doctrine. *Fur'iyah* are contrasted with
usuliyah, which are issues of core doctrine. In contemporary Indonesia, Ahmadiyah's denial of
the finality of the Prophet is considered a question of *usuliyah*.

[62] Federspiel (1995, 10).

[63] Noer (1978, 12–13).

The second issue was that Ahmadiyah Lahore attended. NU questioned why Ahmadiyah was permitted to join the MIAI when leading Muslims from both inside and outside Indonesia had made it clear that the organization was outside Islam.[64] NU published, from 1938 into early 1939, a three-part essay on Ahmadiyah that focused on its collusion with British imperialism and Ghulam Ahmad's claim to prophecy.[65] This brought the issue of Ahmadiyah to a head, and at the 1939 MIAI meeting it was resolved: "During the proceedings of the Second MIAI Executive Council in Jombang, a question arose which demands answering: is the door of the MIAI open to the Achmadijah? To the question, the Executive Council gave the answer: the doors of the MIAI are closed to the Achmadijah."[66]

From 1925 to 1939, then, Muhammadiyah, Persis, and NU pushed Ahmadiyah from the center of Muslim civil society to outside the incipient community united around the MIAI.[67] And while the MIAI lasted only from 1937 to 1943, it profoundly influenced the nationalist movement. As Mizan Sya'roni wrote, "Its establishment marked a turning point in the history of the Indonesian Islamic movement in particular and the nationalist movement in general, since the federation was a pioneer in the drive for Islamic and to some extent national unity."[68] Indeed, the coalition of Islamic organizations established in the MIAI endured through the Islamic political party Masyumi, which, like the MIAI, did not accept Ahmadiyah Lahore when it applied to be a member in the 1950s.[69]

From 1942 to 1943, the occupying Japanese transformed the MIAI from an Islamic federation into the political party Masyumi and embedded it in the institutional structures of the proto-state through the Office of Religious Affairs, which became the MORA. Harry Benda notes that by 1944, "[t]he Masyumi ... had for all intents and purposes become part of the government itself."[70] When the Japanese occupation ended the following year, the Islamic organizations that had formed the MIAI only seven years earlier became the governing religious authorities in the new state. Since the MORA's creation, those organizations' control over the MORA and its penetration into every level of government have allowed it to shape the meaning of religion and its place in public life. The MORA's mission included: (1) to make belief in the

---

[64] "Ma'loemat Officieel tentang moendoernja Delegatie H.B.N.O. dari Al-Islam Congress," *Berita Nahdlatoel-'Oelama* 7, 11 (April 1, 1938): 5–7.

[65] "Achmadijah," *Berita Nahdlatoel-'Oelama* 7, 22 (September 15, 1938): 8–10; continued in 7, 24 (October 15, 1938): 11–12; and 8, 1 (January 1, 1939): 30.

[66] Madjlis Islam A'laa Indonesia, *Soeara Madjlis Islam A'laa Indonesia* (Jakarta, n.d. [1941]).

[67] Not surprisingly, the MIAI's goals were those of an emergent *umma*: to strengthen bonds between Islamic organizations, defend Islam, and promote pan-Islamic ties (Elson 2009a, 28).

[68] Sya'roni (1998), 2.

[69] Noer (1978, 244 n. 106). While the coalition splintered when NU broke off from Masyumi in 1953, its position on Ahmadiyah remained unchanged.

[70] Benda (1958, 166).

One and Only God an operative principle in public life; (2) to be watchful that every inhabitant is free to adhere to his own religion and to worship according to his own religion; and (3) to assist, support, protect, and promote all sound religious movements.[71] The first task is a reference to the national ideology of Pancasila, with belief in God as the first principle. The second professes freedom of religion, but the meaning of the Indonesian word for religion, *agama*, is narrower than its English equivalent. *Agama* was defined in 1952 as a monotheistic religion with belief in the existence of One Supreme God, a holy book, a prophet, and a way of life for its adherents.[72] This definition closely resembled Muhammadiyah's definition of religion.[73] Islam, Roman Catholicism, and Christianity (Protestantism) were recognized as religions in 1951, while Hinduism and Buddhism were later included under pressure from Soekarno (see Chapter 5).[74] The third task suggests the limits of official tolerance – 'unsound' movements such as Ahmadiyah were designated deviant streams (*aliran sesat*, from the Persis designation of 1935) or beliefs (kepercayaan) rather than religions.[75]

Since the 1950s, adherents to deviant streams and faiths have been pressured to join the 'sound' religious movements.[76] In 1954, the MORA set up a special section for the Supervision of Faith Movements in Society (*Pakem*) that monitored heterodox, heretical, and apostate faiths.[77] As I will show in the next section, the policing of heterodoxy got a boost in authority in 1965 when

---

[71] Boland (1982, 108).

[72] Abalahin (2005, 4).

[73] Pimpinan Pusat Muhammadiyah, "Kitab Masalah Lima" (1942), in Asyumuni Abdurrahman and Moelyadi, eds., *Himpunan Putusan Majelis Tarjih Muhammadiyah* (Malang: Pimpinan Pusat Muhammadiyah, 1999), 276–278.

[74] In contrast to its treatment of Ahmadiyah, the MORA worked with Balinese elites to mold their religion into a form of monotheism including a single holy book, a prophet, a system of law, standardized ritual practices, and origins in India. See Geertz (1973, 170–189); Monnig Atkinson (1983); Schiller (1996).

[75] In 1948, the MORA published a book by the traditionalist Muslim author and activist H. Aboebakar, which included an appendix listing the Ahmadiyah as one of seven "false revelations" (1948, 325–328). A delegation of Ahmadiyah leaders protested their inclusion on the list. The response by the MORA was ambiguous. The young NU leader Wahid Hasjim distanced the MORA from the publication of the book and, possibly in response, the 1952 edition was published by a private publisher, Sinar Pudjangga, with an introduction by Aboebakar thanking R. Sunarjo, secretary general of the MORA, for his past support. One month after their protest, however, then secretary general of the MORA, Mohammad Kafrawi, responded to the Ahmadiyah in a letter on August 16, 1951, saying that he had consulted with H. Aboebakar, who defended his conclusions, albeit adding a question mark to the heading "false revelations" in the 1952 edition (1952, 325–328). I am grateful to Kevin Fogg for sharing his notes on this incident. See Wahid Hasjim to Pengurus Besar Djema'at Ahmadiyah Indonesia, July 20, 1951, RA7 Kabinet Presiden, #163, INA; Letter from the Ministry of Religion to Pengurus Besar Djema'at Ahmadiyah Indonesia, August 16, 1951, RA7 Kabinet Presiden, #163, INA.

[76] Mulder (1978, 109).

[77] Abalahin (2005, 134).

President Soekarno affirmed that there were only six recognized religions and declared that any group that threatened these religions should be prohibited.

This history reveals that opposition to Ahmadiyah, as a heterodox faith, stretched across theological and political cleavages in Muslim civil society. To Muhammadiyah, Ahmadiyah was a fifth column within Islam. To Persis, Ahmadiyah stubbornly held onto beliefs that perverted the pillars of Islam. To NU, Ahmadis were apostates and stewards of imperialism. That Ahmadis deny the pillars of Islam while calling themselves Muslim has provoked opposition across the diverse Muslim world;[78] different groups dislike Ahmadiyah for diverse reasons, but nearly everyone agrees on their distaste for the sect. This history further suggests that intolerance is a productive part of the process of transforming a latent identity into one that is politically salient, bringing new attitudes to the fore and enabling new political institutions to emerge. I now turn to showing how these patterns of productive intolerance endure in contemporary, democratic Indonesia.

Productive Intolerance, Part II

The final years of the Soekarno administration were marked by tensions between Indonesia and its neighbor, Malaysia. Soekarno saw Malaysia and its British military bases as an outpost of counterrevolutionary imperialism, and he mobilized the public through a campaign of confrontation (*konfrontasi*), consisting of mass demonstrations, low-level military engagement, and support for revolutionary movements in Southeast Asia. Mass organizations proclaimed their support for Soekarno as the president, leader of the revolution, and commander in chief.[79]

Soekarno also sought to mobilize support as the self-proclaimed leader of the Muslim world. On January 27, 1965, he signed Presidential Order No. 1: "Every person shall be prohibited from deliberately before the public telling, encouraging, or soliciting public support for making an interpretation of a religion adhered to in Indonesia or performing religious activities resembling the activities of such religion when the interpretation and activities are deviant from the principal teachings of such religion."[80] Soekarno's 'blasphemy law' formalized the orthodox definition of religion that the Islamic organizations had long sought.[81] Mystical sects were only marginally tolerated; they were recognized as a category of belief rather than as religions, and were not entitled to resources from or protection by the state.[82]

---

[78] See, for example, Iqbal (1974, 7).

[79] Djakababa (2009, 50, 55).

[80] "Penetapan Presiden No. 1/1965 tentang Pentjegahan Penjalahgun Dan/Atau Penodaan Agama," *Suara Merdeka*, March 9, 1965: 1.

[81] The law has been used to prosecute both blasphemy (offensive speech about sacred matters) and heresy (belief that runs counter to orthodox doctrine).

[82] Howell (2005, 473); Ricklefs (2008, 340).

FIGURE 4.1. Front page of *Suara Merdeka* with headlines, "Bung Karno is Also Leader of the Islamic World" and "Presidential Order No. 1/1965 Regarding the Prevention of Abuse and/or Desecration of Religion."

Six weeks after the signing, the law was publicly announced, flanked by a joint statement by NU, Muhammadiyah, Partai Sarekat Islam Indonesia, the traditionalist group Jamiatul Washliyah, and the Indonesian Joint Trade Union declaring their support for Soekarno's broader agenda of revolution, confrontation, and NASAKOM (Soekarno's shorthand for uniting the streams of national politics: nationalism, religion, and communism).[83] In March 1965, Soekarno hosted a sequel to the 1955 Asia-Africa Conference in Bandung, the international body that became the Non-Aligned Movement. At this Islamic Asia-Africa Conference, leaders from thirty-two countries awarded Soekarno the title "Champion of Islam and Freedom in Asia and Africa."[84] The front page of the newspaper shown in Figure 4.1 encapsulates what Soekarno was trying to do; the right side announces the law against blasphemy, while the left headline introduces Soekarno's speech: "Bung Karno Is Also Leader of the Islamic World." By demarcating the boundaries

---

[83] "Pernjataan Bersama Partai-2 Dan Ormas Islam," NU folder 106, AN. See also "Pernjataan Bersama Partai 2 Dan Ormas Islam," *Berita Antara*, March 18, 1965. NU's youth wing issued a similar statement on March 23: "Putjuk Pimpinan Gerakan Pemuda Anshor," NU folder 106, no. PP/616/B/III/1965, AN.

[84] "Bung Karna Adalah Djuga Pemimpin Dunia Islam," *Suara Merdeka*, March 9, 1965: 1; Fogg (2012, 411).

of tolerance, Soekarno brought together and placed himself at the head of a coalition of organizations, just as the MIAI had done in 1937. In another act of productive intolerance, Soekarno strengthened the framework for godly nationalism put into place by the Muslim organizations, the MIAI, and the MORA.

Since 1965, the organization of godly nationalism has become more formally institutionalized in the state.[85] Laws concerning personal identity are based on membership in one of the six recognized religions inscribed on each individual's identification card. The state privileges recognized religions, and any educational institution under the auspices of the MORA receives funding while being subject to oversight. Other ministry mechanisms for promoting and controlling orthodox religious belief include support for mosques, guidance in Qur'an recitation, and organization of religious ceremonies. Most of the ministry's work focuses on Islamic development, although there are also offices for Protestant, Catholic, and Hindu/Buddhist affairs.[86]

While the institutional structure of religion crystallized in 1965, two new developments have since arisen: the creation of the Indonesian Council of Ulamas (MUI) and the emergence of a new generation of intellectuals. In 1975, Soeharto created the MUI to co-opt domestic organizations and represent the government abroad in the Organization of Islamic States (OIC) and the World Muslim League (Rabit'at al-Alam al-Islami). The MUI was the first state agency to disseminate the views of the OIC. In April 1974, the OIC urged Muslim governments to declare the Ahmadis a non-Muslim minority, which led to anti-Ahmadi resolutions in Jordan, Mauritania, and Mecca, and exacerbated conflicts in Pakistan.[87] The MUI issued its own fatwa ten years later when it decried Ahmadiyah as a heretical sect. In 2005, it reissued its fatwa against Ahmadiyah with the support of vigilante groups FPI and Hizb ut-Tahrir Indonesia, as well as Persis.[88] While the content of MUI sentiment harks back to the 1930s, the current scale of mobilization against Ahmadiyah is greater than ever before.[89]

---

[85] Suharto's attempt to make Pancasila the "sole foundation" (*Azas Tunggal*) for social organization's policies strengthened godly nationalism by making belief in God mandatory, although mass organizations interpreted Pancasila in diverse ways (Ramage 1995, 5–18).

[86] Office for the Research and Development of Religion (1993). Confucianism was recognized by the MORA in 1950 and by President Soekarno in 1965, derecognized by Soeharto in 1979, and then rerecognized in 2000 after democratization. See also Abalahin (2005).

[87] Friedmann (1989, 44).

[88] While in the 1950s the MORA was trying to marginalize the Ahmadiyah, the Ministry of Justice apparently issued a letter of recognition to Ahmadiyah, a point of long-standing frustration to the MUI. See Tim Penyunting Majelis Ulama Indonesia, *Himpunan Fatwa Majelis Ulama Indonesia* (Jakarta: Majelis Ulama Indonesia, 1997), 71, citing Surat Keputusan Menteri Kehakiman RI No JA/23/13, March 13, 1953; Menchik (2007); Hasyim (2011); Ichwan (2013).

[89] Indeed, my conversations with the younger generation of Persis leaders suggest they are more supportive of violence against Ahmadiyah than is the older generation. Author's interviews, Tasikmalaya, September 25–27, 2010.

Since the 1970s, Indonesia has also witnessed a growing presence of intellectuals with liberal leanings, including former Muhammadiyah chairs Syafii Maarif and Amien Rais, former NU chair and former Indonesian president Abdurrahman Wahid, and the Islamic intellectual Nurcholish Madjid.[90] They influenced young scholars who today are prominent in promoting liberal notions of tolerance. These two developments have contributed to polarizing contemporary public opinion even while the origins of intolerance of Ahmadiyah and its institutional manifestation can be traced to the 1930s and 1960s.

In 2001–2002, local government bans on Ahmadiyah and physical attacks on Ahmadiyah mosques launched the most recent debate about heterodoxy.[91] In response, a group of human rights activists began researching legal remedies to the state discrimination against heterodox groups.[92] The activists gained momentum with the involvement of the National Alliance for Freedom of Religion and Belief (AKKBB), a network of interfaith organizations that in May 2008 published an advertisement calling for respect for Ahmadiyah, and held a rally that was attacked by 400 vigilantes.[93] In 2009, the coalition of Indonesian activists submitted a petition to the constitutional court to strike down the 1965 blasphemy law.[94]

In positive legal terms, the activists' petition questioned whether the blasphemy law was consistent with the 1945 constitution. Article 28e, paragraph 1, provides that "Every person shall be free to adhere to a religion and to worship in accordance with his/her religion." Paragraph 2 states, "Every person shall have the right to the freedom to hold a belief, to express his/her thoughts and attitude in accordance with his/her conscience." These obligations are echoed in the International Covenant on Civil and Political Rights, which Indonesia acceded to in 2006. The opponents to the petition – the government and the interested parties who submitted evidence – pointed to clauses in the constitution that recognize the state's right to limit individual rights to promote the community's values. Article 28j, paragraph 2, states, "In exercising his/her rights and freedom, every person must be subject to the restrictions stipulated in laws and regulations with the sole purpose to guarantee the recognition of and the respect for rights and freedom of other persons and to fulfill fair demand in accordance with the considerations of moral and religious values,

---

[90] Kersten (2011).

[91] Two Ahmadiyah mosques in West Java were attacked on December 23, 2002, following the local government's decision to prohibit the activities of Ahmadiyah. Alfitri (2008, 3, n. 15, 23); Crouch (2009, 11).

[92] Uli Parulian Sihombing, interview by the author, Jakarta, February 12, 2010.

[93] Crouch (2009, 13).

[94] The petitioners included the Indonesian Human Rights Monitor, the Institute for Policy Research and Advocacy, the Indonesian Legal Aid and Human Rights Association, the Center for Democracy and Human Rights Studies, the Equal Community Association, Desantara Foundation, the Indonesian Legal Aid Institute Foundation, Abdurrahman Wahid, Prof. Dr. Musdah Mulia, Prof. M. Dawam Rahardjo, and Maman Imanul Haq.

security, and public order in a democratic society." The opponents pointed to laws from 1964, 1970, 2003, 2004, and 2009 that affirm the centrality of belief in the One and Only God by the state. They argued that since 1950–1951, when Mohammad Natsir was prime minister, promoting belief in God had been a part of the educational curriculum for all public institutions, helping to unify the country's diverse groups. While acknowledging that promoting belief in God could limit individual religious freedom, they suggested that only external practices (*forum external*) were limited, not internal faith matters (*forum internal*).[95]

Subsuming the legal arguments was a set of abstract debates: how to govern religion, how to balance protecting religious freedom and promoting belief in God, whether groups can democratically curtail their own rights, and whether determining religious truth is less subjective than other policy issues. The petitioners argued, "The blasphemy law forces the state to determine the proper stream of religion: which is deviant, and which is an acceptable religion. When the state is involved in this decision it is no longer neutral. This is the problem."[96] This second set of debates shows how arguments over the blasphemy law produced a consensus about the proper relationship between God and nation in Indonesia. Heterodoxy is excluded from that relationship.

Although both the AKKBB and the petitioners emphasized the need to expand religious freedom in the country to protect the Ahmadis,[97] no Ahmadis were present in the courtroom. One of the lawyers for the petitioners, Uli Parulian Sihombing, stated that their inclusion would be "too sensitive."[98] His caution was inspired by the presence of vigilantes who dominated the courtroom's second floor and the courthouse's front lawn, and hung banners naming activists that they judged apostates.[99] Figure 4.2 displays how the vigilante groups created a tense atmosphere at the court. Yet an equally important reason for prudence in the court was the petitioners' call for a radical reformulation of the social contract that prominent leaders of civil society believed to be in place.[100] Sihombing called for the state to be neutral in *all* matters of faith; as already described, the contemporary state privileges orthodoxy over heterodoxy. By excluding the Ahmadis, the petitioners hoped to sidestep the thorny question of whether the state must become secular in order to be neutral.

---

[95] For a thorough legal analysis of the decision, see Crouch (2012).

[96] Uli Parulian Sihombing, interview by the author, Jakarta, February 12, 2010.

[97] Author's observation at the petitioners' strategy meeting, Wahid Institute, Jakarta, February 9, 2010.

[98] Uli Parulian Sihombing, interview by the author, April 19, 2010. Representatives from Jemaah Ahmadiyah Indonesia said that Choirul Anam, a petitioner, did not want Ahmadis to testify because he feared the debate would then revolve around them. Jemaah Ahmadiyah Indonesia, interview by the author, Jakarta, September 22, 2010.

[99] Author's observations, Constitutional Court Building, Jakarta, February 10, 17, and 24, and March 3, 10, 12, and 17, 2010.

[100] See Ramage (1995) on the continuing debates over the social contract.

FIGURE 4.2. Vigilante groups at the constitutional court, February 2010.
The photos on the top left and top right show vigilante groups dominating the courthouse's lawn and the courtroom's upper level. The banner on the bottom left reads,
"These are the defenders of heretics: They do not understand religious difference
versus the defamation of religion" and includes photos of prominent activists. Feces
are smeared on the photos, some in the shape of genitalia. The banner on the bottom right reads, "The names below are intellectuals (hypocrites of learning) in favor
of the heretic Ahmadiyah and thereby [they] lead Muslims to deviance.... Let us crush
the AHMADIYAH, AKKBB, AND THEIR PATRONS." The names are the same as
the signatories to the AKKBB petition of 2009. (Photographs by Jeremy Menchik,
Constitutional Court Building, Jakarta, February 10, 2010.)

As a result of their exclusion, the Ahmadis were discussed as an example of
the necessity of promoting proper belief in God. Amidhan from the MUI testified that human rights and religious freedom had nothing to do with the Ahmadi
question because Ahmadiyah was not a recognized religion; if it were, members
would be free to practice their faith.[101] Dr. Atho Mudzhar, professor of Islamic

---

[101] Court transcript, 140/puu-vii/2009, III, 33. The court heard similar testimony from Muhammad
Al Khotob and Wirawan Adnan from Forum Ummat Islam (FUI), Muhammad Al Khaththath
from FUI, and Habib Riziek Shiyab from FPI.

law and head of the Office of Research and Development in the MORA, testified for the government that the Ahmadis were permitted their internal beliefs, but the state was obligated to prohibit the dissemination of deviant religious beliefs in order to promote belief in God.[102] Sudarsono, from the Ministry of Internal Affairs, testified that belief was a matter of internal faith in which the state could not intervene. The expression of faith, however, was a public matter that could be restricted, as with the successful ban on the Ahmadiyah.[103] During brief mentions of violence toward Ahmadiyah by the intellectual Azymardi Azra, as well as Dr. Kunthi Treiewiyanti and Dr. Yunianti Chuzaifah of the National Commission on Women, the crowd on the second floor screamed at the witnesses until the chief justice threatened to clear the gallery and the lawyer for the MUI signaled for his allies to quiet down.[104] In sum, while the petitioners intended to support Ahmadiyah, the witnesses' testimony focused on the state's obligation to promote belief in God and prevent blasphemy.

Ahmadiyah's exclusion allowed the interested parties and the state to proclaim their commitment to a limited form of pluralism without extending religious freedom to heterodox faiths. Muhammadiyah supported maintaining the blasphemy law, and implicitly referenced its support for the ban on Ahmadiyah: "Muhammadiyah believes that freedom of religion or religious freedom is not freedom without limits."[105] Abdul Mu'ti, one of the leading advocates for tolerance in Muslim civil society, read from a "Guide to an Islamic Life for Members of Muhammadiyah" to exemplify Muhammadiyah's commitment to virtuousness with non-Muslim neighbors. The guide is a vivid expression of both the centrality of tolerance to Muhammadiyah's values and how Ahmadiyah falls outside tolerable limits: "Islam teaches mutual respect and freedom to practice, but not by mixing religions and not by insulting the religious beliefs of others."[106]

Mu'ti's scholarship further confirms this relationship. His book *Kristen Muhammadiyah* describes the curriculum of Muhammadiyah schools in areas where the population is overwhelmingly Christian or Buddhist. Teachers of any faith can provide instruction in secular subjects to students of any religion, while the doctrines of each specific religion are taught by a member of that religion.[107] In a 2009 interview, former Muhammadiyah chair Syafii Maarif touted Mu'ti's research as an example of the group's tolerance, while also making it clear that there would never be a book titled *Ahmadiyah Muhammadiyah*.[108]

---

[102] Court transcript, V, 93–95.
[103] Court transcript, X, 14.
[104] Author's observations, Constitutional Court Building, Jakarta, March 10 and 12, 2010.
[105] Court transcript, 140/puu-vii/2009, III, 44–47.
[106] Court transcript, 47–51.
[107] Mu'ti and Riza ul Haq (2009).
[108] Syafii Maarif, interview by the author and Alfred Stepan, Jakarta, September 30, 2009.

In its court testimony, NU also supported pluralism while emphasizing that freedom of religion has limits:

> From the Islamic perspective on well being, religious freedom is not a new thing. Long before the Western world's campaign to guarantee the freedom of religion, Islam has for fifteen centuries guaranteed [religious freedom] using verses of the Qur'an, the Hadith, and practices of the Prophet and his companions demonstrating that granting religious freedom in Muslim society is religiously compulsory, just like religion is obligatory.... But something that should be underlined is that this freedom to express diverse beliefs or practices concerns subjects related to *fur'iyah*, the branches.... The position and attitude of companions of the Prophet and the scholars are clear and firm on matters concerning the *usuliyah*: those differences of opinion or interpretation of religious practices that oppose points of religious doctrine, especially those ideologies and ideas that differ from the main/ basic teachings of religion and are raised in a provocative manner to foment anarchy. If the problem concerns *fur'iyah*, then we will witness a high tolerance and appreciation by scholars against parties who have different views; yet the Islamic scholars will demonstrate an uncompromising attitude in matters of *usuliyah*.[109]

The lawyer for NU, Arsul Sani, built on the *usuliyah/fur'iyah* distinction to argue for democratically delineating the boundary between the two. Under Sani's proposal, witnesses would be able to provide their opinions, lawyers argue their cases, and justices rule in a transparent manner:

> The State has the right to determine if religious groups are deviant and force them to choose among the recognized religions.... The majority can decide in a democratic, transparent manner if a group is outside Islam. Catholics could object to Jehovah's [Witnesses] and ban them, Protestants could object to Mormons and ban them. Each community can regulate themselves.... [The problem of Ahmadiyah] could be solved if they were declared non-Muslim. As it stands, they are not entitled to the protection of being Muslim.[110]

Sani's proposal would allow the state to promote belief in God while creating a system for the definition of orthodoxies that could change over time. It would also allow the state to expand the scope of recognition to other religions; heterodox groups would be able to become orthodox and receive state support and protection (see Chapter 5 for historical precedent). Although illiberal, his proposal attempted to balance the state's mandate to promote belief in God with the protection of minorities.[111]

While the National Protestant Council and National Catholic Council called for the law to be either revoked or revised, most representatives of the country's minority groups supported the law. Matakin, the High Council for

---

[109] Court transcript, 140/puu-vii/2009, IV, 18–20.

[110] Arsul Sani, interview by the author, Jakarta, February 11, 2010.

[111] A spokesperson for Ahmadiyah, however, rejected the proposal on the grounds that their religion is Islam and not Ahmadiyah. Ahmad Masihuddin, interview by the author, Jakarta, September 22, 2010.

the Confucian Religion in Indonesia, advocated maintaining the blasphemy law on the grounds that it helps protect the minority religions, although it also sought to extend the law to include "small religions."[112] The government's witness for the Buddhists, Philip K. Wijaya, argued that the law was important to protect minority religions and maintain peace between sects of the same religion.[113] The representative of the Indonesian Buddhist Community testified that the 1965 law was key to maintaining tolerance in the country.[114] Yanto Jaya of the Indonesian Hinduism Society supported the law on the grounds that its revocation would lead to violence.[115]

As in the 1930s, Persis enthusiastically backed the eradication of heterodoxy. Persis chair Maman Abdurrahman argued that the law was consistent with the values of the republic: "Indonesia is not a secular state that ignores the values of religion in national life and tolerates blasphemy. The founders of the Republic of Indonesia consciously made sure that religion was integral to the founding of the Republic."[116] Persis leader Amin Djamaluddin listed ten examples of deviant sects whose leaders had declared themselves prophets or tried to merge multiple religions into one. He reported these cases to the police, who successfully applied the blasphemy law and imprisoned the leaders.[117] Rather than being unconstitutional, he argued, the blasphemy law was more important than ever.

The trial did include testimony about victims of the 1965 law. Arnold Panahal from one kepercayaan group, the Coordinating Authority for Belief Organisations, described how kepercayaan followers have been discriminated against since the end of the colonial period. They are denied access to funding for their schools, cannot list their religion on their ID cards, are prohibited from entering the military, and often refuse to send their children to school because the state would force them to register and be educated in one of the recognized religions.[118] Representatives of other kepercayaan groups testified that the 1965 law degrades their beliefs, discriminates against them in favor of orthodox faiths, and leads to their stigmatization in society. They pointed to the elucidation of the law that treats kepercayaan associations as problems to be solved rather than beliefs that must be respected.[119]

The response to the testimony of kepercayaan groups played out in a session when the chief justice asked the parties whether faith in God without subscribing to one of the six religions should be recognized. The answer came from Dra. Hj. Nurdiati of the Irena Center Foundation, which is dedicated to

---

[112] Court transcript, 140/puu-vii/2009, IV, 16–18.
[113] Court transcript, VII, 28–30.
[114] Court transcript, VI, 69.
[115] Court transcript, V, 13–15.
[116] Court transcript, VI, 70–73.
[117] Court transcript, VII, 30–35.
[118] Court transcript, VI, 74–78.
[119] Court transcript, XI, 79–85. The interfaith spiritual guru Anand Krishna, atheists, and Shi'ites have been arrested and brought to trial under the same law and could have testified as victims.

preventing religious conversions from Islam: the regulations of the MORA are clear; kepercayaan is not a religion but only a cultural practice. She went on to say that the country had experience with another people without religion: the Indonesian Communist Party (PKI). And just like the PKI, groups that do not believe in religion should be banned and their members socialized into belief in God.[120] Azam from the Indonesian Council for Islamic Propagation said that because kepercayaan consisted of practices stemming from culture rather than religion, their experiences were irrelevant to the law and only germane to the Department of Tourism.[121]

Two routine court practices reinforced the marginality of heterodox groups. At the start of each session, the chief justice asked the day's witnesses what religion they followed and then swore them in under their respective faiths. On March 3, 2010, the petitioners presented a witness, Sardy, who followed a kepercayaan group. When it was time for the swearing-in, the chief justice asked, "What would you like to swear on?" and Sardy replied, "Pancasila." The courtroom erupted in laughter, and there was a moment of confusion while the court figured out what to do. Eventually the chief justice replied, "There is no oath for Pancasila," and proceeded to swear Sardy in on the basis of a personal oath: "I promise to state the truth and nothing but the truth."[122]

Similarly, most witnesses began and ended their statements with greetings from their respective faiths. For example, orthodox Muslims opened their statements with "*Assalamu alaikum*" (peace be unto you), to which the audience reciprocated with "*Waalaikum salam*" (and also unto you). More secular Muslims said both "peace be unto you" and "good morning." The five participants who adhered to kepercayaan began and ended their statements with *rahayu* (a Javanese expression of greeting) and *sangkalangkong* (thank you). While the chief justice reciprocated the kepercayaan greetings on two occasions, none of the other judges or participants acknowledged them. To the contrary, the kepercayaan greetings were challenged. Dr. Eggy Sudjana of the Fraternal Body of the Islamic Scholars for Madura Schools mocked the use of *rahayu* as an artifact of an outdated culture.[123] Only greetings based on religious or secular vernacular were deemed appropriate.

By the end of the trial the outcome was certain; eight of the nine justices and the overwhelming majority of witnesses supported the continued exclusion of heterodox faiths from state recognition. Recognition that the heterodox faiths had been discriminated against would have necessitated a redefinition of the meaning of religion in the state, reorganization of the MORA, redistribution

---

[120] Court transcript, 140/puu-vii/2009 VII, 61. At least 500,000 members of the PKI were killed in a coup orchestrated by Soeharto from 1965 to 1966. It is still illegal to belong to the PKI.

[121] Court transcript, VII, 57–58. The dismissive invocation of ritual as cultural or folkloric has parallels in Turkey, where Alevism has served as the site for contestation over the religious imaginaries of the nation (Tambar 2010).

[122] Author's observation, Jakarta, March 3, 2010; court transcript, 140/puu-vii/2009 VII, 10.

[123] Court transcript, VII, 53–55.

of the state patronage system, and an end to the privileging of religious organizations such as NU and Muhammadiyah as the backbone of civil society. The judges pointed to these organizations as partners of the state:

> Indonesia is a country which upholds the concept that religion is not separated from the state and has the Ministry of Religion which serves and protects the growing and development of religions fairly.... Religious organizations that are deeply rooted and have historical foundation are parent organizations of religions recognized in Indonesia. It is these religious organizations that in the end shall be able to become partners of the state in creating religious social order to respect and tolerate one another.[124]

The decision reaffirmed the existing structure of religion-state relations, and a consensus emerged that the law is vital to promoting the core national value of belief in God. A representative from the Irena Center summarized:

> Honored Justices of the court, my name is named Sulaiman Zachawerus, the son of a mother from Ternate and the father from Sanger Talaud, both of whom were Christian from a family of Christians. The only Muslim in the Zachawerus family is me.... Although the law is being appealed by the petitioners, for us this is a blessing in disguise. Because before now, Act no. 1 of 1965 was lost. But now it is a blessing because laymen everywhere will know that we have a law against blasphemy. And they will know that religion is the ultimate concern of humanity, the preeminent concern of every human being. And after [today], if religion is disgraced, then the cost is their soul.[125]

The consensus that Zachawerus, NU, Muhammadiyah, Persis, the minority religions, and the justices helped constitute is plural, modern, and godly. Outside the courtroom, former NU chair Hasyim Muzadi has been a vocal critic of the vigilante group FPI and has refused its repeated requests to engage in dialogue.[126] Inside the courtroom, FPI and NU were on the same side.

Some of the country's most public proponents of pluralism excluded Ahmadis from the jurisdiction of tolerance and characterized the blasphemy law as irrelevant to freedom of religion even while denying the political quality of this move. In the interview I conducted with Syafii Maarif in 2009, I asked him the following: "Muhammadiyah is vocal in defending the rights of the Christians and Catholics. Why not Ahmadiyah?" Maarif responded: "Because Muhammadiyah sees this as politics! If Muhammadiyah is involved in defending Ahmadiyah, they will be seen as entering partisan politics. Muhammadiyah was fed up with politics in the 1960s when we

---

[124] Constitutional court verdict (2010), 140/puu-vii/2009, 3.58.

[125] Court transcript, 140/puu-vii/2009, VII, 56–57. Zachawerus's belief that the state has jurisdiction over the welfare of the soul hints at support for more aggressive coercion of individual belief than practiced by the MORA, which says individuals must publicly believe in God but possess absolute internal religious freedom.

[126] Asrul Sani, interview by the author, Jakarta, February 11, 2010; Wahid Institute, "Monthly Report on Religious Issues," June (2008): 11, 12.

exited Masyumi."[127] Maarif defines the political in a way that allows him to deny Muhammadiyah's responsibility for the status quo, deny its exclusion of Ahmadiyah, and embrace the liberal injunction to avoid mixing religion and politics. His statement resonates with scholarship on the Islamic revival, in which Saba Mahmood suggests that liberal secularism and Islamism compete on terrain that is often considered apolitical but is crucial for demarcating the influence of these two movements.[128] By excluding the Ahmadis, the discussion in the courtroom shifted from religious freedom and discrimination to a different set of priorities: promoting belief in God, maintaining the state's religious identity while respecting pluralism, distinguishing internal freedom from external freedom, combating deviant beliefs through law rather than violence, and protecting the dignity of religion. This is a vocabulary imbued with commitments to pluralism while differentiated from that of the ostensibly secular West:

> The constitution of the Unitary State of the Republic of Indonesia does not allow any possibility for a campaign for the freedom of non-religion, freedom of anti-religion as well as any possibility to insult or defile religious teaching or holy books serving as sources of religious beliefs or to defile God's name. This element constitutes one of the elements marking the existence of a principal difference between the constitutional state of Indonesia and the constitutional states of the West. Accordingly, in the implementation of state administration, the formation of law, and the implementation of government and judicature, the basis of belief in God and teaching as well as religious values serve as a benchmark to determine whether or not a certain law is good, or even whether or not a certain law is constitutional.[129]

Rather than overturning the law, the case helped create a broad, institutionalized, and durable consensus on the values of state and society as rooted in godly nationalism.

Conclusion

> We have to be able to differentiate between democracy and moral deviation.
> Hasyim Muzadi, Chair of Nahdlatul Ulama from 1999 to 2010[130]

Indonesia's successful transition to democracy has not been accompanied by an increase in individual religious freedom. The promotion of belief in God and the exclusion of heterodox faiths help unify the country's diverse population behind a common theism: the state mobilizes religion against secessionist movements, in favor of economic development through family planning,

[127] Syafii Maarif, interview by the author and Alfred Stepan, Jakarta, September 30, 2009. Muhammadiyah left Masyumi in 1959.
[128] Mahmood (2005, chapter 2).
[129] Constitutional court verdict (2010), 140/puu-vii/2009, 3.34.11.
[130] "NU Opposes Blasphemy Law Review," *Jakarta Post*, February 1, 2010.

against Islamist militants, and in civic education.[131] While the vigilante groups use antidemocratic violence, they share a common goal with those large swaths of civil society seeking to live in a nation where belief in God is part of the "overlapping consensus" necessary for a functioning democracy.[132] Their goal is a polity where individuals, organizations, and the state are partly responsible for one another's moral condition rather than it being the domain of self-determining individuals.[133]

Godly nationalism is not limited to Indonesia. Globally, majorities in over twenty countries say that belief in God is necessary for a person to have good values.[134] These attitudes are not only influential in the private sphere; nine out of ten Americans would vote for a presidential candidate who is Catholic or Jewish and eight out of ten would vote for one who is Mormon, yet only 54 percent would vote for one who is an atheist.[135] Likewise, in a speech to commemorate the 400th anniversary of the King James Bible, British prime minister David Cameron sought to link citizenship in Britain with holding strong religious values, whether Christian or another faith: "Those who say being a Christian country is doing down other faiths simply don't understand that it is easier for people to believe and practise other faiths when Britain has confidence in its Christian identity."[136] Cameron suggests that religious values, like belief in God, underpin national values; here he echoes the arguments of the Indonesian modernist intellectual Mohammed Natsir, who in the 1950s argued that Islamic nationalists, not secular nationalists, provided the best protection of minority Christians due to their shared devotion to God.[137] Cameron, like Natsir, sought to create a system of godly nationalism where diverse faiths are mobilized by the state, and society is bound by a common theism.

Recent work on religious freedom has stressed its place in the production of a global power differential between imperial states and the developing world. Mahmood persuasively argues that the demarcation of groups as "minorities" is both descriptive and useful for projects of Western imperialism.[138] Mahmood's comments elucidate the situation in Indonesia, where Christian missionaries have used the guise of religious freedom as an entry point for the conversion of Muslims.

Yet there is more to the debates over religious freedom and religious blasphemy than imperial domination. The war against blasphemy under way in

[131] Aspinall (2007, 245–263); National Family Planning Coordinating Board (1993).
[132] I borrow the concept of an "overlapping consensus" from Rawls (1993, 134).
[133] For a parallel social account of the role of *nasīha* (advice) in creating a public sphere distinct from that of the liberal tradition, see Asad (1993, chapter 6).
[134] Pew Research Center (2014).
[135] Jones (2012).
[136] Cameron (2012).
[137] Natsir (1954), in Feith and Castles (2007 [1970]).
[138] Mahmood (2012, 418–446).

Indonesia is part of a productive effort by Muslim civil society to further develop a system of godly nationalism and communal tolerance while avoiding the templates of liberal secularism or theocracy. Indonesia's Muslim civil society values the country's religious diversity but does not want to sanitize the public sphere of religion in order to promote liberal values; its vision for a godly democracy aims to balance individual rights, group rights, religious pluralism, and belief in God. Putting this vision into practice is difficult at a time when liberal secularism is equated with tolerance, and religion is synonymous with intolerance, but the rising influence of pious democrats in Tunisia, Turkey, and the United States hints toward a future of godly nations.

5

The Coevolution of Religion and State

According to classical Islamic theology, Muslims should exclude Communists and Hindus from tolerance because they are godless, or possess too many gods, respectively.[1] Yet in contemporary Indonesia, Hindus are seen as similar to Christians, while Communists are the most feared and despised group. Why? This chapter highlights three moments of shifting tolerance in the period from 1950 to 1966: Persis' increased tolerance of Christians, the MORA manufacturing of Balinese Hinduism as a monotheistic religion, and NU's shift to intolerance of Communists and their designation as hypocrites (*munafik*). Drawing on the constructivist argument that state and society are mutually constitutive, these moments bring into relief the coevolution of religion and state in a modern Muslim democracy.

This is one of the underlying assumptions of a historical constructivist approach to the study of religion and politics. This argument stands in contrast to the two dominant approaches to the study of religion and politics. The statists argue that institutions shape the behavior of religious organizations through repeated interactions.[2] The society-centered approach holds that the state is a reflection of social values, and that societies with a high degree of religious observance carry it over into political institutions.[3]

The shortcoming of both positions is their inability to delineate the boundary between state and society.[4] What becomes clear from the history of interactions between Islamic organizations and the Indonesian state is that their

---

[1] "The unsubjugated unbeliever is by definition an enemy [of Islam]" (Lewis 1991, 77). Likewise, "In its crystallized form, Islam would brook no compromise with polytheism of any kind" (Friedmann 2003, 28).

[2] Kalyvas (1996); Pepinsky, Liddle, and Mujani (2010).

[3] Norris and Inglehart (2004); Gill (1998) argues that the social market for religion shapes the political behavior of religious actors and, indirectly, the state.

[4] Mitchell (1991).

(Secular) state   (Islamic) society

(Secular) state	Overlap	(Islamic) society
Security	**Ministry of Religious Affairs**	**Nahdlatul Ulama, Muhammadiyah, Persatuan Islam and others**
Infrastructure	Pesantren and Madrasah curriculum	
Non-Islamic banking	(Non)recognition of religions	Membership
Elections	Hajj management	Management of schools–primary, secondary and university
International affairs	**Ministry of Education**	Connections to political parties
Courts (except Islamic courts)	Religious education in state schools	Informal politics
Food safety	**Attorney General**	Hospitals, health clinics, orphanages
Telecommunications	Coordinating Board for Monitoring Mystical Beliefs in Society	Collection and distribution of zakat
Transportation	**Council of the Ulamas (MUI)**	Moral guidance for members and non-members
Education (non-religious)	Halal food certification	Scouting organizations
Health	Islamic banking	Youth and student organizations
	Ministry of Justice	Paramilitary organizations
	Islamic courts with jurisdiction over family law	Women's organizations
	Control over national symbols (Pancasila)	Environmental organizations
	Some political parties	Labor organizations

FIGURE 5.1. Overlap of the (secular) state and (Islamic) society.

interactions are part of a single contested field where the contours of religion and politics are fluid and evolve together over time. To speak of decisions by religious organizations about their political behavior is to assume that the terrain of their decision making is analytically distinct from the act of implementation. Yet their structure, language, identity, and understanding of their interests are as much a consequence of state action as state interests, actions, identity, and organization are a result of the influence of religious organizations. The subsequent identities and behavior are no less real than before the interactions. Once religious actors enter the public sphere they change it, making a clear distinction between religious society and the secular state increasingly meaningless.[5] Moreover, this overlap is the rule, not the exception to it. Cross-national quantitative work suggests that state entanglement in religion is the norm.[6]

Figure 5.1 provides examples of the institutional basis of this overlap. There are numerous areas of governance that are regulated according to secular law. And there are numerous areas of Islamic civil society where the secular state is relatively uninvolved. Yet there are an equal number of institutional overlaps making it empirically infeasible to draw a clear line between state and society. Theoretically, the division is even more problematic once we recognize the diverse ways in which religion and the secular interpenetrate.

[5] Asad (2003, chapter 6).
[6] Fox (2006).

So far I have shown that local history and context are key to understanding the impact of ideas on behavior, and that Western political concepts such as nationalism need to be reconstructed in order to understand modern politics. This chapter shows that the mutual constitution of religion and politics must be central to the understanding of either. Drawing on archival material from the period 1950–1966, this chapter demonstrates that global concepts such as religion exist within a matrix of power relations that define their boundaries and underlying content.[7] I will show that the definition of religion in the state is a product of the influence of Islamic organizations, which went on to define religion for other groups, notably for Balinese Hindus. The converse is also true. The delineation of boundaries between us and them, Muslims and Communists, Hindus and unbelievers, is a product of the mobilization of religion in the service of the state.

While Christian-Muslim relations were determined by events in the 1930s (Chapter 3) and Indonesian nationalism and Ahmadi relations were shaped by events in the late 1930s and 1940s (Chapter 4), this chapter highlights the role of events in the 1950s and 1960s in shaping contemporary relations between Muslims, Hindus, and Communists.

Persis' Shift toward Tolerance of Christians

As explained in Chapter 3, Persis is sometimes compared to the Muslim Brotherhood in Egypt as well as to Mawdudi's Jamaat-i-Islami in Pakistan.[8] Usually categorized as radical fundamentalist, extreme modernist, literalist or hardline radical, Persis would be predicted by a theological explanation to be perpetually intolerant toward Christian minorities.[9] Yet from 1951 to 1960, prominent Persis leaders made repeated promises to protect the religious and political rights of Christians, even by use of force if necessary. This section highlights the dynamics that shaped Persis leaders' tolerant behavior and discourse toward Christians.

Remember that in the heated debates of the 1930s, Persis leader Mohammed Natsir attacked Christian teaching as distorted. Ahmad Hassan had written a refutation of the divinity of Jesus, *The Divinity of Jesus According to the Bible (Ketoehanan Jesoes Menoeroet Bijbel)*, and critiqued Christian belief in the crucifixion of Christ, and the Christian view of the Trinity.[10] These polemics were in response to the increase in missionary activity in Bandung in the late 1920s as well as the conspicuous Christian polemics against Islam. Later, MIAI asked Hassan to rebut Christian polemics, resulting in a division

---

[7] Asad (1986).
[8] Federspiel (1970, iv); Hefner (2000, 105).
[9] Feith (1978, 136–137); Ricklefs (2008, 212, 217, 226); Hooker (2003, 48); Laffan (2003, 237).
[10] Federspiel (1970, 108–110).

of labor between Islamic organizations with Persis specializing in Islamic defense.[11]

In the intervening years, however, 'Christians in Indonesia' became 'Indonesian Christians'. The 1945–1950 revolutionary war against the Dutch was marked by Christian and Muslim unity in defense of the newly proclaimed homeland.[12] NU and Muhammadiyah jointly declared that defense of the fatherland against the Dutch was a holy war, an obligation for all Muslims.[13] This was in contrast to the 1940s when they refused a Japanese request to declare World War II a holy war.[14] Similarly, as a result of their participation, Indonesian Christians came to be seen as part of the nation instead of foreigners backed by Dutch finances and power.[15] As a result of the war, Muslim leaders, including those from Persis, began to see Christians as allies rather than enemies.

In addition to the perceived shift in the alliances of the Christians, the costs of intolerance toward Christians increased as a consequence of the rising power of the Communists. Remember that in the 1910s and early 1920s, the categories of Muslim and Communist were compatible and even overlapping. Islamic Communism spread through Minangkabau and West Java in the early 1920s.[16] Yet, during the revolutionary years, the Communists and modernist Muslims became bitter enemies. In September 1948, war broke out between nationalist and the PKI forces in Madiun, with the santri Muslims firmly on the side of the nationalists. Although the specific number of Indonesians killed is unknown, santri Muslims and abangan Communists systematically targeted each other for violence.[17] The implications of the Madiun affair and the tumultuous politics of the late revolutionary period were significant. In the early 1950s, the alliance between the Islamic groups and the nationalists was strengthened given their shared animosity toward the PKI. This alliance took precedent over religious leaders' widely held antagonism toward the nationalists' more secular vision. Similarly, the animosity between Masyumi[18] and the PKI was deepened. Modernist Muslims could no longer be Communist, nor

---

[11] The division of labor between Islamic organizations is similar to other religious communities. The American Jewish community is organized around divisions between Jewish defense organizations (the Anti-Defamation League), political lobbying organizations (the American Israel Public Affairs Committee), educational organizations (Hillel), youth organizations, women's organizations (Hadassah), and fundraising bodies (the Jewish Federation) (Goldberg 1996).

[12] This was more true for Java and Sumatra than for East Indonesia. I am grateful to Kevin Fogg for guidance on this point.

[13] Ricklefs (2008, 253).

[14] Ricklefs (2008, 241).

[15] Benda (1958, 176).

[16] Ricklefs (2001, 220).

[17] Ricklefs (2008, 266).

[18] From 1945 to 1952, Persis, Muhammadiyah, and NU formed a collective political party, Masyumi. While NU split off in 1952, Persis and Muhammadiyah remained in Masyumi with Persis figures often leading the organization. For that reason, this chapter refers to Persis and Masyumi interchangeably while specifying the names of specific leaders as often as possible.

vice versa. The polarization of Communists and modernist Muslims forced Persis and Masyumi to look for other potential allies in parliament and society. In other words, the rise of the PKI forced Persis to put aside polemics toward Christians and attempt tolerance.

After democratization in 1950, Persis sought the implementation of an Islamic state. Their opponents in parliament, the Indonesian Nationalist Party (PNI) and the PKI, pointed to Indonesia's religious diversity as the central reason why an Islamic state would be inappropriate. It thus became incumbent on Persis and Masyumi leader Mohammad Natsir to signal Masyumi's tolerance of non-Muslims. Masyumi's shift was clear from discourse regarding Indonesian pluralism as well as from the appointment of Christian politicians in Mohammed Natsir's governing coalition from September 1950 through March 1951, and in successive Masyumi cabinets.

Mohammad Natsir penned an eloquent treatment of Persis' 'Islamic Tolerance' in 1954. Acting in his capacity as the leader of Masyumi, Natsir sought to remove Christians' doubts about the commitment of Islam, and Muslims, to religious freedom for non-Muslims.

> The tenets of Islam uphold a principle, which can serve as a means of solving the problem; the ideas of our faith teach us to respect the diverse cultural patterns in Indonesia where various religious beliefs have been followed for centuries ...
>
> First, it must be emphasized that the attainment of belief in the Oneness of God is, in effect, a spiritual revolution liberating man from the bonds of superstitious fears. With the attainment of belief in the Oneness of God man is brought to an awareness of the Being of God to whom he has surrendered his spirit. But man must come to an awareness of the Being of God without compulsion of any sort. In the teachings of Islam it is insisted that genuine acceptance of religious faith cannot be acquired under constraint.
>
> Second, it is the Muslim view that only a faith held in the way that conforms to the teachings of Islam can be considered as a true religious faith. When the profession of religious belief represents merely a conventional expedience and is not based on a sense of deep-rooted spiritual conviction, there is no question of true religious faith. Again, it may be pointed out that the tenets of Islam specifically reject any forced imposition of religious belief. In the Koran we read, "There is no compulsion in religion." This statement comprises the basis of the Muslim attitude to religious faith.
>
> Third, awareness of the Being of God is a favor conferred by Divine grace, a favor that is to be acquired only through proper teaching, through careful guidance, and through calm and reasoned discussion ... Muslims are commanded to exhort, to persuade with reasoned argument, but to adjure the use of force in seeking to spread the teachings of the Prophet.
>
> Fourth, confronted with the differences of views and the divergences of belief that are encountered in the course of everyday existence, the Muslim must neither remain indifferent nor give way to despair. Rather must every Muslim seek some common feature in the various religious beliefs. It is the duty of every Muslim to promote understanding between the congregations of different faiths by putting into practice the teaching of the Koran ...

Fifth, every Muslim must have an unfailing capacity for self-restraint, never giving way to impulses of passion, in endeavoring to foster better understanding with followers of different faiths. With an unshakeable conviction in the truth of his creed, and strong in the awareness that Allah is the God of all mankind, the Muslim must personify the spirit of tolerance ...

Sixth, the attitude of tolerance emphasized in the teachings of Islam is an attitude of positive action. It is an attitude that calls for a preparedness to seek a basis of conciliation between diverse beliefs. But more than that freedom of religious belief is for a Muslim dearer than life itself. It is the obligation of every Muslim not only to succor those of other faiths who have been deprived of religious freedom with the facilities for worshipping God in their own way, but also, should the need arise, to defend with his life the right of others to liberty of religious belief. The teachings of the Koran require that a Muslim defend those who are driven from their homes for having worshipped God. It is required that a Muslim should defend monasteries, churches, places of prayer, and mosques wherein the name of Allah is spoken ...

If religious liberty is really to be safeguarded, if, in the interests of national unity, real understanding is to be fostered among the various religious communities in Indonesia, obviously, no effort must be spared to inspire the entire Indonesian people with the attitude of tolerance and mutual respect described above.[19]

In seeking to align with Christians as a group, Natsir drew on the notion that they shared the desire for Indonesians to bring their beliefs into the public sphere in contrast to the policies of the PKI and the PNI who viewed religious observance as a private issue with no consequences for public life. He drew on the social ethic of tolerance prescribed by Islamic teaching to convince Christians that a good Muslim was always and foremost a tolerant Muslim.

There are, however, obvious limits to Natsir's vision of tolerance. In sharp contrast to the Rawlsian liberal template, congregations are tolerated and not individuals with heterodox or atheist beliefs; references to monasteries and churches suggest respect for Christianity while the pejorative reference to superstition suggests that animist views are not held at the same level of respect as those of Christians. Similarly, in contrast to liberal neutrality, Natsir promotes Islam as the correct and final faith. Although other beliefs are not condemned, nor individuals of other faiths coerced, neither are those religions honored in the same regard as Islam.

Other Persis leaders also promoted tolerance toward Christians, sometimes in explicit contrast to polemics toward Communists. In an article titled "Russian Methods in Indonesia" (*Tjara Rusia di Indonesia*), Isa Anshary wrote that the Communist PKI wanted to promote religious freedom in the form of new, anarchist religions in order to destroy Islam; this was what the Communists thought of as 'progress.'

From the perspective of Islam and Christianity, these [non-monotheist religions] are imports that have arrived from outside our country ... In the disguise of "national

[19] Natsir (1954).

[interests]" they now demand of the government to create national marriage laws that are not [appropriate] for Muslims or Christians, nor for Buddhists.[20]

Anshary went on to argue that PKI propaganda was fundamentally anti-religion and against peace. Notably, his defense against the PKI entailed grouping together Christians, Muslims, and Buddhists in order to block the Communists, rather than argue that the PKI was anti-Islam as in the polemics of the 1930s.

Another article in the Persis magazine *Aliran Islam*, "Islam and Nationalism" (*Islam dan Nasionalisme*) by someone writing under the name Muhammad Sabil emphasized the areas of commonality between Muslims and non-Muslims as well as the obligations of Muslims to protect Christians and Jews: "Within an Islamic country, churches and Jewish houses of prayer may be there and they should not be harassed but rather must be protected."[21] The author went on to discuss periods in history when Muslims and Christians worked together in harmony and both mosques and churches were safe spaces for believers. These points of commonality, as well as this shared history, were intended to demonstrate that Islam is active, not passive, in protecting religious freedom:

[This history] reveals concretely that among the virtues that make up a true Muslim include the spirit of tolerance, *tasamuh*,[22] or *vedraagzaamheid*[23] toward humans in religion and faith. Tolerance is not rooted in cowardice or fear, but tolerance is born of faith and personal conviction. Nor is tolerance merely passive; it is incumbent upon those who are the people of true Islam to sacrifice themselves wherever necessary in order to protect the life, honor, religion and religious freedom of other people. Freedom of religion, to worship the One Almighty God, is a living value for Muslims: [one that is] more valuable than protecting their own soul ...

Muslims and Christians in Indonesia should return to their glorious history [of cooperation]. Let them honestly realize that they need to live like brothers again, as was once originally the case.

To the Christian community in Indonesia we offer this advice, because we are in a time when the nationalist groups that are "neutral" regarding religion are provoking shock and anxiety among [Christians] regarding the propaganda of Islamic parties who seek the implementation of Islamic law in Indonesia.

Instead of their [the Christian community] siding with the nationalist group that is "neutral" on religion, it would better for them to side with the Muslims who have been outspoken in outlining the foundation for living together in society, and who guarantee both freedom and faith.

In a well-known story, when once there passed by a group of people carrying the corpse of a Jew for a funeral, the Prophet Muhammad stood up. One of his

[20] M. Isa Anshary, "Tjara Rusia di Indonesia," *Aliran Islam*, November–December 1953, 2–4.

[21] Muhammad Sabil, *Aliran Islam*, January 1954, 56, 7–19.

[22] *Tasamuh* is the Arabic term commonly used for tolerance, sometimes translated as patience or peace of mind.

[23] *Vedraagzaamheid* is the Dutch term for tolerance.

friends said that the funeral is only that of a Jewish person. [To which] the Prophet Muhammad replied to his friend with a clear statement: *"Is that not a soul?"*[24]

Using the language of the nationalists – religious freedom (*kemerdekaan beragama*), nationality (*kebangsaan*), tolerance (*toleransi*) – and envisioning the Christians as a community similar to the community of Muslims (*ummat Keristen*), the author echoed Natsir's contention that Islamic values provided an unwavering base of support for the protection of Christians' religious freedom. In making this claim, the author was trying to draw Christians into a political alliance against the groups that were advocating for a more secular government: the PNI and the PKI.

As the 1955 election grew closer, the hostility toward the PKI and the PNI grew alongside expressions of tolerance to Christians. In a fatwa titled "Joining Parties Whose Principles Are Opposed to Islam and Those Whose Character Is Opposed to Islam," the Persis Ulama Council (*Madjelis Ulama Persatuan Islam*) declared that it was prohibited (*haram*) for Muslims to become members of parties (1) that have principles that are opposed to Islam, or (2) whose character/qualities are opposed to Islam like the PKI. In a footnote following point (2), the Islamic principle in question was defined as agreement that Islamic law be followed in society and the state. The footnote following point (2) named the PNI as agreeing with the PKI that Islamic law should not be followed.[25] The rest of the magazine was filled with condemnation of the PKI for the violence in Madiun including a printed, detailed list of names of victims of the 1948 attempted coup.[26] Another issue described the PNI and the PKI as the same,[27] and the subsequent issue featured lengthy discussions of what it meant for the PKI to be hypocrites (*munafik*).[28] Persis' linking of the PKI and the PNI may or may not have delegitimized the communist and nationalist parties in the eyes of some Muslims; it did, however, back Persis into a corner. Without the support of the PNI or the PKI, the Masyumi alone did not have enough votes in parliament to form a cabinet.

In another Persis periodical, *Al-Muslimun*, the editors went beyond publishing the Persis fatwa against voting for the PNI or the PKI and declared in the 'Question and Answer' section of the magazine that anyone choosing a non-Islamic party would be considered a non-Muslim. In doing so, they

---

[24] Muhammad Sabil, *Aliran Islam*, January 1954, 56, 16. The hadith is cited as Muhhafaq 'alaih, R. Sahl bin Hanif: Nailul Authar.

[25] Madjelis Ulama Persatuan Islam, "Fatwa Madjlis Ulama Persatuan Islam Tentang Memasuki Partai-Partai Jang Berpendirian Menentang Islam Dan Jang Bersifat Menentang Islam," *Aliran Islam*, January 1954, 56, 55.

[26] "Daftar Sebagai Ketjil Orang2 mendjadi korban Pemberontakan PKI di Madiun 19 September 1948", *Aliran Islam*, January 1954, 56, 29.

[27] Mudjahid, "PNI Bersama PKI," *Aliran Islam*, October 1953, 53, 60.

[28] Tamar Djaja, "Islam Munafik," *Aliran Islam*, November and December 1953, 54/55, 68; H. Munawar Chalil, "Apakan dan siapakah 'Munafiq' itu?" *Aliran Islam* November and December 1953, 54/55, 69–71.

used a novel translation of Qur'an verse An Nisaa' 144, substituting the word 'friends' for 'leaders':

Arabic:	Indonesian:
O ye who believe!	Oh Ye who believe!
Take not for <u>friends</u>	Do not take people who are unbelievers
Unbelievers rather than	as your <u>leaders</u>
Believers: do ye wish	since actually they are not
To offer God an open	of the family of Muslims.[30]
Proof against yourself?[29]	

Other scholars of Persis have noted their resourcefulness when translating the Qur'an into Indonesian.[31] Although they provide the original Arabic text, most of their readers could not translate Arabic. By shifting the focus of the verse from friends to leaders, they strengthened their appeal against the PNI and the PKI. The author went on to define unbelievers as: (1) those who are not Muslim; (2) those who think that Islamic law is not good, or correct, as the law for the state; (3) those who believe that there is any law which is better than the law of Allah; and (4) others who are like the groups in (1), (2), or (3). The article ended with a similarly unusual translation of the Qur'an:

Arabic:	Indonesian:
Your (real) <u>friends</u> are	Your real <u>leader</u> is
(No less than) God,	None other than Allah,
His Apostle, and the (Fellowship Of)	His Apostle,
Believers, – those who	and those who have faith,
Establish regular prayers	Those who establish regular prayers,
And regular charity,	And give out zakat,
And they bow	and they bow humbly.[33]
Down humbly (in worship).[32]	

As before, the author substituted 'leaders' for 'friends' in the Indonesian translation. The next issue of the magazine, in May 1954, continued the polemics against the PNI and the PKI with specific definitions of unbelievers. The author of the section Question and Answer defined four types of unbelievers:

1. *Kafir Inkar*, those who deny, refuse, or reject Allah like Pharaoh (*Fir'aun*), Karl Marx, Lenin, Stalin, and other Communists.
2. *Kafir Nifaq*, those hypocrites who accept Islam but their goal is to distort/ mix [with other ideas] Islam and its followers, like the followers of the PKI.

[29] Qur'an 4:144, using translation by Ali (1987).
[30] *Al-Muslimun*, "Memilih Pemimpin Jang Bukan Islam," 1:1 April 1954, 3.
[31] Federspiel (1977).
[32] Qur'an 5 (Al Maa-idah): 55.
[33] *Al-Muslimun*, "Memilih Pemimpin Jang Bukan Islam," 1:1 April 1954, 3.

3. *Kafir 'Inaad*, those who fight the truth. They know the truth of Islam, but do not have the confidence [in Islam], like those of the PNI who know the Qur'an but do not want it for the foundation of the state.
4. *Kafir Djumud*, those who are static, frozen, and contradictory. They know Allah but do not want to listen, like *Iblis* [the leader of the demons in hell].[34]

Doing so further pushed the PNI and the PKI away from Persis, while increasing expressions of tolerance toward Christians.

Though Persis did not call for violence against the PKI, it came remarkably close. In the Question and Answer section of the January 1955 issue of *Al-Muslimun*, the editors asked whether it was permissible in a country of law to oppose people from the PKI, or to (physically) slap those from the PKI who have overstepped the bounds of appropriate conduct. While the question was vague, the answer was clear. "And kill them wherever you meet them."[35] The author went on to explain that the verse made obligatory the destruction of those who fight Muslims. And while the Qur'an gave many reasons to justify a jihad against the PKI as long as there was evidence, attacking people from the PKI was prohibited without evidence. Not surprisingly, in a subsequent issue, marriage to a Communist was prohibited since members of the PKI were considered disbelievers (*kufur*), and marriage to a disbeliever rendered one an disbeliever as well.[36]

Meanwhile, working in a church or working for Christians was embraced as long as it did not entail compromising one's faith. In the same issue of the magazine, in response to the question of whether a Muslim can work in a church, the author wrote that it would be permitted as long as it was not necessary to kneel in front of a statue of Jesus (*Nabi 'Isa*) or Mary (*Sitti Marjam*). Working for an unbeliever in other ways would also be permissible.[37] In sum, while Persis' attacks on the PKI and the PNI came closer to prescribing outright violence, their recommendations for relations with Christians improved.

The 1957–1960 issues of *Al-Muslimun* provide a helpful glimpse into the ideational origins of Persis' views: Al-Ustadz Abul A'la Al-Maududi of Pakistan and his model of an Islamic state as a "theo-democracy" with limited popular sovereignty,[38] Said Ramadan of Egypt, the son-in-law of Muslim Brotherhood founder Hassan al-Banna and progenitor of the World Islamic League on Islamic constitutionalism,[39] and Muhammad Asad on Islamic constitutionalism and the head of state in an Islamic government.[40] Yet none of these Islamists

---

[34] *Al-Muslimun*, "Kafir," 2:1 May 1954, 8.
[35] *Al-Muslimun*, "Menempeleng Orang P.K.I.," January 1955, 1:10, 4, citing Qur'an 1 (Al-Baqarah): 191.
[36] *Al-Muslimun*, "Kawin Dengan Orang Komunis," 1:12 no date, 7–8.
[37] *Al-Muslimun*, "Bekerdja Digeredga," January 1955, 1:10, 5.
[38] *Al-Muslimun*, "Negara Islam," June 1956, 3:27, 19.
[39] *Al-Muslimun*, "Program Perjuangan," no date, 4:42, 20.
[40] *Al-Muslimun*, "Negara Islam," July 1956, 3:29, 18–19.

provide an explanation for why Persis' rhetoric toward the Christians changed so drastically from the 1930s to the 1950s. To explain the shift, it is necessary to look at the political alignments of the 1950s. The PKI was growing in power, and often aligning with the nationalist PNI. In response, Persis and Masyumi looked increasingly to the Christians as potential allies in parliament and in public debates concerning the role of religion in the new state. Natsir and Anshary made repeated signals to the Christians for them to join with Muslims and form a kind of "Alliance of the Faithful" and anti-Communist front.[41]

Once in power, Natsir rewarded Christian leaders with seats in the cabinet. The Natsir cabinet allocated two seats to non-Muslims: one to the Indonesian Christian Party, Parkindo, and one to the Catholic Party of the Republic of Indonesia, Partai Katholik. While Natsir had tried initially to form a cabinet with the PNI, disagreements over cabinet portfolios, particularly Education and Interior, prevented agreement, leaving Natsir to draw from leaders outside of both the PKI and the PNI.[42] Subsequent Masyumi-led cabinets continued this pattern: the Sukiman cabinet (April 1951–February 1952) and the Burhanuddin cabinet (August 1955–March 1956) both included the Catholics and Parkindo. Sukiman's cabinet, unlike Natsir's, also included the PNI, which again included the Masyumi, Parkindo, and Catholics in the subsequent Wilopo cabinet. The only change in this pattern was in the first Sastoamidjojo cabinet from July 1953 to July 1955.

The reason for this change was that Masyumi splintered in 1952. Recall that Masyumi was a coalition of santri groups – Muhammadiyah, Persis, NU, and others – and originated in cooperative efforts in the mid-1930s. Factionalism between the santri peaked in 1952 owing to struggles over leadership of Masyumi. NU leaders felt that they were underrepresented in the Central Leadership Council relative to their strength in the regions and centrality to the Revolution.[43] Another concern was control over the Department of Religion, which NU held from 1946 and which managed core aspects of Islamic life: religious education, regulation of marriage, inheritance and divorce laws, the definition of religion, and supervision of *hajj* affairs. NU also used the Department of Religion in order to develop patronage networks and businesses. Moreover, unlike Masyumi, NU leaders lacked the education to manage most other ministries; only the Department of Religion provided a pathway into the state for those with traditional santri education. NU's loss of control of the Department of Religion to the modernist Fakih Usman in the Wilopo cabinet was one of the key factors leading to its secession from Masyumi.[44]

---

[41] Federspiel (1970, 181).

[42] Feith (1978 [1962], 148–155).

[43] Federspiel (1970, 160); Feith (1978 [1962], 223–237).

[44] Fealy (1998, 78–105). By splintering the 'Muslim vote' and failing to push its agenda through parliament, Masyumi fits the pattern of Islamist parties in other Muslim-majority states that have not experienced great success in formal politics, but have had more of an impact in transforming the state bureaucracy and social norms. Islamists in Egypt (Hirschkind 2001;

The secession of NU from Masyumi marked the reemergence of the intra-santri cleavages that were conspicuous in the politics of the 1920s and 1930s. And, as an independent party, NU was able to make alliances with parties that Masyumi would not. The Sastoamidjojo cabinet included the PNI, the new NU party, two Communist-sympathizing parties, the Progressive Faction, and the Indonesian Peasant Front (*Barisan Tani Indonesia*), as well as Dr. Ong Eng Die of the PNI, who was also thought to be close to the PKI.[45] Meanwhile, the Masyumi remained outside of the cabinet along with the Christian parties.[46] For the next few years NU and Masyumi maintained radically different relationships with the Communists.

While Isa Anshary and the Masyumi lambasted the PKI as polytheists (*musyrik*) and non-Muslims (*kafir*), NU cooperated with the PKI as part of the first Sastoamidjojo cabinet, then again in the Soekarno government's Gotong-Royong Parliament (Mutual Cooperation), and again in Soekarno's Guided Democracy organized around the ideology of Nasakom (an acronym based on *NASionalisme, Agama* (religion), and *KOMunisme* (Communism)).[47] In the following section, I explain NU's willingness to cooperate with the Communists in the 1950s, its role in the Communist purge of the 1960s, and the reasons for its switch from tolerance to intolerance of the Communists. In the subsequent years, Persis' attitudes toward Christians would also revert back to its intolerance of the 1930s. The failure of Natsir's tenure, the dissolving of Guided Democracy, and the unwillingness of the Christian parties to support Masyumi meant that its shift to tolerance was short-lived.

That Persis' tolerance was short-lived does not mean that its intolerance it was inevitable. In contrast to relations with the Christians, relations between Hindus and Muslims in Indonesia were brokered not by party alliances but by the strong involvement of the Ministry of Religion (MORA), which shaped how Islamic organizations see Balinese religion. As the next section makes clear, this brokerage has shaped levels of tolerance in contemporary Indonesia.

Manufacturing Monotheism from Balinese Hinduism

From 1953 to 1964 the MORA worked with Balinese elites to mold their religion into a form of monotheism including a holy book, prophet, system of laws, and standardized rituals, with its origins plotted in India.[48] This process of rationalizing and modernizing religious practices in Bali has continued

Mahmood 2005; Moustafa 2000), Tunisia (Sadiki 2007), Jordan (Wiktorowicz 2001; Brown and Hamzawy 2010), and Turkey (Mecham 2004; White 2002) have had similar trajectories. On the origins of political Islam's failure in formal Indonesian politics, see Feillard (1999); Fealy (2005); Jones (1980).

[45] Feith (1978 [1962], 337–339).
[46] Feith (1978 [1962], 338).
[47] Fealy (1998, 222).
[48] Geertz (1973, 170–189); Monnig Atkinson (1983); Picard (1997); Schiller (1996).

into the present day. This is not merely an invented tradition, although the interaction between Balinese elites and Jakarta has certainly changed the language with which Balinese describe themselves. Nor is the process of receiving state recognition merely a bureaucratic project of naming and reimaging the contours of religion, with little consequence for the population in Bali. The Balinese appropriation of the language of the ministry, their lobbying efforts, and their willingness to construct multiple, often contradictory visions of their religion are also not merely an act of resistance against the sanitizing and homogenizing impulses of the central state. All these observations are true, but incomplete. Instead, the manufacturing of Balinese religion into a world religion, and then a monotheistic religion, demonstrates the mutual constitution of state and religion in twentieth-century Indonesia.

Late-nineteenth-century descriptions of religion in Bali portray an overlapping array of ritual, divine caste structures headed by a royal king, local temple worship, ecstatic dance and art, and legal norms governing social distinctions between nobility and the common people. These practices stem from at least two sources. One is the Hindu-Javanese kingdom of Majapahit, which ruled Java from 1293 to 1527. When the Islamic sultanate of Demak defeated the rulers in 1527, a large number of artisans, priests, and members of the royal family are thought to have fled to Bali bringing Javanese and Hindu traditions. The second is the Buddhist and Hindu influences that arrived in Bali between 800 and 1343 and are today linked to small villages that have practices distinct from the Javanese, called Original Bali or *Bali Aga*.

Major changes in religious practices began with the Dutch administration of Bali starting in 1850. At first the Dutch attempted to convert the Balinese to Christianity, which failed, and then they turned to a policy of *Baliseering*, the traditionalization or Balinization of Bali.[49] Balinization aimed to return the island to how the Dutch imagined Bali to be prior to the arrival of the Javanese, even while it was politically domesticated under colonial rule. This entailed strengthening the tradition of customary law (*adat*) organized around caste (the Brahama, Satria, Wesia, and Sudra castes, whose parallel in Indian Hinduism are Brahmin, Kshatriya, Vaishya, and Sudra). These caste distinctions were intended to be a bulwark against both Indonesian nationalism and Islam, which were viewed as threatening to Dutch control over the island.[50] Alongside the political administration, the Dutch sought to produce a renaissance of Balinese culture for the youth. The policy ensured that Balinese society and state would be oriented to matters of interpretation of tradition through mass education in culture, religion, and caste.

By the 1920s, Balinese religion was a hybrid of traditional custom, culture, religion, ethnicity, and artistic practice. Balinese religion was not chosen or sustained through belief; participation was a consequence of membership in

[49] Howell (2005, 18).
[50] Picard (1999, 20–21).

a local community and descent group. Picard notes that "Unlike the world religions that have a core of abstract basic tenets and symbols meaningful to people of diverse cultural backgrounds, Balinese religion is highly localized: it consists of rites relating specific to groups of people to one another, to their ancestors, and to their territory."[51] Religion for the Balinese was not regarded as something distinct from the broader traditions of the island.

The transformation of Balinese religion from a multifaceted tradition to a modern, rationalized religion occurred during the 1920s–1950s as a result of negotiations between elites in Bali, and later, the MORA in Jakarta. The first issue to be settled was the name of their faith. At the end of the 1920s, the following names for Balinese religion were commonplace: *Agama Bali, Agama Tirta, Agama Sirta, Agama Siwa, Agama Siwa Tirta, Agama Budha, Agama Siwa-Budha, Agama Trimurti, Agama Hindu Bali, Agama Bali Hindu, Agama Hindu*. The name of the religion's God was similarly diverse: *Bhatara Siaw, Sanghyang Tunggal, Sanghyang Suksma, Sanghyang Widi, Sanghyang Widi Was a, Sanghyang Widi Wisesa, Sanghyang Parama Wiesa, Tuhan, Tuhan Esa, Allah*.[52]

It should be no surprise then that an attempt by Balinese in 1937 to compile a holy book for their religion failed after three years of effort because religion (*agama*) could not be separated from tradition (*adat*), adat differed from one village to the next, and the priests could not agree on a canon for the island.[53] In 1945, a delegation of Balinese priests (*pendanda*) were gathered by the Japanese to strengthen their religion, and chose the name *Agama Siwa* and their highest God Siwa the Sun God, as a way of affiliating Balinese religion with Shintoism.[54] In 1948, another association of priests aligned against the Republican administration was established to unify the *Agama Siwa-Budha*.[55] And in 1949 a larger gathering of priests and kings met for two days of debate before settling on *Agama Tirtha*. There was no resolution by 1950, when after independence, the Republic of Indonesia established a provincial office for religious affairs (Kantor Urusan Agama Propinsi Nusa Tenggara) and a regional office (Kantor Urusan Agama Daerah Bali). Neither office recognized Balinese religion.[56]

Once the MORA was established, the task of defining Balinese practices in religious terms became more urgent. As Chapter 4 established, while the constitution guaranteed Indonesian citizens the freedom of religion, the available choices were constrained by the MORA to those with divine revelation recorded by a prophet in a holy book, a system of law for the community of believers, congregational worship, and a belief in the One and Only God. Bali's

---

[51] Picard (1999, 31).
[52] Picard (1999, 49 n. 28).
[53] Picard (1999, 41).
[54] Picard (2011, 486–487).
[55] Picard (2011, 487).
[56] Picard (2011, 488).

local, ritual-oriented, and descent-based practices were excluded from recognition. The Balinese were said not to profess a proper religion, but only beliefs (*kepercayaan*). As a result, the Balinese were open to Christian and Islamic proselytizing, and would not receive support for the teaching of their beliefs in national schools, acknowledgment of their holy days, or recognition by the state as a religion on par with Islam or Christianity.[57] The challenge for the Balinese thus became twofold: to distinguish their religion from customary traditions in order to unify the elite around a single definition, and to meet the rigidly monotheist, scriptural definition of a religion promulgated by the state.

In 1950, the name Balinese Hinduism (*Agama Hindu Bali*) was chosen by the regional government official I Gusti Bagus Sugriwa when he requested that the provincial government recognize the Balinese religion on par with the other religions.[58] Sugriwa explained that Balinese religion consisted of Hinduism of the Siwa sect and Buddhism of the Mahayana sect, which explained the profuse number of priests and prophets. In accordance with the constitution and Pancasila, Sugriwa claimed that Balinese worshiped a single God, *Sanghjang Tunggal*.[59] The request was apparently denied.

By the early 1950s, there were four distinct religious organizations on Bali, each taking a different stance on the nature of their religion. The *Paruman Para Pandita* argued for the distinctness of Balinese religion apart from other faiths and in particular the authority of the priests. The *Wiwada Sastra Sabha* represented the cultural traditions of the island, in particular the arts, dance, and music, which were inseparable from religion. The *Panti Agama Hindu Bali* wanted to modernize their religion but retain the Balinese practices. And the *Madjelis Hinduisme* aimed to conform religious practices to Indian Hinduism; they even established ties to India and educational programs there.[60] In June 1951, representatives of these organizations wrote to the minister of religion and other government officials in Jakarta and the province to request recognition in all religious affairs offices, support for priests, support for temples, and support for the artistic traditions that accompanied religious practices. Again the request was denied and the MORA insisted on an official name for the Balinese religion.[61]

A committee of the main organizations came together with the Dutch Orientalist Roelof Goris to comply with the ministry's request. The Balinese religion was called *Agama Hindu Bali*. Three holy books were chosen from the Hindu and Balinese traditions. A profession of faith to a single God was chosen, similar to the Islamic sahadat: *Om tat sat, ekam ewa dwityam* (We believe

---

[57] Picard (2011, 483–484).
[58] Picard (2011, 488). This was despite the word *Hindu* only being known in Bali in the twentieth century (Picard 2004).
[59] Picard (2011, 489).
[60] Picard (2011, 490).
[61] Picard (2011, 490–491).

in the One God, almighty and eternal). In response, a Hindu Bali section was established in the provincial government. This representation was expanded to the provision of specific services in 1955: religious affairs, religious information, and religious education. But Balinese Hinduism was still not recognized in Jakarta.[62]

In July 1952, the MORA stipulated that in order to receive recognition *Agama Hindu Bali* must be monotheistic, have a codified legal system, possess a holy book and a prophet, enjoy international recognition, and not be limited to a single ethnic group.[63] The response in Bali was manifold. Some argued that Balinese religion had no need for a prophet or holy book, as these were distinctive features of Islam and Christianity, not Hinduism or Buddhism. Others denounced the demands of the state as unwarranted interference in religious affairs. Others defended Balinese Hinduism as predating the arrival of both Christianity and Islam in Indonesia and not needing recognition from the new arrivals.[64] In February 1953, the MORA followed up by designating Balinese Hinduism as a religious current or movement and not a proper religion.

By 1957, the Balinese had grown closer in their shared opposition to Islam and the national government. Dutch attempts at conversion, as well as the growing mobilization of Islamic movements in Java forced the Balinese to see their identity as a religious one distinct from Islam and Christianity.[65] The name of their faith, Balinese Hinduism, was no longer seriously contested. The necessity for national representation was agreed on. The continued denial of the national ministry for recognition brought together the Balinese.[66] In 1958, a movement to demand the establishment of a Balinese sect of Hinduism was launched by Wedastera to put pressure on the minister of religion, the prime minister, the president of the Republic, and the authorities at the provincial and regional levels. The major Balinese organizations met in June 1958 and adopted a resolution calling for full recognition and incorporation. This resolution was presented personally to President Soekarno, whose mother was Balinese.

Soekarno summoned the minister of religion to Bali to articulate his support for the Balinese and three months later a Balinese Hinduism section was established within the ministry.[67] By this point Balinese Hinduism had been transformed, by the process of recognition, into a religion with an emphasis on texts, theology, a single God, a holy book, standardization of ritual, ethical injunctions, a prophet, and universal application. The Balinese created contacts with India to establish credibility as Hindus and translated classical studies of Hindu theology into Indonesian, Indian teachers were invited to Bali to teach their religion, and scholarships to study in India were granted to young

[62] Picard (2011, 491).
[63] Picard (2011, 497).
[64] Picard (2011, 499).
[65] Picard (1999, 31); Vickers (1987, 35).
[66] Picard (2011, 501).
[67] Picard (2011, 501–502).

Balinese.[68] In 1959, the multiple representatives of religion in Bali merged under the Hindu Balinese Council (Parisada Dharma Hindu Bali [PDHB]), which became the official liaison between Hindu Balinese and the MORA. The council compiled theological dogma to standardize ritual practice and normalize the priesthood.[69]

After recognition, the movement of religious rationalization continued. The PDHB promoted the use of a single holy book, standardized religious rites, formalized priesthood, and a religious education curriculum. In 1964, due to interest in Hinduism from Java, the council changed its name again to Parisada Hindu Dharma (PHD), thus completing the connection to a universal religion, Hinduism. This is the name that was recognized by Soekarno in the 1965 blasphemy law.

In the subsequent years, the shift toward rationalized Hinduism moved from the Jakarta bureaucracy into Bali's classrooms, households, and temples. PHDI (the word Indonesia was added to the name in 1986) has increasingly controlled religious education in schools and narrowed the diversity of Balinese religion. In 100 years, the religion of Bali went from a local, ritual-based mix of tradition, culture, art, and belief to a universal, scriptural religion originating in Hinduism, tied to India, separate from local cultural practices of art-making and dance, and in contrast to Islam.[70]

This process of rationalization has shaped how Islamic organizations see Hindus. Rather than polytheists, Islamic organizations see a monotheist faith. Remember that NU controlled the MORA in the early 1950s, and both NU and Muhammadiyah strongly backed the 1965 law, as did their various youth wings. State recognition changed religious practice, even as religious ideas, particularly the Islamic definition of a religion, forced their way into state practice.

NU Integrates with the Military

While Persis declared the PKI an enemy in the 1950s, and Muhammadiyah published repeated polemics against Communism, NU became hostile to the Communists only in the 1960s. As discussed in Chapter 3, NU was formed in 1926 in order to defend traditionalist Islam, the rural syncretism practiced by many Indonesian Muslims. Traditionalists seek to preserve the authority of classical Islamic scholarship and tend to be tolerant of local religious customs like the veneration of saints.[71] Under the leadership of Abdurrahman Wahid (Gus Dur) in the 1980s and 1990s, NU was at the forefront of efforts to promote pluralism, democracy, and toleration. Yet, while NU's leadership during the 1980s professed high levels of tolerance, it is no less likely to change policies

---

[68] Picard (1997, 194).
[69] Picard (1997, 194).
[70] Picard (1999, 44–45).
[71] Fealy and Hooker (2006, 40).

than other organizations. As a result, there is empirical value to Indonesian studies in correcting the selection bias of research that has overemphasized NU's tolerance. This section focuses on the period from 1957 to 1966, when NU changed its policies toward the Communists as the result of a political alliance with the military against the PKI and its program of land reform.

In the 1950s, NU was the only one of the leading Islamic parties willing to cooperate with the Communists during parliamentary democracy. Although this was an anxious, reluctant form of tolerance, it stood in stark contrast to Persis and Muhammadiyah. Recall that in 1954 Persis denounced Communists as polytheists (*musyrik*) and non-Muslims (*kafir*). Muhammadiyah, similarly, derided Muslim Communists as ignorant. The December 1953 issue of *Suara Muhammadiyah* described a mass conversion of 6,000 people in Sungai Pagu who, under the banner of Masyumi, returned to Islam. Muhammadiyah explained how such incidents often happen in areas where people are unaware. As soon as other Indonesians were taught the differences between their religion and Communism, Muhammadiyah noted, they would likewise return to Islam.[72]

After NU's split from Masyumi in 1952, it quickly differentiated itself from the other Muslim parties despite publicly proclaiming solidarity. Feith and Fealy rightly note that from early 1953, NU often had more in common with the PNI than with Masyumi: both were anti-imperialist, strongest in Java rather than the outer islands, and ardent nationalists.[73] NU also worked to find points of commonality with the PKI. A news article from *Berita Antara* for March 4, 1953, describes a joint seminar led by Secretary of the Central Board of Nahdlatul Ulama (PBNU) Idham Chalid and H. A. Notosoetardjo from the Department of Foreign Affairs on the value of socialism as a tool for developing the nation. Notosoetardjo emphasized the points of commonality between socialism and Islam, including social justice for all, unity among mankind, and the compatibility of socialism with belief in God. He went on to argue that those who feared Islam or socialism failed to understand Soekarno's Revolutionary Doctrine. Although Chalid's participation should not be seen as an endorsement of socialism and certainly not of communism, it would have been a clear signal that NU was open to working with parties with other ideological commitments.

The PBNU's behavior made this stance explicit in the coming years. After the fall of the Wilopo cabinet in June 1953, NU vacillated between public declarations of Islamic solidarity and private negotiations with the PNI about a joint cabinet. The result was that NU eventually joined the Ali Sastroamidjojo cabinet while Masyumi was excluded. NU was given three ministries where previously it held only one, greatly expanding opportunities for its students to fill the ranks of the bureaucracy and for the organization to offer material

---

[72] Muhammadiyah, "Ada-Ada Saja," *Suara Muhammadiyah* No. 39, December, 1953: 529.
[73] Feith (1978 [1962], 325); Fealy (1998, 121).

rewards to supporters. Indeed, over the next few months NU began a campaign of 'NU-ization' within the national and provincial branches of the Religious Affairs offices.[74]

NU's decision was not without controversy, and the central board proffered repeated justifications to its branches for their willingness to join a cabinet dependent on the Communists for support and against Masyumi. A June 1954 letter from Vice Chair of the Executive Board K. H. Moh Dahlan and Secretary Achmad Sjahri to the Jakarta branch of Ansor notes that NU needed to be flexible in advancing its goals, even working with groups (*aliran*) with whom it disagreed, such as the Communists.[75] Not surprisingly, NU leaders faced criticism both within the party and outside of it for failing to defend the interests of the Muslim community.[76] Less controversial, apparently, was NU's purge of Masyumi members from the Department of Religion. Fealy notes that "In many sections of the party there was deepening mistrust of modernists which, on occasions, bordered on vengeance. NU leaders were under constant pressure to purge Masyumi members from politically sensitive positions."[77]

NU's also showed its flexibility through its enthusiastic cooperation with President Soekarno, who became increasingly important in the mid-to-late 1950s. NU was Soekarno's strongest supporter among the Muslim organizations and in contrast to Isa Anshary from Persis/Masyumi, NU refrained from harsh criticism of the president even on core areas of disagreement such as the establishment of an Islamic state. When Soekarno moved to establish "Guided Democracy" on March 14, 1957, with the proclamation of martial law, NU was reluctantly supportive. Soekarno's template was a concept/plan (*konsepsi*) that included the formation of a Mutual Cooperation (*Gotong-Royong*) cabinet of NU, Masyumi, the PKI and the PNI. The PKI welcomed the konsepsi, the PNI was noncommittal, and the Masyumi and the Catholic Party were opposed. NU was initially opposed, but in a March 6 meeting, Soekarno asked an NU delegation of K. H. Abdul Chasbullah, K. H. Idham Chalid, K. H. Masjkur, and H. Zainal 'Arifin to study and support the konsepsi. Soekarno's direct appeal worked, and NU issued a statement saying that in order to preserve 'the prestige of Bung Karno' it would back the president. "The prestige of Bung Karno is a central psychological concern [for the country]; if the leader fails, it will be very bad for the country." NU also seemed concerned that without its support, Soekarno might form a coalition with the PKI and no Islamic party. "[In] the proposal of Bung Karno, NU is equal [to the PNI], and [we] have to weigh the idea that otherwise Bung Karno might be in the cabinet alone with the PKI." NU furthermore seemed to think that it would be able to gain the

[74] Fealy (1998, 123–129).
[75] 3044/VI/1954 Surat PBNU Kepada Dewan Harian PP GS Ansor Tentang Sikap Tegas Terhadap Komunisme, INA.
[76] Fealy (1998, 132).
[77] Fealy (1998, 130).

formateurship and that one of its members might be prime minister. With the formateurship, it also could put into place its own *Konsepsi NU* comprising a cabinet of the PNI, Soekarno, NU, and Masyumi and without the PKI.[78]

NU was ultimately tricked by Soekarno, who rather than appointing an NU leader as formateur appointed Suwirjo from the PNI, and then appointed himself after the Suwirjo-led cabinet failed to materialize. Eventually Soekarno appointed a cabinet of four ministers from the PNI, four from NU, and three who were Communist sympathizers.[79] Fealy notes that NU's participation in the cabinet signaled a departure from earlier policies. NU had declared its commitment to parliamentary democracy but was now in a cabinet formed through questionable means; NU had declared support for Muslim solidarity, yet was the only Muslim party willing to serve in the cabinet; and most importantly for this chapter, NU had declared its opposition to the PKI involvement, yet accepted the inclusion of known Communist sympathizers.[80] Indeed NU defended its cooperation with the PNI and the PKI on the grounds that national unity was necessary in times of crisis, proclaiming, "A nation divided against itself cannot stand!"[81]

Greg Fealy explains NU's willingness to accommodate Soekarno, the end of guided democracy, and the establishment of military rule along with NU's willingness to abandon their alliance with the other Muslim parties and to work alongside the PKI as "classic Sunni quietism."[82] NU stressed the need for caution, realism, and compromise with superior force to protect the Muslim community and especially its followers, the *ahlus sunnah wal-jama'ah*. Defending democracy, defeating communism, and supporting modernist Muslims were secondary to protecting its faith and followers. It is on this basis that Fealy argues throughout his dissertation that the key to explaining NU's behavior is its religio-political ideology of quietism. "This quietism was expressed and codified in NU's political discourse largely through jurisprudential principles and maxims which enjoined risk minimization, flexibility, the pursuit of benefit, and the avoidance of extremes."[83]

Fealy's targets of critique were the studies of the 1950s–1960s that explained NU's behavior on the basis of crass materialism and opportunism.[84] In that respect, his argument is a welcome corrective as well as an impressive marshaling of empirical evidence. Yet there is a subtle tension between Fealy's argument and NU's behavior. In at least two periods its alleged preference for

[78] 171/Tanf/III-1957 Surat PBNU Kepada PWNU dan PCNU seluruh Indonesia tentang Penyerahan Mandat Kebinet Ali-Idham Chalid, INA. See also Fealy (1998, 184–185).

[79] Fealy (1998, 187 n. 25).

[80] Fealy (1998, 188).

[81] March 1957/Surat PBNU Kepada PCNU Kab Nias, INA; Kom GP Ansor Wil Sulawesi; dan PB Partai NU Kab Bandung tentang Sekitar Konsepsi Bung Karno. INA.

[82] Fealy (1998, 192).

[83] Fealy (1998, 77).

[84] For example, Samson (1968, 1002); Lev (1966, 105).

quietism has been abandoned in favor of extremism and the taking on of risk. NU was quietist toward Dutch rule throughout the 1930s, but was a leader of physical opposition to the Dutch return in 1945 when, Fealy notes, "in a dramatic early act" it issued a 'Resolusi Jihad' obligating Muslims to fight against the Dutch.[85] Similarly, NU's flexibility in cooperating with the PKI in the 1950s was abandoned from October 1965 through 1966, when NU leaders from Matraman preceded the army in accusing the PKI of attempting a coup on Soekarno, were the first to call for the PKI's banning, and drew up plans for mass rallies on October 13 followed by attacks on PKI buildings and the killing of PKI supporters.[86]

Fealy recognizes this tension in Chapter 7 of his dissertation, which departs from the theoretical emphasis on Sunni quietism to focus on the disconnect between the 'accommodationist' leadership in Jakarta and younger 'militants' who led new suborganizations within NU: the Ansor Multi-Purpose Brigade (Barisan Serba Guna Ansor [Banser]), Ansor, and the NU Students Association (Ikatan Pelajar Nahdlatul Ulama [IPNU]). Instead of explaining NU's behavior from 1963 to 1967 on the basis of Sunni quietism, he emphasizes the competing streams that alternated in leading NU. "Accommodationists and militants pursued their respective approaches to achieving the party's goals, the former collaborative and irenic, and the latter activist and confrontational."[87] Rather than reconcile the militants' behavior with Sunni quietism, Fealy argues that the divergence served the ultimate goals of flexibility and safeguarding the Muslim community.

Another way to explain the shift in the behavior of NU, however, is to look beyond ideas and focus on the leadership switch as an endogenous organizational mechanism for policy change. It is clear that the shift between tolerance and intolerance toward the Communists was prompted by pressure from the military and Communist Party policy. The mechanism for the shift was the emergence within the organization of leaders with alliances to the state. The 'accommodationists' were led by Wahab, Idham, Saifuddin Zuhri, and Masjkur and were highly loyal to Soekarno. M. Munasir, Jusef Hasjim, Subchan, and Bisri Syansuri led the new generation of 'militants.' This group had closer links to anti-Communists in the military and led the new NU militia units. Its strength grew in 1963 and 1964 when the PKI launched its 'unilateral actions' to begin land reform and quickly ran into resistance from local NU leaders. While the accommodationists professed support for Soekarno, who backed land reform, the militants mobilized swift attacks on *aksi sepihak* (unilateral actions) squads and replaced accommodationist NU leaders in the regions with other hardliners.[88] By 1965, the militants were sufficiently well organized to lead NU's response to the events of September 30, 1965.

---

[85] Fealy (1998, 42).
[86] Fealy (1998, 248–252).
[87] Fealy (1998, 269).
[88] Fealy (1998, 242–244).

Although the concept of a leadership shift has not been clearly articulated in the literature on Islam and politics, its occurrence is common. Quinn Mecham argues that the Welfare (*Refah*) and Virtue (*Fazilet*) parties in Turkey moderated their platforms in response to strategic interaction in a political system that rewards political entrepreneurship, the presence of institutional constraints on the Islamist movement's behavior, and incentives for the movement to provide costly signals about its intentions. Yet key to Mecham's story is the switch from the old parties' elites, Recaï Kutan and Necmettin Erbakan, to the new leaders, Recep Tayyip Erdogan and Abdullah Gül.[89] Edward Aspinall explains the transformation of the Islamist Darul Islam rebellion into a secular, ethnically Achenese movement on the basis of national identity construction and differentiation. Yet key to Aspinall's story is the changing leadership of the movement from the chiefly caste, the *uleebalang*, to the Islamic *ulama* and then to more secular Achenese nationalists.[90] Muhammadiyah's split from Ahmadiyah in the late 1920s featured a similar dynamic when Djojosoegito and Tjokroaminoto were pushed aside by Fachruddin, Hadji Ibrahim, and Hadsi Sudjak.[91] The split anticipated the break from Ahmadiyah and marked the onset of Muhammadiyah polemics toward the Ahmadis.

While the accommodationist leadership of NU allied with Soekarno, the militants created a close partnership with the military that was mobilized in the service of mass killings. NU militants performed two key functions: religious sanctions for mass violence and integration into the armed forces. Before detailing how this occurred, it is first necessary to map out why land reform posed such a danger to NU and to describe the precipitating events of September 30, 1965.

NU's rural schools (*pesantren*) were built on a simple economic model. The students cultivated labor-intensive crops like rice and soybeans as well as undertaking craftwork like cigarette making or tailoring in exchange for room, board, and religious instruction from the teachers. Students would move from pesantren to pesantren in order to obtain an education and, if they continued their studies, find a niche within the Islamic sciences in astronomy, Qur'anic exegesis, or some other field. Often their travels included studying abroad in Mecca or Cairo and sometimes the students would settle at a single pesantren for many years, even marrying into the family of the *kiai* (religious scholar) and taking on responsibilities for religious instruction.[92]

Land reform, if fully implemented, would have posed an existential challenge to NU. Many of the large land holdings in rural Java were controlled by santri families and pesantren, and *madrasah* (Islamic boarding schools that also

---

[89] Mecham (2004, 345–347, 354, 359).
[90] Aspinall (2007, 248, 253–254).
[91] Alfian (1989, 221–229).
[92] Interview with kiai at Pesantren al-Musri, Ciganjur, October 9, 2010; interview with Ulil Abshar-Abdalla, June 9, 2009; see also Geertz (1960, 177–180).

incorporated secular education) relied on large tracts of land to support the students.[93] Land owners and santri families were already in crisis due to general economic stagnation since 1962 and the drought of 1963–1964. Economic output from food crops declined from 1960 to 1961, again from 1962 to 1963, and then again from 1964 to 1965. GDP per capita declined from 1961 to 1964, and again from 1965 to 1968.[94] Not surprisingly relations between NU and the PKI began to seriously deteriorate in 1964 and 1965 when the PKI launched its "unilateral actions" (*aksi pihak*) to bring about land reform.

On September 30, a small group of palace guard officers launched a preemptive coup to protect Soekarno from a supposed military takeover of the state. The officers kidnapped seven leading army figures including the commander of the army, executed them, and dumped their bodies in a well. The attempted coup was marked by incompetence and confusion and is still considered one of the most enigmatic moments in Indonesian history. This confusion is due in part to the briefness of the coup attempt, which ended before most Indonesians or even the leaders of the movement understood its goals.[95]

The significance of the attempted coup lies not in its origins but in its immediate aftermath. The same day as the coup, General Soeharto took control of the army and launched a counterattack against the rebel troops. All the rebels were either caught or killed by October 3, only a few short days later.[96] Soeharto then used the Thirtieth of September Movement (G30S or *Gerakan 30 September*) as an excuse to systematically crush the PKI through violence, media manipulation, and presidential orders. Soeharto's mobile hit squads recruited NU youth from the countryside and slaughtered PKI members across the archipelago. The army used the media to create a hysterical atmosphere, scaring non-Communists into believing their lives were in danger. A combination of public demonstrations against Soekarno and the PKI, and presidential directives from Soeharto, slowly led to public calls for Soekarno to step down from office. Soekarno was slowly weaned from power through a combination of force, media-induced public hysteria, and careful planning.[97]

There is an extensive literature on the coup attempt, the mass killings, and Soeharto's consolidation of power that is not necessary to describe here. Rather, I want to focus on NU and the military's formation of hit squads and their role in sanctioning the violence. The first contact between the military and NU took place in the evening of October 1, when one NU militant, Subchan, along with student leaders, contacted two military leaders close to Soeharto, Major General Umar Wirahadikusumah and Brigadier General Sutjipto. Subchan was informed of the kidnapping of the generals and the Communists' role in

---

[93] Fealy (1998, 240–241); Mortimer (1972).
[94] van der Eng (2006).
[95] Roosa (2006, 3).
[96] Roosa (2006, 4).
[97] Roosa (2006, 197–201).

the coup, and NU's cooperation was sought to defeat G30S. The Ansor board quickly issued a press release declaring that the party had no connection to G30S, using the same wording as Soeharto's evening radio broadcast.[98] Two days later PBNU formed the Organization Security Coordinating Body (Badan Koordinasi Keamanan Djama'ah Nahdlaul Ulama [BKKDJNU]) to coordinate action by NU and the military 'to restore order in the country.' The body included Dr. K. H. Idham Chalid, K. H. Moh Dahlan on planning and external relations, H. A. Sjaichu as coordinator for politics and operations, H. M. Subchan Z. E. as coordinator of logistics and coordination of autonomous bodies by, H. Moh Munasir as head of staff, H. Sullam Sjamsu as vice head of staff, and assistants from among the leaders of the branches and other organizations.[99] Fealy argues that while Chalid and the other accommodationists held nominal positions, the authority was in the hands of Munasir, Dachlan, Subchan, and Sjaichu.[100]

PBNU openly called for the dissolution of the PKI along with the other 'counterrevolutionary movements.' PBNU specifically asked for the Muslim community and supporters of the revolution to help the military to stop the disorder brought about by G30S, and the statement was signed by the major NU bodies: Ansor, Muslimat NU, Pergerakan Mahasiswa Indonesia, Serikat Buruh Muslimin Indonesia, Pertanian NU, Fatayat NU, Serikat Nelayan Muslim Indonesia, and Lesbumi. The statement was broadcast on Radio Republic Indonesia, circulated to NU branches, and published on October 6 in major newspapers.[101]

Large-scale violence involving NU members began the next week. By the end of the month, NU, Muhammadiyah, Catholic, and other anti-Communist youth groups were conducting systematic killings of suspected Communists, known Communists, and Communist sympathizers. Of the upwards of 500,000 people killed, the majority died at the hands of NU and Ansor groups.[102] Yet there was careful coordination with the military.

NU's archives from October and November 1965 contain hundreds of letters from NU branch offices to the central office in Jakarta reporting on their coordination with ABRI in dissolving the PKI often along with signatures of support from local Catholic and Protestant leaders. Some NU branches requested arms from Jakarta such as the Banser unit in Palembang.[103] A memo from the Belitang branch details the operational structure of its 'Komando' unit: the public coordinator, Bachtier Jusufy, was head of NU for the branch, with seven assistants from Ansor, GP Ansor, NU's department of economic affairs, and

[98] Fealy (1998, 247 n. 59).
[99] No. 3302/Tanf/B/X-'65, October 3, 1965, NU folder 182, INA.
[100] Fealy (1998, 248 n. 65).
[101] *Berita Yudha* October 6, 1965; Fealy (1998, 250).
[102] Fealy (1998, 253).
[103] NU folder 115/10/KKNU/XI-1965 from Palembang November 17, INA.

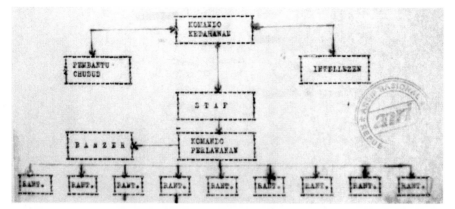

FIGURE 5.2. Structure of the Balikpapan hit squad. Indonesian National Archives, NU folder 116.

other bodies.[104] Figure 5.2 is from a document outlining the structure and division of labor of a NU hit squad in Balikpapan, Kalimantan:

Commander (*Komando*) of the Resistance: Abd Hamid Th
Chief of Staff (*Kepala Staff*): Stijono
Vice Chief of Staff (*Wakil Kepala Staff*): Mohmas
Special Assistants (*Pembantu Chusus*): Puang Ali, Djailani, Abdullah, Moh Dardjad, Get Hamsjah, Djohanis, Abd Kadir Tamin, Hamzah Abu
Intelligence (*Intelozen*): All Islamic Organizations within NU
Commander of the Opposition (*Komando Perlawanan*): Ansor, Lesbumi, Serbamusi, Pertanu, IPNU
Para-Military Brigade (*Banser*): Ansor, Sarbumusi, IPNU, and others
Branches (*Ranting-Ranting*): Islamic society within their respective neighborhoods.[105]

NU's hit squads coordinated their actions with the military, which approved plans, helped compile lists of local PKI members, and in some cases left NU and other civilian groups to do the killings.[106] In doing so, NU functioned as a partner and a structurally integrated wing of the military. The archival record of NU-military cooperation suggests a highly coordinated purge of the PKI.

In addition to performing the mass killings, NU provided the moral sanction for the purge. NU kiai issued fatwas declaring that the PKI were unbelievers who were belligerent toward Islam (*kafir harbi*), and rebels against a legitimate government (*bughat*).[107] While the NU archives do not contain the

---

[104] NU folder 115/00372/XS-1965, INA.
[105] NU folder 116/030/Taaf/x/K/65 Laporan Susunan Kohandjenu (Komando Pertahanan Djemaah NU) Kotapradjo Balikpapan, INA.
[106] Fealy (1998, 253).
[107] Fealy (1998, 255).

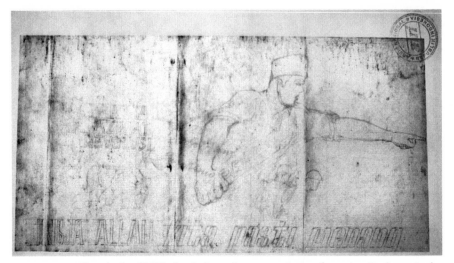

FIGURE 5.3. First draft of NU's fortieth anniversary painting featuring Soekarno's slogan "Five Charms of the Revolution" (*Panitia Tanzimat Revolusi*) and "If God Wills It
We Surely Will Be Victorious." Indonesian National Archives, NU folder 117.

fatwas, correspondence from the regions cites the decision of the NU Syuriah
board that it was obligatory (*wajib*) to ban the PKI since the PKI was a danger
to the government and should be considered kafir harbi.[108] While the conflict
began as a secular military coup, NU framed the violence in sectarian terms.

A series of three drafts of a poster created to commemorate NU's fortieth
anniversary in January 1966 provide a dramatic illustration of NU's role in
transforming the events of late 1965 into a religious struggle.[109] Figure 5.3
is a preliminary draft of the poster, created by the committee for the fortieth
anniversary of NU in Indramayu, West Java. The poster depicts a man wearing a black-velvet skullcap (a *peci*) pointing to the right, presumably forward.
In his hands is a quotation from Soekarno, and in the background is the slogan "*Panitia Tanzimat Revolusi*," which referred to Soekarno's Five Charms
of the Indonesian Revolution: *Nasakom* (the guiding state principle of com-
bining nationalism, religion, and communism), *Pancasila* (belief in one God,
humanity, nationalism, democracy, and social justice), *Manipol* (Soekarno's
political manifesto of 1959), *Usdek* (Soekarno's acronym for the constitution
of 1945, Indonesian-style socialism, guided democracy, guided economy, and
Indonesian self-identity), *Trisakti* (complete national sovereignty, self-sufficient

[108] NU folder 110/Surat dari Rapat Pimpinan Wilayah Partai Nahdlatul Ulama bersama Ormas2/
Badan Autonom dan Pimpinan Tjabang Partai Nahdlatul Ulama dan Gerakan Pemuda Ansor
jang berlangsung pada hari Djumat dan Sabtu tanggal 5 dan November 6, 1965, INA.

[109] NU folder 117/Committee for the 40th Anniversary of NU Indramayu/12 and December 30,
1965, INA.

FIGURE 5.4. Revised version of NU's fortieth anniversary painting: "If God Wills It We Surely Will be Victorious." Indonesian National Archives, NU folder 117.

economy, national self-identity), and *Berdikari* (standing on one's own feet was Soekarno's principle of national economic self-sufficiency).[110] At the bottom is the slogan "If God Wills It We Surely Will Be Victorious" (*Inshallah Kita Pasti Menang*). A group of three soldiers appear under the man's arm, moving in the direction he points. The picture is laden with references to Soekarno's political coalition of the PNI, the PKI, and NU and the ideological synthesis that he tried to engineer.

The second painting, a completed version (Figure 5.4), presents a marked shift in content and tone. "If God Wills It We Surely Will Be Victorious" is now the headline with no reference to Soekarno. Instead, the central figure is larger, with a muscular forearm and elongated fist. The background is dark green with a small banner of an Indonesian flag. Alongside the man is an older woman dressed in green with a loosely worn headscarf. Replacing *Panitia Tanzimat Revolusi* is *Hari Ulang Tahun ke 40 NU* (NU's fortieth anniversary) atop an exploding yellow sun. The shift in reference from Soekarno to NU suggests that 'we' signified NU's struggle and success, rather than Soekarno's or the state's struggle. NU's logo is prominent in front of the man and woman, leading the way forward. Religious symbols, with NU at the center, are prominent and central to the painting.

The third and final painting, Figure 5.5, features the same NU man and woman striding forward surrounded by people and landmarks. The slogan on the bottom, "Fighting, Worshipping, the Duty of the Ummat to Worship God." synthesizes the fight against the PKI with the broader community's obligation

---

[110] Roosa (2006, 274).

FIGURE 5.5. Final version of NU's fortieth anniversary painting, "Fighting, Worshipping, the Duty of the Ummat to Worship God." Indonesian National Archives, NU folder 117.

to God. The anniversary of NU is again displayed, but in a small green box off to one side rather than atop an exploding sun. The central figures are flanked by a nurse, two women wearing traditional Javanese dress and painting batik, a female dressed in military garb, workers on a machine, soldiers with a rifle pointed in the same direction as the central man, and three men with what appear to be welding irons. Emanating from the man's right arm are flames, while he points toward a mosque and minaret. His white shirt is unbuttoned and his bare chest visible above white pants. While the woman in the previous painting was matronly, here she is young, her head uncovered, her hair in a single braid and her white shirt open to the base of her neck. In the background, the Indonesian flag is interwoven with NU's flag.

Taken together, the paintings help to narrate NU's transformation from October 1965 to January 1966. The first draft features only a man and many references to Soekarno. The second is darker, more muscular, with only NU at the center. The third painting is assertive and puts NU back at the center of a broader constellation of actors. The men are conspicuously phallicized, with three shooting flames and a fourth pointing a rifle. Where the second painting was dark, this one is bright, with the sun shining from the top right corner in the direction of progress, rather than exploding from behind. The slogan at the bottom is distinctly religious in content and tone, yet not exclusionary, using the monotheistic 'God' rather than 'Allah' and the term 'ummat' but without identifying it as solely Muslim. In other documents from the period, NU spoke of a 'ummat Christian' as well as an 'ummat Muslim.' As such, where the first 'we' signaled allegiance to Soekarno and the second only to NU, the third is a plural 'we' where NU is interwoven into the fabric of the country providing the path forward through unity and piety.

The first image portrays NU before the violence, the second is during it, and the third depicts the newly invigorated NU leading the nation forward on the basis of diligence and piety rather than submission to Nationalism, Religion, and Communism, *Nasakom*. The paintings document NU's reassertion of the place of Islam in the public sphere and the centrality of Islam to the narrative of violence. The paintings also demonstrate that NU's switch from tolerance of the Communists to violent intolerance was central to the envisioning of a post-Soekarno, post-Communist Indonesia, and the creation of a new community.

Central to that new community was the exclusion of the Communists. Muhammadiyah celebrated life without the Communists: "After PKI is no more, every aspect of life, such as society, politics, culture, and education will proceed smoothly. No more insults thrown at religion, no more attempts to separate religion from the state, no more leaders who only talk and do nothing, no more people who accumulate wealth for their own sake."[111]

Soekarno's new regime was built upon this act of mobilization and mass killing of his political opposition in 1965–1966.[112] Like the exclusion of the Ahmadiyah in the 1940s, the exclusion of the Communists was a productive act that instituted one of the most capable, durable regimes in modern history.

This similarity between Ahmadiyah and Communists points to the most important reason why intolerance toward Ahmadiyah and Communists has persisted for decades; state policy with the backing of NU and Muhammadiyah. Muhammadiyah fused the idea that eradicating Communists was an act embodying loyalty with the idea that eradicating Communists was an act of adherence to Islamic law: "The G30S incident is an act of betrayal to the Indonesian Revolution: committed by Atheists, disbanded forums/conferences, and going against the concept of One Almighty God and the Sovereignty of the People. No matter how the PKI always acts in favor of Pancasila, their actions are clearly going against the Pancasila teachings, hence they are *Pancasilais munafik*."[113] Like NU, Muhammadiyah transformed a secular conflict into a positive duty of undertaking jihad. The duties of national citizenship became synonymous with those of faith.

Not surprisingly, despite the effective eradication of the Communists from contemporary Indonesia, their ideational exclusion from social and political life continues in the present. The survey that I conducted contains only one question that addresses all minority groups. Table 5.1 demonstrates that on the question of who may be mayor in Jakarta, Christians are the most tolerated,

---

[111] Muhammadiyah, "Lebih Baik Tanpa PKI," *Suara Muhammadiyah* 1–2, January 1966, 3.

[112] Slater and Ziblatt (2013); Siegel (1998).

[113] Italics mine. Muhammadiyah, "Laksanakan Fungsi Muhammadiyah Sebagai Abdi Tuhan dalam Negara Pancasila," *Suara Muhammadiyah* No. 4–5, February–March 1966, 12.

TABLE 5.1. *Leaders' tolerance toward recognized/nonrecognized groups*

Survey Question	N = 1,000 (%)
Should Christians be permitted to ...	
... become the mayor in Jakarta?	40
Should Hindus be permitted to ...	
... become the mayor in Jakarta?	35
Should Ahmadis be permitted to ...	
... become the mayor in Jakarta?	22
Should Communists be permitted to ...	
... become the mayor in Jakarta?	11

Note: Means are different at the level of significance of $p < 0.01$ using a two-sample test of proportions.
Percentage refers to tolerant response.

followed by Hindus, followed by Ahmadis, followed by Communists. In contemporary Indonesia, Christians and Hindus are accorded similar levels of tolerance, while Ahmadis and Communists are the least tolerated groups.

Conclusion

How and why do Islamic organizations change their policies of tolerance over time? The period from 1945 to 1966 provides three examples of shifts in the policies of Islamic organizations and the centrality of the state to the evolution of Islamic organizations' attitudes and behavior. Rather than the state simply shaping the preferences of Islamic organizations or Islamic organizations simply shaping the institutions of the state, it is clear that the two are mutually constitutive and coevolve over time.

Inclusion in democratic elections created incentives for Masyumi to signal its tolerance of Christians, who were being simultaneously courted by the nationalist PNI. Masyumi's outreach was not without impact. Mohammad Natsir appointed Christians to his cabinet, and Masyumi, Parkindo, and Partai Katholik supported one another in political coalitions throughout the decade. A further incentive to work together was their common enemy, the PKI.

The manufacturing of Balinese religion into a form of universal, Hindu, monotheism brought it recognition by the state and support from Soekarno. Incorporation into the state changed the way the Balinese were perceived by other religious groups to the point that they are now seen as similar to Christians, despite theological beliefs that should put them outside the bounds of Islamic toleration.

With the PKI land reform in 1963 and the coup d'état in 1965 that brought new political power to Jakarta, traditionalist Muslims and Communists became mutually exclusive categories despite having theoretical overlap and despite the political cooperation between NU and the PKI in the previous forty years.[114] Before then, the rhetoric of NU, Soekarno, and the PKI suggests that an amalgam of ideologies was no less likely than their polarization. Within NU, a new generation of leaders with close connections to the military and strong anti-Communist sentiments drove the push from reluctant cooperation with Communists to violent intolerance against Communists.

Interestingly, NU's public pronouncement that the PKI was non-Muslim, belligerent to a legitimate state, and obligatory to kill followed the onset of violence rather than preceding it. This suggests that intolerance may not be a major cause of violence. Similarly, in the case of Ahmadiyah, theological differences prompted the break from Muhammadiyah and debates with Persis, but the political marginalization and state intolerance of the Ahmadis were launched as a way of unifying the santri, rather than as an outcome of attitudes themselves. This finding resonates with other studies of mass violence, which have found that ethnic hatred and racist beliefs play a relatively minor role in instigating violence.[115]

And yet vocal intolerance enabled the violence to take place. Once underway, sanction from the leadership of PBNU, the demonization of the Communists, and the presence of militants within NU made the killings possible. This finding is consistent with the work on Rwanda, where Hutus who responded to the hardliner's call and took the initiative to kill were those who had fewer preexisting ties with Tutsis and looked more unfavorably on them. Likewise, Jewish communities in interwar central and Eastern Europe were more likely to be subject to mass killings when their political and civic ties to non-Jews were weaker.[116] It also accords with the leadership switches of NU. The leaders with strong ties to Communists and Soekarno were not the same leaders as the ones that led the call for and implementation of the mass killings. In other words, theories of primordial identity or intolerant ideologies do not predict behavior toward non-Muslims. But once violence begins, those with preexisting hatreds are more likely to implement violent policies. In Indonesia, intolerance toward Communists became a pillar of both state and society and remains salient in contemporary attitudes.

[114] Ricklefs (2001, 332).
[115] Straus (2006, chapter 5).
[116] Kopstein and Wittenberg (2011); Dumitru and Johnson (2011).

6

Communal Tolerance

Islam teaches mutual respect and freedom to practice, but not by mixing religions and not by insulting the religious beliefs of others.

Abdul Mu'ti, Muhammadiyah Central Board[1]

How do Islamic organizations envision the accommodation of religious difference in social and state practices? My goal in previous chapters was to demonstrate that a focus on ideas in explaining tolerance overlooks the historical and political conditions that give rise to civic virtues. In this chapter I shift the focus back to ideas, specifically to ideas within Indonesian Islamic political thought. By doing so, I advance the goals of the book: explaining the origins of a normatively valued outcome, delineating the boundaries of tolerance in Islamic organizations, explaining how those boundaries evolved, and expanding the jurisdiction of tolerance beyond the secular-liberal conception that dominates scholarship on religious pluralism.

Drawing on comparative political theory and survey research, this chapter explains the meaning of tolerance to NU and Muhammadiyah. On the basis of key texts in Indonesian Islamic political thought, I suggest that these organizations are tolerant of religious minorities based on social and state rules that differ from John Locke and John Rawls' model of secular-liberal tolerance rooted in individual rights, the separation of church and state, and state neutrality toward religion. These organizations support tolerance based on group rights, legal pluralism, and the separation of religious and social affairs. Together, I call this set of values 'communal tolerance.' I then use survey data to demonstrate that the concept of communal tolerance derived from comparative political theory accords with the attitudes of municipal-level leaders of NU and Muhammadiyah. I end by suggesting that instead of asking whether Islam

---

[1] Court transcript, no. 140/puu-vii/2009, III, 47–51.

TABLE 6.1. *Leaders' tolerance toward Christians, Ahmadis, Hindus, and Communists*

Survey Question	NU (n = 379) (%)	Muh. (n = 387) (%)	Persis (n = 234) (%)	Sig. (%)
Should Christians be permitted to ...				
... become the mayor in Jakarta?	52	43	16	***
Should Hindus be permitted to ...				
... become the mayor in Jakarta?	47	37	13	***
Should Ahmadis be permitted to ...				
... become the mayor in Jakarta?	36	20	6	***
Should Communists be permitted to ...				
... become the mayor in Jakarta?	15	10	5	**

Significance (Sig.): ***$p < 0.01$; **$p < 0.05$; *$p < 0.1$; n/s – not significant. The significance of the difference between group means is measured using Pearson's χ2 tests.
Percentage refers to tolerant response.

is compatible with democracy, researchers should investigate what kind of democracy Muslims prefer; NU and Muhammadiyah favor a communal and religious democracy that is similar to the vision of strong multiculturalists and is marked by a convergence of liberal individual rights and group-differentiated rights within a system of legal pluralism.

The previous chapters established that understanding the levels of tolerance in Islamic organizations requires separating the targets, actors, and time period in order to explain the push-and-pull factors that underpin social attitudes. Table 6.1 summarizes levels of tolerance among leaders of all three organizations toward the four minority groups included in the survey.

Persis is omitted from this chapter because in contemporary Indonesia it is intolerant of religious minorities using most indicators. See Table 6.1 as well as previous chapters. Persis' attitudes stem from a deep cleavage with Christians in West Java, an ethnic identity that overlaps with a religious identity, and long-standing alliances with other Islamist groups. Although Mohammad Natsir penned an eloquent conception of "Islamic Tolerance" in 1954 (Chapter 5), his overtures to Christians were not reciprocated and the survey data demonstrates that Persis leaders' attitudes do not accord with Natsir's vision. In contrast to Muhammadiyah and NU, Persis prioritizes the purification of religious belief over tolerance of other faiths.

At the same time, however, these preferences do not make Persis a militant organization; in interviews Persis leaders stressed that they disagree with the crass (*keras*) behavior of vigilante groups such as Front Pembela Islam. The rise of these new Islamists has pushed Persis to moderate its stance regarding Christians and the legitimacy of the state. It has recently joined interfaith dialogue groups and sought to build bridges with the government, leading Indonesian President Susilo Bambang Yudhoyono to attend the 2010 Muktamar and to Persis Chair Maman Abdurrahman to proclaim that "*Dakwah* is more effective when we are close to the palace."[2]

Yet even with this moderation, Persis' values are incompatible with the civic virtues necessary to making democracy work: recognition of religious pluralism, religious equality, and support for popular sovereignty. Persis leaders say that they feel like an isolated minority in Indonesia, unable to implement their sincerely held aspiration for an Islamic state. Persis' small size compared to NU and Muhammadiyah suggests that its values do not resonate with the broader public; from the perspective of democratic theory, its isolation is good for the consolidation of democracy.

Comparative Political Theory

Up until now, I have treated tolerance as a discrete hierarchical variable ranging from complete intolerance to complete tolerance, applying separately to each target, varying by each organization, and changing over time. I explained the variation based on structural factors. Here I want to explore how Islamic organizations think differently about tolerance. By integrating comparative political theory with concept formation and survey research, scholars can explain more attitudes and outcomes than by relying on concepts originating in European political thought. After all, political science categories such as power, democracy, nationalism, and agency manifest differently around the globe.[3] While there is a thriving literature on democracy and authoritarianism in comparative perspective, there is relatively little research on comparative understandings of the civic values that support democracy. I move that effort forward by drawing on scholarship that makes distinctions between different modes of tolerance.

Such comparisons of cultural values have suffered a bad reputation ever since former prime minister of Singapore Lee Kwan Yew proclaimed that "Asian values" rendered international human rights norms inapplicable to Asia. Lee was rightly denounced for his homogenous conception of Asian culture and for using cultural values to justify authoritarian practices. My task

---

[2] Interview with the author, Garut, September 26, 2010.
[3] For the leading statement on this subject see Chakrabarty (2008). On power see Anderson (1972) and Euben (1999); on democracy see Schaffer (1998) and Wedeen (2008); on nationalism see Cheah (2003) and Laffan (2003); on agency see Mahmood (2005).

is less grandiose. I seek to understand the values of the leaders of NU and Muhammadiyah rather than the values of all Indonesians, or all Muslims, or even all Indonesian Muslims. I do so because these are actors and values that are important for understanding democracy in the Muslim world, but that are often overlooked. Even within Indonesian studies, research on NU and Muhammadiyah pales in comparison to research on small, militant organizations such as Jemaah Islamiyah. Instead of the margins, I examine the heart of mainstream Islam in order to understand NU and Muhammadiyah's visions for the accommodation of religious difference.

Secular-Liberal Tolerance

Secular-liberal tolerance derives from the writings of John Locke, who penned *A Letter Concerning Toleration* while in exile in Amsterdam. The letter reflected Locke's station; the arguments for toleration symbolized a treaty that would liberate Protestants from the persecution of the Anglican church and British state. Locke laid out the basis for toleration by separating private faith from public action. He limited the jurisdiction of the state to liberty, health, lands, houses, and other material concerns.[4] When the state attempted to compel private matters, it would inevitably produce insincere belief or martyrdom. In order to avoid both, Locke affirmed that the state should tolerate all private beliefs.

Locke also laid out detailed policy prescriptions. First, churches were defined as voluntary organizations that individuals were free to enter or exit. Second, the state could not make rules delineating approved and unapproved churches. Third, excommunication, while the right of the church, had no civil ramifications for individuals. Fourth, the church had no voice in worldly matters. In addition to separating religion from public matters, Locke banished the church to the private realm. Fifth, equality was the right of most men in matters of religion. There were boundaries to tolerance, however. Since atheists did not believe in an afterlife, they lacked the motivation to act morally and could not be tolerated. Catholics, meanwhile, held an allegiance to the pope that rendered them unreliable citizens. Locke's view of Catholics reflected his fear that Charles II might align with France and introduce absolutism.[5]

Secular-liberal tolerance has broadened considerably in the ensuing years. The most influential recent work is by John Rawls, whose "political liberalism" argues that in order to accommodate plurality, liberal democracies should seek an "overlapping consensus": a set of basic principles to which all reasonable comprehensive doctrines can agree based on reasons derived from their own framework, but justified publicly. This mutual agreement can regulate cooperation, while not requiring homogeneity.[6] With this model, Rawls seeks to provide

---

[4] Locke (1983 [1689], 26).
[5] Tully (1983, 8).
[6] Rawls (1993, 59).

a moral foundation for a just society while excluding 'unreasonable' doctrines that are unable to reciprocate the recognition of shared values, consensus, and public forms of reasoning that are widely accessible to a diverse public.

Rawls' emphasis on public reasoning and public justifications has been heavily criticized for excluding religious reasoning and religious values, since it forces religious actors to either change their doctrine, dissimulate, confront the public in order to change the parameters of public debate, or supplement their private reasons with public ones. Murphy suggests that forcing others into a mode of reasoning that they do not accept is highly intolerant, on par with forcing individuals to affirm an alien religious or philosophical creed.[7] In that respect, Locke and Rawls' demand that arguments follow the public/private split exposes their sectarian attachments to the particularism of Protestantism instead of liberalism's often-professed claim to universalism. As Jeffrey Spinner-Halev notes, "Liberal toleration is a sectarian doctrine. It also arose in a specific historical context that allowed the state to reduce the public presence of religion."[8]

It is difficult to see how Rawls' conception of tolerance could be used to map the attitudes of religious organizations that are unapologetically in the public sphere. As Muhammadiyah Chair Din Syamsuddin made clear in a speech in 2010,

> Muhammadiyah's relationship to the Indonesian nation is like the sun to the earth. The sun shines down on the earth to give it sustenance and growth. The earth does not look down on the sun. Muhammadiyah is a moral voice in this country, and in the world as the largest modernist organization. And so if the government is moral, if the government follows the laws and the constitution of the country then Muhammadiyah will support the government. But this balance will be upset if the government is off balance. And while Muhammadiyah is also working for the development of the Indonesian people, that does not mean following the government blindly. After all, Muhammadiyah was here before there was an Indonesian government.[9]

In other words, Muhammadiyah has a voice in worldly matters. It has public policies on corruption, education, public health, economic development, and how to promote tolerance.

As a brief aside, it is important to note that Muhammadiyah and NU do not see their options for influencing policy as limited to party politics. Differentiating between their engagement in *politics* and *party politics* is important to understanding their views; they engage in the former but not necessarily the latter. This distinction may seem disingenuous to scholars who

---

[7] Murphy (1998, 261).

[8] Spinner-Halev (2005, 46). The exception is scholarship on democratic theories of multicultural-ism that go beyond individualism and the public/private distinction. These are addressed in the following section.

[9] Speech by Din Syamsuddin, Muhammadiyah Muktamar, Yogyakarta, July 3, 2010.

support Locke's prescription that religious organizations have no place in public affairs. But it is an important distinction for accurately describing the views of Islamic organizations. For example, while former Muhammadiyah Chair Amien Rais created the National Mandate Party (PAN), PAN is not formally connected to the organization and there are numerous policy differences between the two organizations. PAN has supported raising taxes while Muhammadiyah has opposed it. Muhammadiyah has banned smoking in its schools, universities, and hospitals while PAN has been silent about laws that might ban smoking in government buildings. That difference is not surprising; to NU and Muhammadiyah, getting involved in party politics means supporting one party. NU and Muhammadiyah do have close connections to PAN and the National Awakening Party (PKB), and those connections can be important (and unimportant) in shaping electoral outcomes. But their political influence is broader than parliament, and their social influence is deeper than that of a political party. As such, my focus is on Muhammadiyah's and NU's views, not just the views of PAN or PKB, and not just the organizations' visions for the accommodation of difference through the state.

Hinduism and Tolerance in India

Protestantism and its secular-liberal heir do not provide the only ideational blueprint for tolerance. In an important article, Spinnner-Halev contrasts Protestantism with Hinduism, which has no church hierarchy, is rooted in ritual practices, holds no pretense of having a single truth, and defines membership by birth rather than belief. He argues that as a syncretic religion, Hinduism is highly tolerant of other *external* religions since there is an acknowledged multiplicity of pathways to God(s). Hinduism is less *internally* tolerant, however, to untouchables and member of lower castes.[10]

This distinction between internal and external tolerance has been important for explaining the Indian state's support for minority rights, including differential treatment for internal minorities such as Scheduled Castes (Untouchables) and Other Backward Classes (low-caste groups). Liberal ideas about respect for difference cannot account for these policies; even the most expansive liberal visions for group rights remain hostile to claims based on the amelioration of disadvantage rather than the recognition of cultural difference.[11] Rochana Bajpai persuasively argues that the state has synthesized ideas about liberal rights, group rights, and nationalist appeals to social justice.[12] And democratic theorists argue that this form of muscular multinationalism has been pivotal to understanding India's democratic success.[13] In sum, in order to understand the values that bolster democracy and pluralism in postcolonial states such

[10] Spinner-Halev (2005, 38).
[11] Bajpai (2011, 292), critiquing Kymlicka (1989, 1995).
[12] Bajpai (2011, 23, 194, 291–292).
[13] Stepan, Linz, and Yadav (2011, 5).

as India and Indonesia, it is necessary to think beyond liberal visions for the accommodation of difference.

The Skeptical Humanist Defense of Tolerance

The skeptical humanist defense of tolerance is grounded in two principles: (1) there are certain fundamental ideas or values that undergird the commonwealth and (2) tolerance should serve the common good.[14] Erasmus differentiated between certain religious knowledge and uncertain knowledge, known as the *adiaphora*. He argues that the fundamentals of faith are uncontested while the adiaphora are contested but unresolvable. Since actors cannot be certain of adiaphora, they cannot persecute minority perspectives.

The skeptical humanist distinction between certain and uncertain knowledge runs parallel to a similar distinction in Islamic law between matters of consensus (*ijma*) and disagreement (*fur'iyah or furu*). Matters of fur'iyah are subject to disagreement among scholars of Islamic law and there is widespread recognition that these differences should be tolerated. This distinction has had political effects in Indonesia. In 1935, NU founder Wahid Hasjim called for disputes between traditionalists and modernists to be set aside as furu: "Do not make the differences in fur'iyah a reason for disunity, discord, treachery ... while our religion is one and the same, Islam!"[15] More recently, a representative for the NU Central Board testified at the constitutional court that this distinction has strengthened intrafaith tolerance, within limits:

> [S]omething that should be underlined is that this freedom to express diverse beliefs or practices concerns subjects related to *furu*, the branches.... If the problem concerns *furu*, then we will witness a high tolerance and appreciation by scholars against parties who have different views; yet the Islamic scholars will demonstrate an uncompromising attitude in matters of *usuliyah*.[16]

Like Erasmus, NU does not tolerate disagreements about fundamental values (Chapter 4), while it does tolerate disagreements regarding furu (the adiaphora). In moving beyond Locke and Rawls' conception of tolerance, understanding the boundaries between usul and furu will be crucial to seeing NU's vision for religious accommodation.

Pragmatic Tolerance

Pragmatic tolerance is based on the willingness to put up with those things one finds disagreeable for the sake of stability. For example, Barkey notes that "In its broad outlines the Ottoman state organized and administered a system of religious and communal rule that instituted religious boundaries, marking difference, yet allowing for enough space, movement and parallel

---

[14] Remer (1992, 33).
[15] Noer (1978, 241).
[16] Court transcript, 140/puu-vii/2009, IV, 18–20.

alternative structures to maintain a divided, yet cohesive and tolerant imperial society."[17] The Ottomans' *millet* system was organized along religious lines; each quasi-autonomous community of Jews, Greek Orthodox, and Armenian Orthodox were subject to their own laws in matters of religion and personal status while Islamic law governed disputes between communities. The legal traditions, religious practices, and internal affairs of minorities were generally respected and enforced throughout the empire.[18] In this model, tolerance is not a virtue but a strategy for social control.

István Bejczy suggests a similar logic was at work in the medieval concept of *tolerantia*. Tolerantia refers to putting up with something that is unpleasant. A large sin demands greater tolerance than a small sin; thus a small sin may be tolerated, while a large one may not be. Jewish rites, for example, were considered an evil that must be tolerated so as to prevent the forced conversion of the Jews, since conversion to Christianity had to be a matter of free will.[19] Major ills, however, such as heresy, were not tolerated since they threatened the core of Christian civilization. As with the Ottomans, tolerantia does not celebrate difference as a value, but puts up with it as a pragmatic means to other ends.

Does pragmatic tolerance, or tolerantia, help us to understand the beliefs of NU and Muhammadiyah? Certainly the concept resonates in Indonesia. Under Soeharto, a narrow brand of cultural diversity was protected by the state under the Sanskrit saying "unity in diversity" (*bhinneka tunggal ika*) as a pragmatic way of dealing with difference while promoting economic development. This diversity was expressed through state celebrations of regional dances and songs, as well as architectural renderings of each 'culture' in sites such as the amusement park Taman Mini Indonesia Indah. This pragmatist accommodation of difference, however, should not be conflated with tolerance in any meaningful sense of the term. Suharto's vision of tolerance left no space for ethnic political movements, religious mobilization, or even public discussion of group identity.

Soeharto's policies have had long-term effects. Both Muhammadiyah and NU oppose religious practices by the minority or majority that could lead to instability, even when that means truncating individual rights. They are even willing to see their own political goals frustrated if realizing them would entail the use of violence by the state or society. For example, even though NU believes Ahmadiyah to be apostates that should be banned, it does not want Ahmadis to be attacked or imprisoned. Rather, it believes that Ahmadiyah should be educated into proper belief and its teachings prohibited. In September 2005, the Central Board of Nahdlatul Ulama (PBNU) stated:

1. Ahmadiyah is a deviant sect and outside of Islam for not recognizing Prophet Muhammad as the last messenger of Allah as clearly explained in the Qur'an,

---

[17] Barkey (2005, 15).
[18] Barkey (2005); Kymlicka (1992); Lewis (1984, 125–128).
[19] Bejczy (1997, 372).

the Sunnah, and the consensus of ulema. Though it is a true fact, people may not commit anarchic acts against Ahmadiyah. The ban on Ahmadiyah teachings and activities is in the hand of government and its legal officials and not the authority of individuals or groups.

2. When objecting to the continuation of Ahmadiyah activities, people are expected to use peaceful and elegant methods [of protest].

3. We call on all Muslims to be able to study Islam comprehensively to avoid any misunderstanding and error in interpreting religious teachings.

4. The government is expected to stand firm and be consistent in dealing with the existence of Ahmadiyah in Indonesia.[20]

NU's solution for acts that are not tolerated is to implore the state to educate Ahmadiyah into remedying its false beliefs. NU's position is a pragmatic balance between imprisonment for Ahmadiyah (the preference of hardline groups) and allowing deviant sects to persist (the preference of secularists and liberals). While it is normatively difficult for Western scholars to celebrate NU's understanding of tolerance, it is causally important to understand why NU and Muhammadiyah have supported limits on the rights of 'anarchic' groups such as Ahmadiyah while still promoting a truncated version of religious pluralism; the two organizations are often more pragmatically tolerant than they are tolerant in the Rawlsian or Lockean sense of the term.

Mystical Tolerance

Masroori lays out arguments for mystical tolerance based on the work of the Sufi Muhammad Jalal al-Din Balkhi also known as Rumi. Rumi presents one of the most encompassing Sufi theories of toleration, anticipating modern theories of tolerance by four centuries. Rumi's arguments for toleration are both internal to Islam and external to non-Muslims, exceeding the boundaries of both the Hindu model and tolerantia.[21] Rumi makes five arguments in defense of toleration. First, God created both nonbelievers and heretics. Thus, both blasphemy and faith are God's creation and have worth in the eyes of God. Second, while Muhammad is considered the last and final prophet, God has sent others, and their differences are merely variations on a single divine truth. Third, like other Sufis, Rumi is skeptical of the ability of reason to discover universal truth. And given its inadequacy at discerning truth, reason cannot be used to delineate truth from false tenets of faith, nor can coercion generate true belief from falsehood. Fourth, toleration anticipates and encourages conversion to Islam. Fifth, diversity is God's creation and divinely given. Given the value of diversity, persecution cannot be permitted.

Masroori rightly contrasts the expansiveness of Rumi's inclusiveness with Locke, who excludes Catholics from toleration on pragmatic grounds. Rooted in the universal truth of God's salvation rather than skepticism, relativism, or

---

[20] NU (2008).

[21] Masroori (2010, 243).

pragmatism, Rumi provides strong claims for tolerance from a public, religious perspective. That said, it is difficult to translate arguments for mysticism into practice. Rumi does not flatten the liminal and syncretic commonalities between individuals or groups in the way that is implicit to the modern concept of difference.[22] Likewise, although NU has been influenced by Sufi mystical practices (*tasawwuf*), they are more historical than contemporary; the major Sufi orders have become less important over the twentieth century as rational exegesis has gained influence. In that respect, the main barrier to seeing the salience of Rumi's conception of tolerance in contemporary Indonesia is not the fact that it is anchored in the sacred, but that it is not modern.

Communal Functionalist Argument for Tolerance

Rumi's mystical arguments for tolerance are based on epistemological skepticism. The communal functionalist argument is radically different. Nederman's communal functionalist argument is based on a modern conception of the community as made up of functionally distinct parts, each of which is necessary for the well-being of the whole. This model of segmented cooperation identifies the common good through the participation of all the members in the political process, while exclusion of any members damages the realization of the common good.[23]

In detailing the communal functionalist argument for tolerance, Nederman makes a pivotal move toward resolving a long-standing communitarian critique of liberalism; privileging individuals over the community is socially alienating and psychologically implausible. Nederman usefully suggests the value of communal functionalism as a bridge between liberal and communitarian visions of toleration. For example, Orthodox believers may refrain from contact with infidels in matters of worship, but not in civil affairs.[24] Differences are inevitable and inalterable; communal functionalism acknowledges and even legitimizes these differences in order to form a common civic union.

The communal functionalist argument parallels NU and Muhammadiyah's understanding of the social and political system for the accommodation of religious difference. As NU's Ahmad Siddiq notes, "NU accepts that the nature of human relations is based on distinctive group bonds; any inter-group relations should be based on toleration, understanding, and respect."[25] Note that groups of religious believers, rather than individuals, form the unit of analysis for tolerance. As we saw in Chapter 4, in 1954 and 1955 Masyumi embraced the Christian community in exactly these same terms, as an *umma Kristen*. And as we will see in the survey data, NU and Muhammadiyah are tolerant according to a logic of group rights.

---

[22] I am grateful to Rebecca Gould for this point.
[23] Nederman (1994, 903).
[24] Nederman (1994, 912).
[25] Siddiq (2006 [1979], 63–66).

This system for tolerance is not purely theoretical: consociational states such as the Netherlands, South Africa, Nigeria, Belgium, Switzerland, Cyprus, and Lebanon are organized around both groups and individuals. Unlike the Ottoman millet system where coexistence was dictated from above, consociationalism is maintained by agreement between multiple parties who agree to form a union with goods distributed based on the size and strength of the associated communities. This arrangement allows each community to have autonomy over its own affairs including language, education, and religion while also ensuring political representation.[26] Proponents of consociationalism argue that carefully configured institutional engineering (including power dividing, federacy, and decentralization) can give identity groups a greater stake in the political system without exacerbating intergroup conflict.[27]

Islamic Tolerance in Islamic Law

The Ottoman system emerged both as a pragmatic strategy for imperial rule and because of the structure of tolerance inherited from Islamic jurisprudence *(fiqh)*. In the first five years of the hijra calendar (622–626 CE) when the Prophet Muhammed led the Muslim community in Medina, he began to think of the new faith as providing his followers with laws similar to those in the other Abrahamic faiths of Christianity and Judaism.[28] The constitution of Medina was written as a pact between the Muslims who had emigrated with Muhammad, their Arab hosts who had become Muslims, the polytheists in their federated clans, and their Jewish client clans and allies. Mohammed recognized three communities: the Muslim community, the Jewish community of Moses, and the Christian community of Jesus.[29] Arjomand argues that this moment marked the origins of the institutional basis for religious pluralism in Islam, which later developed into Qur'anic verses[30] and fiqh.

The framework for tolerance in Medina and in classical fiqh was based on group rights, like that of communal functionalism. That said, recognition was limited to the monotheistic religions of Judaism and Christianity as People of the Book *(ahl al-Kitab)* while animists and polytheists *(musyrikun)* were not protected. The People of the Book, however, were not equal to Muslims; relations between Muslims and other monotheists were based on the concept of *dhimmi*, which according to the Hanafi and Maliki schools of law were protected only on condition of their recognition of the superiority

---

[26] Lijphart (2004, 105).

[27] Lijphart (1996); Liu and Baird (2010); Lublin (2012); Norris (2008); Reynolds (2010); Stepan, Linz, and Yadav (2011); Wolff (2007); for research arguing that power-sharing increases conflict see Selway and Templeman (2012) and Wilkinson (2000), among others.

[28] Hallaq (2005, 20–22).

[29] Arjomand (2009, 571).

[30] Arjomand (2009, 568); Q2:62, Q2:148, Q2:213, Q3:23, Q2:256, Q4:58, Q4:105, Q5:44, Q6:35, Q7:87, Q10:109, Q24:48.

of Islam.[31] Dhimmis retained religious freedom based on the principle of no compulsion in religion (Q2: 256) but were also required to pay a tax (*jizyah*) for unbelief.[32] The dhimmi contract provided non-Muslims with security and religious autonomy, but along lines and to a degree that is not recognizable by contemporary metrics of liberty, religious freedom, and political representation.

Does the model of tolerance from fiqh capture the views of Muhammadiyah and NU? As discussed in Chapter 4, religion is a privileged status in Indonesia, defined in 1942 by Muhammadiyah as having eight specific characteristics.[33] In 1952, the MORA, staffed by leaders of Muhammadiyah, narrowed that definition to a faith with: guidelines for its adherents, belief in the existence of the One Supreme God, a holy book, and a prophet.[34] This definition has been used by the state to marginalize heterodox, syncretic, animist and liminal faiths such as *kejawen*, *kebathinan*, and Ahmadiyah. This is a model of religious tolerance with strong resemblance to fiqh.

Nonetheless, the MORA's model of tolerance is as different from fiqh as it is similar. The MORA has recognized Buddhism and Confucianism as religions despite only superficially manufacturing them into monotheist faiths. Similarly, in a book of Qur'anic exegesis specifically devoted to social relationships between religions (*hubungan social antarumat beragama*), Muhammadiyah argues that the concept of ahl al-Kitab should be understood beyond the narrow meaning of the fiqh: "in a modern era such as this, the concept of Ahli Kitab must be understood as a universal concept, far-reaching and transcending historical boundaries as well as literal meanings."[35] This means that "Ahli Kitab consists of Jews, Christians, *Majusi*, and Sabians, and even can be extended to Confucians, Hindus and Buddhists."[36] Similarly, in the ten years I spent doing research on NU and Muhammadiyah and in reading a century of their publications, I never once read or heard them use the term dhimmi.[37] The term does not appear in the leading Indonesian-English dictionary nor in Michael Feener's canonical text on Muslim legal thought in

---

[31] Scott (2007, 2–3).

[32] Some scholars contend that the jizyah was the non-Muslim equivalent of the zakat or a substitute for military service.

[33] Muhammadiyah (1942, 11–14).

[34] Abalahin (2005, 121); Mulder (1978, 4).

[35] Muhammadiyah (2000, 129).

[36] Muhammadiyah (2000, 151). 'Majusi' refers to the Persian or Zoroastrian religion. Asad (2003, 21 fn. 49) notes that Sabians were a monotheistic group between Judaism and Christianity, most likely followers of John the Baptist and related to the contemporary community of Mandaeans in Iraq. Like Muhammadiyah, subsequent legal interpreters used the inclusion of the vaguely identified Sabians to grant tolerance to other established religions such as Hindus in India (Lewis 1984, 20).

[37] The only mentions of dhimmi were by Islamic liberals who denounced the concept, by militant groups such as Laskar Jihad, and by former PKS president Hidayat Nur Wahid where he upheld the prophet as a model of tolerance due to his respectful relations with dhimmis.

Indonesia.[38] The same is true for the jizyah. In fact, a concept of solidarity or brotherhood (*ukhuwah*) has had far greater resonance than dhimmi.

Against the conservative Islamists' promotion of Muslim solidarity (*ukhuwah Islamiah*), Kiai Siddiq of NU has drawn on Islamic law to propose more inclusive forms of solidarity such as national solidarity (*ukhuwwah wathaniyyah*) and human solidarity (*ukhuwwah bassyariyyah*).[39] These ideas have had practical effects: Kiai Siddiq's embrace of pluralism was influential in NU chair Abdurrahman Wahid's support for Pancasila, rather than Islamic law, being the ideological foundation for the Indonesian state.[40] Wahid also invoked the Medina constitution as the origin for an Islamic theory of religious pluralism and equal citizenship rather than unequal status for non-Muslims.[41] Insofar as the model of Medina from Islamic law does have resonance in NU and Muhammadiyah's values, it is in an abstract sense and not as a set of specific legal codes. "[T]he Quran states that there is an appreciation of the concept of religious pluralism (*pluralisme agama*) by acknowledging that each community has their own perceptions, orientation, and ... religious practices."[42] Instead, concepts from the Qur'an, fiqh, and Islamic history are deployed in order to celebrate the principle of religious pluralism and equal citizenship.

New Islamist Tolerance

NU's Kiai Siddiq is not the only political theorist to mine the Islamic legal tradition for resources to promote a vision for religious accommodation. The Egyptian Islamist Fahmī Huwaydī notes that the term dhimmi is not mentioned in the Qur'an, and was used by Arab tribes before the coming of Islam. Instead of being a valid principle in Islamic law, then, he suggests that it was projected onto the Prophet through the Hadith.[43] Like other Islamists, Huwaydī advocates returning to the Qur'an to define how non-Muslims should be accommodated today. And like Muḥammad al-Awwa, Rashid al-Ghannushi, Ṭāriq al-Bishrī and the other 'New Islamists,' Huwaydī argues that dhimmi can be discarded in favor of the concept of citizenship.

Al-Awwa and al-Bishrī argue that contemporary Muslim-majority states are based on logics of citizenship rooted in historic social contracts; the shared struggle of Muslims and Christians against British colonialism made everyone an equal citizen in Egypt.[44] The logic of shared struggle producing a social

Although I suspect that the concept appears elsewhere, I am confident that it has little resonance in NU and Muhammadiyah.
[38] Feener (2007); Echols and Shadily (1989).
[39] Mujani (2003, 73).
[40] Noeh and Mastuki (2002, 126).
[41] Hefner (2000).
[42] Muhammadiyah (2000, 17).
[43] Scott (2007, 7).
[44] Scott (2007, 10).

contract has shaped Indonesian Islamic organizations' views, too. As noted in Chapter 5, the 1945–1950 revolutionary war against the Dutch was marked by Christian and Muslim unity in defense of the newly proclaimed homeland. As a result of their participation, Indonesian Christians came to be seen as part of the nation.[45] Muslim leaders, including prominent Islamists such as Mohammad Natsir, came to see Christians as citizens rather than as dhimmis or ahl al-Kitab.

This shared history has shaped how the new Islamists interpret the more intolerant verses of the Qur'an, like Q58:22, which has been interpreted to forbid friendship with non-Muslims: "Thou wilt not find any people who believe in Allah and the Last Day, loving those who resist Allah and His Apostle, even though they were their fathers or their sons, or their brothers, or their Kindred." Al-Awwa argues that the verse applies only to non-Muslims who harbor enmity to the Islamic community.[46] Similarly, Muhammadiyah says such verses should be understood as applying only at that moment in time, and not more generally: "The verses that prohibit friendship with non-Muslims do not represent a permanent relationship in the Qur'an with non-Muslims."[47] Likewise, NU states that interactions with non-Muslims should be based on respect; as Achmad Siddiq notes, "Enmity towards another group is allowed only for those who [are] obviously against Islam."[48] Like the influential al-Azhar scholar Yusuf al-Qaradawi, who maintains that all Egyptians are equal citizens based on the principles of national solidarity and neighborliness (*al-jiwār*),[49] NU and Muhammadiyah's baseline since the early 1980s has been that non-Muslims are no different from Muslims in terms of citizenship. As a result, while the model of tolerance from the new Islamists parallels views of Muhammadiyah and NU, it appears to bolster national solidarity more than intolerance.

Beyond Tolerance

Normative critics of liberalism have sought models for pluralism that go beyond tolerance toward active respect for difference, recognition of identity's fluidity, and the elimination of both cultural and economic exclusion.

Iris Young's *Justice and the Politics of Difference* articulates a theory of justice in democracy that addresses both redistribution and recognition through policies that help minimize and combat oppression, defined as the "institutional constraint on self-development."[50] Those social groups suffering from oppression merit policies that counteract cultural exclusion or economic marginalization. Young describes five kinds of oppression:

---

[45] Benda (1958, 176).
[46] Scott (2007, 7).
[47] Muhammadiyah (2000, 93); see also 65.
[48] Siddiq (2006 [1979], 63–66).
[49] Warren and Gilmore (2013).
[50] Young (2005, 37).

exploitation, marginalization, powerlessness, cultural imperialism, and violence.[51]

Young argues that a democratic public should provide mechanisms for recognition and representation of oppressed groups, not just individuals. Like Bajpai, she finds that even the most expansive liberal visions for group rights remain hostile to claims based on the amelioration of disadvantage rather than the recognition of cultural difference. To Young, relieving oppression means (1) self-organization of group members so that they achieve collective empowerment, understanding of their collective experience, and understanding of their interests in society; (2) group analyses and group generation of policy proposals in institutionalized contexts; (3) group veto power regarding specific policies that affect the group directly, such as land use for Native American reservations. Young argues that group representation is better than individual representation as it promotes justice in procedure, sets the public agenda, and assures a voice for the oppressed.

Young's framework goes beyond tolerance and can be used as a standard for normative democratic politics broadly. But her framework is surprisingly restrictive, too; she is explicit that group representation does not imply interest groups or ideological groups. Only social groups, defined as "A collective of people who have affinity with one another because of a set of practices or way of life; they differentiate themselves from or are differentiated by at least one other group according to these cultural forms."[52] Also, only oppressed groups or disadvantaged groups are supported. Privileged groups are already represented.

In the Indonesian case, it is implausible to argue that NU or Muhammadiyah is oppressed. They run their own schools, have access to political representation, have the ability to associate freely, speak and move freely, and are not oppressed according to any of Young's five criteria. To the contrary, their size and influence make them dominant, not subordinate. From the perspective of normative democratic theory, the more appropriate question to ask is: to what extent should the santri's prescriptions for tolerance be accommodated in order to strengthen democracy without oppressing the nonsantri? This question will be addressed in the concluding chapter.

Nahdlatul Ulama on Tolerance

NU is the most tolerant of the three Islamic organizations, its behavior stemming from an alliance with Christians against modernist Muslims, close ties to the state, and its Javanese roots. Its tolerance does not extend to Ahmadis or Communists. As discussed in Chapter 5, its intolerance toward Communists was mobilized in the service of the mass killings of 1965–1966. Here I want to discuss how NU's values strengthen and structure its tolerance.

---

[51] Young (2005, 48–62).
[52] Young (2005, 97).

NU's beliefs are organized around a set of common values and principles rather than adherence to a single set of legal codes from fiqh as the guide to appropriate behavior and belief. Like Locke, NU's orientation stems from its origins: it emerged as a response to the growing influence of modernist Muslims on Java and the coming to power of Ibn Sa'ud in the hijaz, whose alliance with Salafi ulama led to prohibitions on traditionally sanctioned Islamic practices. NU is organized around prominent ulama, pesantren, and membership, not a single mission like Muhammadiyah. As one NU leader noted, "NU is like a cartel, with a common view of *usul* [core matters of Islamic faith] but with different applications."[53] Similar to a cartel, NU's collective interests are to prevent the dominance of the modernists and preserve respect for religious traditions that were common at the turn of the century: the Sunni mazhabs, local religious beliefs like the veneration of the nine saints of Java *(wali songo)*, and Islamic mystical sects *(tarekat)*. This diversity of opinions makes it difficult to specify NU policies toward non-Muslims with precision, but it does allow us to identify common values of the members of NU (the *Nadhliyah*).

In an influential book written in 1979, *Goals of the Members of Nahdlatul Ulama (Khittah Nadhliyah)*, Achmad Siddiq, the head of the Islamic law board *(Syuriyah)* of NU from 1983 to 1989, explained NU's values as based on moderation *(al-tawāssut)*, justice *(al-i'tidāl)*, and balance *(al-tawāzun)*. These values are based on select Qur'an verses:

> Q2:143: "And thus we have made you a *just community* that you will be witness over the people and the Messenger will be witness over you."
>
> Q5:9: "Allah has promised that those who believe and do *righteous deeds* [that] for them there is forgiveness and great reward."
>
> Q57:25: "We have already sent Our messengers with clear evidences and sent down with them the Scripture and the *balance* that the people may maintain [their affairs] in justice."

The most important value for understanding NU's attitudes toward non-Muslims is moderation, which Siddiq says guides NU in intergroup relations, Islamic legal interpretation, faith, and culture.

Earlier, we saw that when applying the principle of moderation to interfaith relations Siddiq used the group, rather than the individual, as the unit of analysis: "Inter-group relations should be based on toleration, understanding, and respect."[54] Similarly, in applying the principle of moderation to Islamic law, Siddiq says: "In *dzanniyyat* problems [uncertain issues in Islamic law, contrasted with definitive issues, *qath'iyyat*], [NU] highly tolerates the differences from other groups as long as they are not against or in violation of Islamic principles." Here Siddiq recognizes the uncertainty that accompanies

---

[53] Arsul Sani, interview by author, Jakarta, February 11, 2010.
[54] Siddiq (2006 [1979]; this and following quotations are from pages 63–66.

interpretations of Islamic law. Like the skeptical humanist approach to the adiaphora, while some principles are settled, others are open to interpretation, and that interpretation is tolerated. This principle also guides NU's approach to Muslims who are not part of NU, such as modernist Muslims. Uncertainty does not, however, apply to settled matters such as the Ahmadi belief that there is another prophet. Such beliefs are beyond the pale.

In applying the principle of moderation to matters of Islamic theology (*akidah*), Siddiq writes, "(NU) does not act in haste to judge a person or a group as *musyrik* [polytheist] or *kafir* [non-Muslim], since they may have not purified their beliefs due to many reasons." Here, too, like Rumi's Mystical Tolerance, Siddiq suggests that even the most deviant groups merit tolerance because they may resolve their mistakes and come to understand the correct interpretation of Islam. NU places the onus of resolving improper understanding of Islam on each religious community in cooperation with the state. NU calls on the state to use peaceful methods of education rather than coercion in order to bring about proper belief. It is incumbent upon each individual to purify their faith and understanding of religion while the broader community may act as a guide.

In applying the principle of moderation to matters of culture, Siddiq professes tolerance for change and diversity, even while guarding against negative influences:

> Culture which includes custom, dressing manner, art, etc., is the result of human civilization which should be put in a proper place for religious adherents. Culture should be valued and measured using religious norms, laws, and teachings. Any good culture – according to religious norms – should be accepted and developed, regardless of where it might originate. On the contrary, any bad and immoral culture should be banned and left wherever it comes from.

This explanation is remarkably consistent with NU's fatwa from the 1920s, in which the central board said Muslims could wear Western dress such as suits and ties as long as their goal was to foster positive social or economic interaction and not to emulate the religious beliefs of non-Muslims.[55] The metric for cultural acceptance is not freedom but rather the degree to which cultural innovation contributes to religious values such as balance, moderation, and justice.

In the same text as he writes that moderation should guide the behavior of NU, Siddiq turns his attention to the threats facing NU, particularly the intersecting threats from Western Orientalists, Muslim modernists, and *Muktazilah* (an Islamic group that believed reason to be the supreme value of Islam). He accuses non-Muslim Orientalists of trying to destroy Islam by raising doubts about the validity of Hadith, emphasizing reason over adherence to tradition, and indoctrinating Muslims into secularism, which privileges worldly

---

[55] NU (2007, 34–35).

over other-worldly matters in order to diminish the importance of religion to daily life. He criticizes Muslims for fanatical adherence to particular religious doctrine, for the use of reason, for the split between Shia and Sunni Muslims, for hostility to traditional practices, and for infighting that can give fuel to Orientalists:

> In the last decades, dangerous matters have threatened Islam. This latent threat appears in the form that is known as Orientalists. Orientalists are highly educated people who devote serious attention to Eastern matters, but their studies are not sincerely dedicated to the East and Islam. On the contrary, they attempt to destroy the East and Islam. They learn about Islam and they also learn Arabic and other Oriental languages together with other aspects of Islam including its history, sociology, law, and customs. From a scientific point of view they might understand Islam better than Muslim scholars. Unfortunately, they only have one intention; destroying Islam as the continuation of their groups' efforts during the Crusade. Physically, the Crusade has been over for hundreds of years, but politically, ideologically, and culturally it has continued afterwards (and is still continuing nowadays and will always continue forever). Their battlefields are wide and vast and they harm the purity of Islam. Their main weapons and tools are their knowledge about Islam and Islamic matters.
>
> Using their knowledge, they attempt to: 1) Blur and unsettle the second main source of Islam, i.e. al-Hadith. They disrupt the certainty of Abu Hurairah (one of the Prophet's Companions) to record Hadith. They make uncertain the ability of Imam Zuhri to compile the scattered Hadith. Finally, they try to shake Muslims' faith by the absence of Hadith Shahih [the most accurate Hadith], which came from and were said by the Prophet. If Muslims have "lost Hadith" due to this uncertainty, this means that they (Muslims) have lost the main path to the Qur'an. 2) Actively campaign to promote the use of reason, arguing that Islam appreciates the use of rationality and individual reasoning. They promote the idea that human reason and individual rationality are adequate to regulate everything. Their goal is to make Muslims prefer their own mind and reason, and [therefore to] neglect their religion. If this goal is achieved, they will be able to wash the brains of Muslims with theories, doctrines, and concepts (isms), including: (a) intellectualism, which emphasizes the use of reason to achieve life goals; (b) materialism, which says that property and wealth determine the quality of human life; (c) secularism, which separates worldly matters (which are their main goal) and the other-worldly matters (which are uncertain).
>
> Threat does not come merely from the Orientalists – an external threat – but from other Muslim groups, which are an internal threat. The threat appears in several forms: 1) Fanaticism toward a person or a group of people with political or other motives.... Fanaticism began in the time of the Caliphate 'Utsman ibn 'Affan[56] and the Caliphate 'Ali ibn Abi Thalib[57] and has continued to recent days with the emergence of Shia and Khawarij groups. 2) The influence of Greece philosophy that causes the emergence of *Mu'tazilah* and other groups.

---

[56] The third ruler of the early Muslim community after the death of Muhammad. His assassination marked the onset of the split between the Sunni and Shia sects.

[57] A cousin of Muhammad, the fourth Caliph, and the spiritual ancestor of the Shia.

3) The existence of old beliefs such as *Israiliyyat* [Judaism], *Majusi* [Persian or Zoroastrian religion], etc. These beliefs are whipped up by *Munafiqin* [Muslim hypocrites]. In places where Islam is not an indigenous religion, the remnants of old beliefs can be a serious threat toward the purity of Islamic teachings, and Indonesia is no exception. 4) Excessive attitude of "against the old" which results in the attitudes like anti-*madzhab* [schools of jurisprudence], anti-*taqlid* [adherence to the mazhabs], anti-grave pilgrimage, etc. All weaknesses within the Muslim community will be used by Orientalists to disturb the purity of Islam.

Siddiq's caution is a useful reminder that NU's principle of moderation stems not from NU's adherence to liberal principles but from a desire to safeguard a way of life.[58] Highly defensive, NU's principles provide the organization a great degree of fluidity and support for social harmony. In addition to moderation, justice, and balance, a similar NU value is *al-amr bi al-ma'rūf wa nahy 'an al-munkar* (do the good and forbid the bad). In a recent statement, the central board of NU reaffirmed the role that these principles play in guiding the members of NU, often called *ahlus sunnah wal-jama'ah* (*Aswaja*, followers of the Sunnah): "Based on the principles of Aswaja, NU rejects and is against any form of fundamentalism, extremism, liberalism, and all deviant sects and groups. Based on the principles of Aswaja, this rejection is firmly addressed, but in persuasive ways through dialogue."[59]

NU's values illustrate that it hews to a moderate approach in accommodating religious minorities. Figure 6.1 illustrates this point with a banner at the 2010 NU Congress in Makassar warning the organization's leaders to beware the influence of fundamentalism, radicalism, and liberalism. NU's values are so broad that it is difficult to discern precise policies about *how* minority groups should be tolerated. While clearly opposed to persecution of minorities, NU is not supportive of individual religious freedom. Instead, it favors a mix of tolerance of some minority rights but not others, and in some policy areas but not others. As we will see, this entails avoiding the more 'extreme' ideas about minority accommodation.

Muhammadiyah on Tolerance
Muhammadiyah is the second most tolerant of the three organizations, with its tolerance stemming from a late cleavage with Christians in Central Java, a Javanese ethnicity, and close ties to the Ministry of Education. Like NU, its tolerance does not extend to members of Ahmadiyah or Communists, although the organization was not formally mobilized by the military against the Communists. Here I want to discuss how its values strengthen its tolerance.

[58] The list of scholars who have misattributed NU's tolerant attitudes to liberal ideology is lengthy: Barton (1996) and Kunkler (2013) are the most egregious. This explanation puts scholars in the awkward position of having to explain NU's reoccurring 'deviations' from liberalism including NU's repeated polemics against secularism, Ahmadiyah, deviant Islamic groups, Islamic reformism (which they pejoratively call Wahhabism), and Communism.

[59] NU (2004, 140).

FIGURE 6.1. Banner at the 2010 NU Congress: "Save NU from the Influence of Fundamentalism, Radicalism, and Liberalism."

The mission of Muhammadiyah Chair Din Syamsuddin's NGO, the Center for Dialogue and Cooperation among Civilizations (CDCC), is to promote mutual respect between religious groups.

> CDCC aims to promote better understanding and peaceful relations among religions, cultures, nations, and civilizations at large.... Rather than viewing diversity as a threat and civilizations as always in clash, CDCC embraces the view that diversity is an opportunity, richness and an integral component for growth, in order to create a peaceful world.... There is an urgent need for a global movement to bridge that gap and promote dialogue, greater understanding and mutual respect between cultures and civilizations.[60]

In 2010, Abdul Mu'ti, a member of the Muhammadiyah central board and the executive director of the CDCC, testified at the constitutional court that Muhammadiyah has long recognized and celebrated religious diversity. He read the "Guide to an Islamic Life for Members of Muhammadiyah" issued by the Central Executive Board of Muhammadiyah in order to demonstrate Muhammadiyah's tolerance. The guidebook provides a window into how Islamic values buttress Muhammadiyah's tolerance and is worth quoting at length:

> First, for an Islamic life, members of Muhammadiyah should know that Islam teaches that every Muslim should establish brotherhood and goodness with others, such as with neighbors and other community members in order to protect the rights and honor of both fellow Muslims and non-Muslims. Islam specifies an area of 40 houses that are categorized as neighbors and whose rights must be protected.
>
> Second, every family member of Muhammadiyah must demonstrate exemplary behavior: be nice to your neighbors, maintain the respect and honor of your neighbors, be generous to neighbors who entrust you with goods or property, check if your neighbors are sick, love your neighbor as you love your own family, express joy and happiness when neighbors obtain success, support and give sympathetic attention when your neighbor is in distress, visit or mourn when your neighbor dies and take care of your neighbor's needs as required, be forgiving and gentle when the neighbor is wrong, do not search or investigate your neighbor's vices, provide food or souvenirs to your neighbors, do not hurt your neighbors,

---

[60] Center for Dialogue and Cooperation among Civilisations (2013).

be affectionate and graceful, abstain from all disputes and disgraceful behavior, visit and provide aid, and enjoin wrongdoing in a way that is appropriate and prudent.

Third, in a neighborhood where there are different religions, you are also instructed to be kind and fair. They are entitled to their rights and dignity as neighbors, and to food that is *halal* [permissible to eat according to Islamic law] and you may also receive food from them in order to promote tolerance in accordance with the principles taught by Islam.

Fourth, in regards to broader social relations, every member of Muhammadiyah as an individual, family, congregation, community or organization must demonstrate social attitudes based on the principle of upholding the values of human dignity, fostering a sense of brotherhood and humanity, realizing that the cooperation of humanity is essential for physical and spiritual prosperity, nurturing the soul of tolerance, respecting the freedom of others, enforcing trust and fairness, giving equal treatment, keeping promises and instilling the value of compassion and preventing harm, making society into one that is pious and responsible for the good and forbidding wrongdoing, trying to be useful and benefiting people, aiding in the prosperity of the mosque, promoting respect and love between the old and the young, having no prejudice for others, caring for the poor and orphans, not taking the rights of others, and competing in goodness and in other social relationships.[61]

The guide is a vivid demonstration of the centrality of tolerance to the values of Muhammadiyah. The term "brotherhood" (*persaudaraan*) is often used by Muhammadiyah to describe the virtue of fostering warm, supportive human relationships (*persaudaraan sesama mahluk*) as well for promoting intra-Muslim unity (*persaudaraan seagama*). Mu'ti's scholarship further confirms this value; his book, *KrisMuha* (a short form of the words for "Christian" and "Muhammadiyah") describes the curriculum of Muhammadiyah schools in Flores, West Kalimantan and North Sumatra where the students are majority Christian or Buddhists. Teachers of any faith provide instruction in math, history, English, and other secular subjects to students of any religion. Doctrine is taught according to religious identity. These schools and curriculum date back to the 1970s, before the central government required that religious education be given in accordance with the religion of the students and by a teacher of the same religion.[62]

Yet, Muhammadiyah's tolerance does not extend to Ahmadiyah. Former Muhammadiyah chair Syafii Maarif touted Mu'ti's research as an example of Muhammadiyah's tolerance, while also making clear that there would never be a book on *AhMuha* (a short form of the words for "Ahmadiyah" and "Muhammadiyah").[63] Muhammadiyah, like NU, draws the boundary of tolerance at interactions that corrupt or undermine Muslims' faith. Brotherhood

---

[61] Court transcript, 140/puu-vii/2009, III, 47–51.
[62] Dr. Abdul Mu'ti, interview with the author, Jakarta, October 1, 2009.
[63] Syafii Maarif, interview with the author and Alfred Stepan, Jakarta, September 30, 2009.

does not extend to matters that might confuse respect for other religious people with admiration for beliefs that are inferior to Islam:

> The attitude of Islam towards other religions which do not show enmity to Islam or Muslims is that difference should not prevent Muslims from performing good deeds in social matters such as paying respect to the dead, visiting the sick, etc. based on a verse: "Allah forbids you not, with regard to those who fight you not for (your) faith nor drive you out of your homes, from dealing kindly and justly with them: for Allah loveth those who are just" (Al-Mumtahanah: 8). About matters which relate to religious rituals, however, it is prohibited for Muslims to follow them, since the infidels of Quraisy[64] proposed such a compromise to the Prophet by performing prayer in the Mosque every Friday and in the Church every Sunday, and the verses in Letter Al-Kafirun were revealed to ban this proposal.[65]

Muhammadiyah believes Islam to be the most perfect faith while other faiths are incorrect, even if they are to be tolerated. Its distinction between permissive interactions in social matters and curtailed interaction in matters of faith stems from its commitment to the primacy of belief over other values such as individual freedom. Although other beliefs are not condemned, nor are individuals of other faiths coerced, those religions are not held in the same esteem as Islam. Any interactions that might lead Muslims to devalue their own faith, confuse the tenets of their faith with those of another faith, or convert to the other faith should be avoided. This issue arose in 1981 when Majelis Ulama Indonesia (MUI) issued a fatwa calling on Muslims to refrain from saying "Merry Christmas" to Christians, and from attending Christmas celebrations. Muhammadiyah agreed with the fatwa:

> Islam teaches its adherents to avoid *syubhat* [uncertain matters in Islamic law] and Allah's prohibitions, and to prioritize rejecting damage over gaining benefits. This is based on a Hadith transmitted by Muslim explaining that halal [permitted] and haram [forbidden] matters are obviously clear, and between these two matters are syubhat.... Based on such considerations, MUI issued a fatwa: A) Christmas celebration in Indonesia, because it is aimed at celebrating and respecting the Prophet Isa [Jesus] peace be upon him, cannot be separated from faith matters; B) Joining celebration of Christmas for Muslims is forbidden; C) It is suggested that Muslims avoid syubhat and Allah's prohibitions, and not join any activities of Christmas celebration.[66]

The point is not that Muhammadiyah is opposed to cooperation with non-Muslims. The point is that by privileging faith over brotherhood, Muhammadiyah is cautious about sanctioning activity that might corrupt the beliefs of its members.

This caution extends to the hiring of teachers in Muhammadiyah schools. As Mu'ti detailed, Muhammadiyah created a framework for including Christian

---

[64] A tribe that resisted Islam and worked against it during the time of Muhammad's prophethood.
[65] Abdurrahman and Moelyadi (1992, 3).
[66] Abdurrahman and Moelyadi (1992, 236–237).

students in the schools long before the government provided guidelines for segmented religious education. Having non-Muslim teachers does not present a problem as long as the subject is not related to faith. Yet it is also clear that it would be better to have teachers from inside Muhammadiyah.[67] Alongside the primacy of religion, Muhammadiyah supports religious self-governance, with each faith tending after its flock. The often-referenced line from the Qur'an, "to you your religion, and to me mine" (*lakum dinukum waliyadin*) appears in many Muhammadiyah publications about how to balance relations with non-Muslims.

Another reason for advocating mutual respect is the danger of persecution, which is similar to the justification for the medieval concept of tolerantia. Persecution can elicit hatred toward Muslims and even toward Allah. As a fatwa from Muhammadiyah notes,

> As humans Muslims are obligated to respect other people, and to associate with other people. This includes relations with non-Muslims, and we should not insult or promote animosity toward other religions, in accordance with Allah's command "Revile not ye those whom they call upon besides Allah, lest they out of spite revile Allah in their ignorance. Thus have We made alluring to each people its own doings. In the end they will return to their Lord, and We shall then tell them the truth of all that they did."[68]

Here Muhammadiyah prizes tolerance as a way to prevent hatred emerging toward Allah or Muslims. While self-interested, like mystical tolerance, Muhammadiyah's commitment to the promotion of Islam may aid in the establishment and extension of the value of tolerance.

The Concept of Communal Tolerance

NU and Muhammadiyah's visions for religious accommodation are similar in four ways that differentiate them from Locke and Rawls' model. These four ways are: an emphasis on communal rather than individual rights, support for communal self-governance through legal pluralism, a separation between social and religious affairs, and the primacy of faith over other values. Together, this set of values can be called communal tolerance. Communal tolerance is defined as the willingness to 'put up' with ideas or groups that one rejects, with rights defined by group membership. In emphasizing group rights rather than individual rights, communal tolerance is similar to the principles underpinning communal functionalism and consociationalism. Similarly, in its support of communal self-governance through legal pluralism rather than legal centralism, communal tolerance is similar to the Indian model of religious pluralism as well as models in other postcolonial states where family law is administered according to identity-group-specific legal codes. Communal tolerance also

---

[67] Abdurrahman and Moelyadi (1992, 246).
[68] Abdurrahman and Moelyadi (1992, 215–216).

resembles the model of strong multiculturalism, where those groups have some autonomy over their affairs.[69] Communal tolerance is dissimilar to the other templates, however, in stressing the primacy of religious belief over other values and in sharply differentiating between minority rights in social and religious affairs. The communal tolerance model can best be understood through these four categorical distinctions. I will further examine each distinction in turn.

First, communal choice is privileged over individual choice. In sharp contrast to the secular-liberal model, communal tolerance does not recognize unlimited individual freedom of conscience. This is most apparent in the restrictions on deviant sects within faiths, in the enforcement of orthodoxy, and in the restrictions on the mixing of faiths.[70] While individual rights are embedded in the Indonesian constitution and are valued by the santri, they mostly see interreligious relations as based on group rights and obligations.

Second, the legal system for the communal tolerance model is plural rather than unitary and secular. In the Ottoman model, the millets maintained autonomy over matters of marriage, inheritance, religious practice, worship, education, and any other internal affairs. In the Indonesian model, Islamic law governs issues of marriage, divorce, reconciliation, inheritance, property use regarding religion, and dietary issues related to halal food certification. As the constitutional court notes,

> At the level of state administration practice, the State established a dedicated ministry in administrating religious affairs, namely the Ministry of Religious Affairs. Religious celebrations are respected in state administration practices. Likewise, the religious law, in this case Islamic laws relating to marriage, divorce (*talak*), reconciliation, inheritance, grants, wills, property donated for religious or community use (*wakaf*), shari'a economy, etc. have become state law, particularly applicable to the followers of Islam.[71]

Legal pluralism is the implicit legal system underpinning communal tolerance. Indonesia's legal system is complicated by other systems of law; local customary law (*adat*) and national secular law overlap with religious law, which varies in application and content by region.[72]

Third, NU and Muhammadiyah want religious accommodation in matters of faith to be subject to a different set of criteria than matters of social relations. This belief stems from a key distinction in classical fiqh and modernist understandings of Islamic law between issues of social relations (*mu'amalat*), faith (*akidah*), and worship (*ibadah*). NU and Muhammadiyah are highly tolerant of minority rights in matters of social relations such as commerce. But when minority group behavior interferes in issues of faith or worship, they are

[69] Spinner-Halev (2001); Shachar (2001).

[70] The problem of in-group rights violations is well recognized by advocates for strong multiculturalism. I discuss remedies in the next chapter, on communal tolerance and democracy.

[71] Court verdict 2010, 140/puu-vii/2009, 3.34.8.

[72] Lev (1972); Bowen (2003).

highly intolerant. NU and Muhammadiyah believe that non-Muslims should not be permitted to demonstrate about issues having to do with Islamic law, that churches and mosques can be built only in areas where the community is of the same faith, and that proselytizing should be forbidden.[73] They are also intolerant of Muslims interfering in the faith matters of Christians and Hindus; in matters of faith and worship, NU and Muhammadiyah feel that each community should govern its own internal relations, while external relations are to be highly regulated by the state. This administration of public religious life is one of the hallmarks of their vision of communal tolerance. In contrast to secular-liberal tolerance, the line between public and private is blurred; in fact this distinction is unhelpful for mapping NU and Muhammadiyah's vision for peaceful coexistence.

Fourth, and finally, NU and Muhammadiyah do not hold individual freedom as their most important value. NU and Muhammadiyah are most dedicated to the promotion of their faith and the interests of the Muslim umma. Belief in God, support for the welfare of their members, and support for the broader Islamic community (sometimes superficially) take precedence over interfaith tolerance. This does not mean that they endorse coercing Muslims to be observant nor that they support forced conversion of non-Muslims. Likewise, it does not follow that NU and Muhammadiyah want Islamic law to be state law. But it does mean that while Islamic organizations are largely tolerant, their support for minority rights is especially truncated on maximalist issues of religious freedom for non-Muslims, whose interests are often subordinate to those of the Muslim umma.

Indicators of Communal Tolerance

In this section, I validate the concept of communal tolerance using micro-level survey data. This also allows me to test whether the values of NU and Muhammadiyah as derived from comparative political theory resonate with their members at the municipal level. Communal tolerance is the 'basic-level' concept, the 'noun with adjectives' that forms the broadest possible meaning of the concept but is more specific than higher rungs on the ladder of abstraction.[74] The secondary level possesses the ontological attribute that gives the concept meaning. Note that the definitions of individual and communal tolerance are similar; the difference between the two is at the third level, the indicator level (see Figure 6.2).

Following other survey research on tolerance, indicators of communal tolerance in this study focus on education, worship, speech, political representation, and recognition. Yet as discussed in Chapter 2, the indicators used by the World Values Survey and General Social Survey are narrowly rooted in liberal political theory, particularly Locke's distinction between public and private

---

[73] Proselytizing is the practice of trying to bring over members of another religion into one's own. *Dakwah* is the Islamic equivalent, and a core practice of the Islamic revival.

[74] Goertz (2006, 50–53).

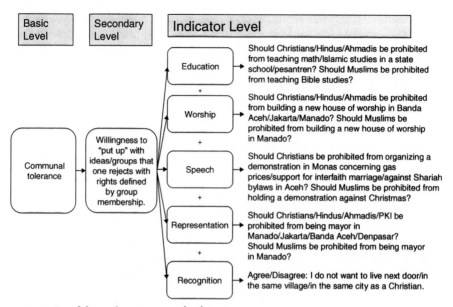

FIGURE 6.2. Measuring communal tolerance.

and the assumption of a public sphere undifferentiated by demographics.[75] For that reason, I developed an alternative set of indicators.

Education is the area where the structure of communal tolerance is most obvious. To measure communal tolerance, I use the question, "Should a [target] be prohibited from teaching [math, Islamic/Christian studies] in a [state school, Islamic boarding school]?" In a system of communal tolerance, each group should be permitted to teach religious material to students sharing their faith, but not to students of other faiths. Likewise, each religious group should be permitted to teach secular subjects such as math. This should be the case regardless of whether the school is in the public or the private sphere. For example, a Christian should be permitted to teach math in a public school or Islamic boarding school. They should not, however, be permitted to teach Islamic studies. Likewise, a Muslim should not be permitted to teach Christian studies in a public school.

Religious worship is a second area where the structure of communal tolerance is especially different from the liberal model. To measure communal tolerance, I use the question, "Should a new [church, temple, mosque] be prohibited from being built in [Aceh, Manado, Jakarta, Denpasar]?" These regions were chosen based on demographic characteristics. According to the 2010 census, Aceh is 98.2 percent Muslim, Jakarta is 85.4 percent Muslim, North Sulawesi is 30.9 percent Muslim (63.6 percent Christian) with the capital city of Manado having an overwhelming Christian majority, and Bali is 83.5 percent Hindu. In

---

[75] For an extended discussion of survey research studies of tolerance, their elision of comparative political theory, and the problem of path dependency, see Menchik (2011, chapter 2).

the communal tolerance model, respondents should permit a Christian church to be built in Manado or Jakarta, but not in Aceh while a Hindu temple should be permitted in Denpasar, Bali, but not in Aceh. Likewise, individual respondents should be less willing to permit a new mosque to be built in Manado.

Minority groups' ability to speak and demonstrate is a third area where the structure of communal tolerance differs from the secular-liberal model. To measure communal tolerance in the area of speech and demonstration, I chose a single location that has a heterogeneous population and is the site of frequent protests. The Indonesia National Monument (Monas) in Jakarta is home to frequent political and religious events. I use the question, "Christians should be prohibited from demonstrating in Monas (Jakarta) [about the price of gasoline, in favor of interfaith marriage, against the Shari'a bylaws in Aceh]?" In the communal tolerance model, respondents should be willing to permit Christians to demonstrate on social matters such as the price of gasoline, less willing on faith matters such as marriage, and unwilling to permit demonstration on issues that should affect only Muslims, such as the Shari'a bylaws in Aceh. Likewise, respondents should oppose Muslims' demonstrating against Christian holidays such as Christmas.

Representation refers to the ability of minority groups to contest and hold public office. Existing World Values Survey indicators of tolerance ask whether the target group should be permitted to hold public office or to become president. Both measures are problematic. The former is limited in that the location, duties and level of public office are not specified, while the latter is limited to a single, highly symbolic office undifferentiated by demography. To measure communal tolerance on representation, I use questions that address the office and demographics of the region. "[Target] should be prohibited from becoming the mayor in [Manado, Jakarta, Banda Aceh, Denpasar]." I also use one question about a Christian becoming president to see whether the level of political office affects the respondents' level of tolerance. In the communal tolerance model, respondents should permit Christians to be mayor in Manado or Jakarta, but not in Banda Aceh. Hindus should be permitted to be mayor in Denpasar but not Jakarta. Likewise, respondents should be unwilling to permit Muslims to become mayor in Christian Manado.

Recognition refers to the ability of minority groups to exist within Indonesian society as citizens. To measure communal tolerance on recognition, I asked whether respondents agree or disagree with the statement, "I would not want to live [next door to, in the same village as, in the same city as] Christians." In the communal tolerance model, as explicitly specified by Muhammadiyah, respondents should be willing to live next door to a minority without restriction. Having fully conceptualized communal tolerance and delineated concrete indicators for both tolerance and intolerance, in the next section I use a newly collected semirandom sample of surveys of municipal-level leaders of NU and Muhammadiyah to demonstrate that the concept of communal tolerance accords with their views.

TABLE 6.2. *Tolerance and group rights I*

Survey Question	NU and Muhammadiyah Elites
Should Christians be permitted to ...	
... hold government office?	86% (747)
... become the mayor in Manado, North Sulawesi?	77% (742)
... become the mayor in Jakarta?	47% (738)
... become the president of Indonesia?	29% (739)
... become the mayor in Banda Aceh?	20% (739)

Note: Differences between regions are significant at p <0.01 using a two-sample test of proportions. Percentage refers to tolerant (positive) response. Sample size is in parentheses.

TABLE 6.3. *Tolerance and group rights II*

Survey Question	NU and Muhammadiyah Elites
Should Hindus be permitted to ...	
... become the mayor in Denpasar, Bali?	83% (739)
... become the mayor in Jakarta?	41% (732)

Note: Differences between regions are significant at p <0.01 using a two-sample test of proportions.
Percentage refers to tolerant (positive) response. Sample size is in parentheses.

Group Rights

How well do these indicators capture the views of the santri? Their writings on tolerance suggest that group distinctions between Muslims and non-Muslims should affect the rights of both minorities and the majority. Since rights are based on group membership, individuals living in areas where they are different from the majority may have fewer rights than in areas where they share the identity of the group. The underlying logic is that people of a given religion should be represented in government by someone who shares that religion.

NU and Muhammadiyah leaders are likely to be tolerant of Christians as elected leader in a predominantly Christian area and somewhat tolerant in the heterogeneous area of Jakarta. But they are less likely to tolerate Christian mayors in a predominantly Muslim area. Similarly, the presidency of a country that is almost 90 percent Muslim, a highly symbolic seat, is likely to be seen as appropriate only for a Muslim. During the constitutional debates of 1945, NU chair Wahid Hasyim and other Islamic leaders wanted written guarantees that the head of state would always be Muslim.[76] Tables 6.2 and 6.3 illustrate how the principle of rights based on group membership, not individual freedom, helps explain contemporary attitudes. Muslim leaders

---

[76] Elson (2009a, 115, 118).

TABLE 6.4. *Tolerance and legal pluralism in public education*

Survey Question	NU and Muhammadiyah Elites
Should Christians be permitted to ...	
... teach in public schools?	85% (745)
... teach math in public schools?	91% (748)
... teach Islamic studies in public schools?	10% (743)

Note: Differences between activities are significant at $p < 0.05$ using a two-sample test of proportions.
Percentage refers to tolerant (positive) response. Sample size is in parentheses.

are intolerant of Christians holding office in overwhelmingly Muslim areas and somewhat tolerant of Christians and Hindus holding political office in heterogeneous areas. They are tolerant of Christians and Hindus holding office in areas where they are the majority; in these areas, we find that Muslim leaders have levels of tolerance similar to citizens in wealthy, industrialized, consolidated democracies.

Legal Pluralism

The next area where communal tolerance is manifested differently from secular-liberal tolerance is in legal pluralism. In the liberal tolerance model, anyone should be permitted to teach any subject in the public schools. And using the WVS question, "Christians should be prohibited from teaching in public schools," Indonesian Muslim elites appear highly tolerant (85 percent disagree). Yet, questions that differentiate the teaching of particular subjects reveal that elites are tolerant within the communal tolerance framework. Christians are not permitted to teach Islamic studies. Likewise, Muslims should not be permitted to teach Bible studies in a public school. The communal tolerance model differentiates the subject that is being taught and proscribes mixing of faiths.[77] Table 6.4 examines communal tolerance in matters of education.

As noted, Muslim elites are somewhat tolerant of Christians teaching secular subjects but not matters of akidah or ibadah. This applies to both public state schools and Islamic boarding schools. NU and Muhammadiyah are somewhat tolerant of Christians and Hindus, and to a lesser degree tolerant of Ahmadis working in an Islamic boarding school when teaching a secular subject. Table 6.5 demonstrates that the public/private division built into the concept of liberal tolerance is unhelpful for understanding Islamic elites' attitudes regarding tolerance in education.

---

[77] In interviews my informants would frequently joke that different religions should not be combined like "gado-gado," a mixed vegetable salad with peanut sauce.

TABLE 6.5. *Tolerance and legal pluralism in private education*

Survey Question	NU and Muhammadiyah Elites
Should Christians be permitted to teach in a pesantren?	33% (745)
Should Christians be permitted to teach math in a pesantren?	67% (753)
Should Hindus be permitted to teach math in a pesantren?	66% (748)
Should Ahmadis be permitted to teach math in a pesantren?	49% (749)

Note: Differences between activities are significant at $p < 0.01$ using a two-sample test of proportions. Percentage refers to tolerant (positive) response. Sample size is in parentheses.

TABLE 6.6. *The separation of religious and social affairs in demonstration*

Survey Question	NU and Muhammadiyah Elites
Should Christians be permitted to...	
... demonstrate in Monas (Jakarta) about the price of gasoline?	82% (746)
... demonstrate?	74% (743)
... demonstrate in Monas (Jakarta) in favor of interfaith marriage?	37% (747)
... demonstrate in Monas (Jakarta) against the Shari'a laws in Aceh?	29% (746)

Note: Differences between activities are significant at $p < 0.01$ using a two-sample test of proportions. Percentage refers to tolerant (positive) response. Sample size is in parentheses.

The Separation of Religious and Social Affairs

Islamic elites are unwilling to tolerate political behavior by minority groups that interferes in religious affairs. They are unwilling to put up with demonstrations by Christians that interfere in matters of Islamic marriage or Islamic community governance. Table 6.6 demonstrates the limits of the right to political demonstration as interpreted by Muslim elites. A series of questions address the extent to which Muslim elites tolerate demonstrations by Christians. On the question of demonstrating on an unspecified topic, and about a topic of broad social interest – gas prices – Islamic elites are willing to tolerate demonstrations. This tolerance dwindles, however, when the subject is religious. Demonstrations in favor of interfaith marriage or against Islamic law in the region of Aceh are not tolerated.

The Primacy of Faith

NU and Muhammadiyah do not hold individual freedom as their most important value. Even after decades of political inclusion and moderation they are not liberals, nor are they likely to become liberals.[78] Even while their interpretation and application of those values varies, as does their geographic

---

[78] For a similar critique of the "inclusion-moderation" thesis, see Schwedler (2011).

TABLE 6.7. *The primacy of faith over tolerance*

Survey Question	NU and Muhammadiyah Elites
I would not want to live next door to a Christian[a]	82% (749)
Should Christians be permitted to ...	
... hold government office?[b]	86% (747)
... teach in public schools?[b]	85% (745)
... teach in pesantren? [b]	33% (745)
... build a church in my neighborhood?[b]	20% (744)

Note: Differences between activities are significant at p <0.1 using a two-sample test of proportions.
[a] Percentage refers to a tolerant (negative) response.
[b] Percentage refers to tolerant (positive) response. Sample size is in parentheses.

conception of the Muslim community, NU and Muhammadiyah are primarily dedicated to the promotion of Islamic values and the interests of their community. Table 6.7 demonstrates how this stance is manifest in the attitudes of Islamic leaders. Islamic leaders are willing to live next door to Christians at a high rate of 82 percent. This is a high level of tolerance similar to that of citizens in wealthy, industrialized, consolidated democracies; WVS pooled data for the question, "Would you object to having neighbors of a different religion?" shows the United States at 87 percent, the United Kingdom at 86 percent, Sweden at 85 percent, and the Netherlands at 86 percent tolerant. Likewise, WVS survey data for Indonesia (not Muslim elites) shows 84 percent tolerance. The same is true for their willingness to have Christians hold unspecified positions of authority in the government and teach in public schools. Yet, there is a marked decrease in tolerance as soon as the subject is religious. Islamic leaders are unwilling to allow Christians to teach an unspecified subject in a private Islamic boarding school, nor are they willing to tolerate the building of a church in an Muslim neighborhood. Again, Table 6.7 suggests that Muslim elites are tolerant but not in the secular-liberal sense.

Majority Domination
Finally, the logic of legal pluralism and group rights implies the restriction of the rights of the majority, not just the minority. To see whether Muslim elites would be willing to self-restrict, I asked a series of questions about Muslims being mayor in a Christian area, building a mosque in a Christian neighborhood, holding a demonstration against Christmas, and teaching Christian studies in public schools. As Table 6.8 demonstrates, on the latter two questions the majority heavily self-restricts, which is a sign there is more going on here than majority domination. The majority is also somewhat willing to disallow Muslims from building a mosque in a majority Christian neighborhood. But there is also evidence of majority domination, with respondents saying

TABLE 6.8. *Majority domination*

Survey Question	NU and Muhammadiyah Elites
Should Muslims be permitted to ...	
... be Mayor in Manado, North Sulawesi?	81% (735)
... build a mosque in a majority Christian neighborhood?	58% (732)
... hold a demonstration in Monas (Jakarta) against Christmas?	46% (737)
... teach Christian studies in a public school?	18% (737)

Note: Differences between activities are significant at $p < 0.01$ using a two-sample test of proportions.
Percentage refers to tolerant (positive) response. Sample size is in parentheses.

that Muslims should be allowed to be mayor in a majority Christian area, a right they do not extend to the minority.

Conclusion

Communal tolerance is not simply a civic value; it is also a set of administrative regulations promulgated by the contemporary Indonesian state to protect community rights. As the constitutional courts noted, "In the name of freedom, a person or a group cannot erode the religiosity of the community, whose values underpin the basis of laws and regulations in Indonesia."[79] These regulations include mandatory religious education for students of each recognized religion, official identification cards listing religious affiliation, the requirement of proving membership in a recognized religion for those who want to enter the military or public service, extensive requirements for the building of new houses of worship including signatures from sixty local community members of a different faith and a written recommendation from the regional or municipal MORA, and prohibitions on the proselytization of individuals and groups who already possess an officially recognized religion, including restrictions on foreign missionaries.[80] The restrictions on blasphemy, discussed in Chapter 4, are one of the most visible signals of how these policies may privilege the promotion of belief in God above individual freedom, and some (but not all) individual rights. In doing so, the constitutional court is both explicit and unapologetic:

> Accordingly, in the implementation of state administration, the formation of law, the implementation of government and judicature, the basis of Belief in God and teaching as well as religious values serve as a benchmark to determine whether or not a certain law is good, or even whether or not a certain law is constitutional. In the framework of thought as described above, the restriction of human rights based on the consideration of "religious values" as set forth in Article 28J

[79] Constitutional court verdict, 2010, 140/puu-vii/2009, 3.34.5.
[80] See Ali-Fauzi et al. (2011); Crouch (2007).

paragraph (2) of the 1945 Constitution constitutes one of the considerations to restrict the exercise of human rights.[81]

Although these explicit restrictions on individual rights may be normatively discomforting to many scholars, it would be a mistake to repudiate communal tolerance as being illiberal or inconsistent with democracy. Instead, like godly nationalism, communal tolerance is an attempt to find a middle ground between individual rights, communal rights, and sacred and secular laws.

Communal tolerance is not simply an abstract virtue; it is also an informal institution that shapes behavior. This point is most obvious through NU and Muhammadiyah's behavior around Christmas. In a full page notice in the November–December 1950 edition of the MORA periodical *Mimbar Agama*, the young NU leader and Minister of Religious Affairs Wahid Hasjim wrote, "Congratulations (*mengutjapkan selamat*) on the Celebration of Christmas to all Christian organizations inside and outside the Ministry of Religion, including the Christian councils, their leaders, and the Christian people, hopefully God (*tuhan*) will bring peace to all in your community. –Minister of Religion, K.H.A Wahid Hasjim, Secretary General R. Moh Kafrawi, and everyone at the MORA and the editors of *Mimbar Agama*." Is this greeting inconsistent with NU's professed desire to separate social and religious affairs? On a research trip to Bangil, the self-proclaimed 'City of Santri' and a stronghold of NU, I posed this question to the municipal NU leaders Syamsul Maarif and Shodiq S.H. Mhum. Maarif replied that rather than being inconsistent, the wording of the greeting confirmed the distinction: "You can say congratulations [*megucapkan selamat*] to a Christian but not recognize their god. This is a very important difference. Notice that Hasjim [pointing to the notice in *Mimbar Agama*] says 'tuhan' and not 'allah' because he is only congratulating them on their holiday. It is okay to do this for Christian people but we cannot say *assalamu alaikum* [peace be unto you] to Christians. We can offer congratulations but not blessings."[82] Here Maarif attempts to differentiate secular recognition of Christians' holiday from matters of akidah, which might pollute the substance of Muslims' faith. He notes that the same is true for interfaith prayer: "If we pray for humanity there is no problem. But if we pray for akidah then we have problems. The same is true for tauhid [oneness of God]."[83] Likewise, the distinguished Kiai Soleh Bahruddin of Pesantren Darul Taqwa notes that he would often attend Christmas celebrations and Christians would often attend his Ramadan celebrations, but would never mix religious beliefs,

---

[81] Constitutional court verdict, 2010, 140/puu-vii/2009, 3.34.11.

[82] Syamsul Maarif and Shodiq SH Mhum, interview with the author, July 29, 2010, Bangil, Indonesia. Interestingly, in its tafsir on interfaith relations, Muhammadiyah notes that it is not prohibited to respond to Islamic greetings said by non-Muslims to Muslims (Muhammadiyah 2000, 74).

[83] Syamsul Maarif and Shodiq SH Mhum, interview with the author, July 29, 2010, Bangil, Indonesia.

"You cannot mix wife and husband. So too you cannot mix religions!"[84] Such a stance is often interpreted as intolerant. When MUI issued a fatwa in 1981 saying it was prohibited for Muslims to attend Christmas celebrations, it was interpreted as evidence of its opposition to interfaith tolerance.

What this interpretation ignores, however, is that opposition to mixing matters of akidah and ibadah by attending Christmas celebration is complemented by the positive obligation to protect Christmas celebrations and Christians' right to worship. A few days before Christmas in 2005, Muhammadiyah chair Din Syamsuddin stated that all buildings and facilities belonging to Muhammadiyah, except mosques, could be used for Christmas services.[85] The offer came during an interfaith meeting during which Christians lamented their difficulty in finding adequate space to hold Christian services. Such behavior is not new. During Persis' outreach to Christians in 1954, Mohammed Natsir noted: "[F]reedom of religious belief is for a Muslim dearer than life itself. It is the obligation of every Muslim not only to succor those of other faiths who have been deprived of religious freedom with the facilities for worshipping God in their own way, but also, should the need arise, to defend with his life the right of others to liberty of religious belief. The teachings of the Koran require that a Muslim defend those who are driven from their homes for having worshipped God. It is required that a Muslim should defend monasteries, churches, places of prayer, and mosques wherein the name of Allah is spoken."[86] While Muhammadiyah has done more to directly aid Christians, and NU regularly protects Christian churches, even the mostly intolerant Persis affirms and works to protect Christians' right to celebrate their holidays (although they prefer Muslims stay outside).

For the past twenty years, scholars have been debating how to 'reconcile' Islam and democracy in order to address the democratic underdevelopment of the Muslim-majority countries of the Middle East. They have devoted less attention, however, to the more important (and less polemical) question: *what kind of democracy do Muslims want?* I suggest that NU and Muhammadiyah favor a consociational form of democracy that is similar to the vision of strong multiculturalists such as Benhabib, Bajpai, and Shahar.[87] Indonesian Islamic organizations seek a state and society where each recognized community has religious freedom, but is not free to interfere in the faith matters of others. This vision echoes the synthesis of liberal rights, group rights, legal pluralism, and muscular multinationalism found in contemporary India, although organized around religious groups rather than ethnic groups or castes, and based on a strong separation of religious/social affairs rather than public/private affairs.

---

[84] Kiyai Soleh Bahruddin, interview with the author, July 20, 2010, Pesantren Darul Taqwa. Pasuruan, Indonesia.

[85] Burhani (2011, 334).

[86] Natsir (1954) in Feith and Castles (2007).

[87] Benhabib (2002); Bajpai (2011); Shahar (2001).

Insofar as NU and Muhammadiyah have helped Indonesian democracy consolidate, and in comparative perspective Indonesia is a democratic overachiever, this chapter suggests that communal tolerance is consistent with democracy and can actually help strengthen democracy, albeit not secular democracy. And in that respect, Indonesia is a model for other Muslim-majority democracies, mixing group and individual rights, and religious and secular laws, at the same time that it resembles other postcolonial democracies such as India, which has been developing a system of multiculturalism for the past sixty years. With the growing involvement of Muslim democrats in Turkey, Senegal, and Tunisia, we are likely to see examples of the communal tolerance model being incorporated into state law. While the communal tolerance model truncates some individual rights, it also enables certain rights – for example, restrictions on non-Christians interfering in matters of faith for Christians – that are not protected in the Rawlsian and Lockean model. More broadly, it provides a democratic template for governance in policies where belief in God and communal affiliation are major priorities for civil society and the state. In the next chapter, I further describe some of the normative benefits and problems with this model of democracy.

In more theoretical terms, this chapter suggests that by integrating comparative political theory into causal analysis, we can better understand the attitudes of religious organizations, see opportunities for the expansion of cooperation, and see the issues around which conflicts may emerge. For expansion of cooperation, social relations such as trade, business, secular education, neighborhood relations, and godly nationalism are areas of high tolerance and are key areas for potential increases in cooperation. Communal tolerance thus provides a template for those activists who want to promote democracy, belief in God, and minority rights. For the conflicts, we are likely to see red lines drawn around non-Muslims' political or social involvement in issues of ibadah or akidah including interfaith marriage, education, proselytization, and non-Muslims' building houses of worship or holding political office in areas that are overwhelmingly Muslim; these issues are likely to provoke a backlash regardless of whether the country is democratic or authoritarian or whether the action is in the 'public' or 'private' sphere. As I will demonstrate in the next chapter, however, these conflicts are not inevitable. From the perspective of democratic theory, many of NU and Muhammadiyah's views, such as their desire for restrictions on interfaith proselytizing and for religious education by a teacher of the same faith, may become state law without violating the rights of the minority. As we will see, NU and Muhammadiyah's vision resonates with democrats elsewhere who have tried to reconcile the rights of the minority with the promotion of piety.

7

Religion and Democracy

Is NU and Muhammadiyah's desire for a convergence of liberal individual rights and group-differentiated rights within a system of legal pluralism compatible with modern democracy? To what extent should the santri's prescriptions for tolerance be accommodated in order to strengthen democratic institutions? In this chapter I demonstrate that while these policies are at odds with American-style secular government, they are common among democracies in Africa, Asia, and Eastern Europe.

More theoretically, this chapter suggests that the study of religion and politics should go beyond the recognition that most politics exist in the grey zone between secularism and theocracy and examine the evolution, manifestations, and implications of the regulation of religion. Notice that this move is distinct from the varieties of secularism literature. We now have prototypes of assertive secularism (Turkey and France), passive secularism (the United States), benevolent secularism (Ireland, Philippines, Senegal), contextual secularism (India), separatist secularism (France, United States, Turkey), positive accommodation secularism (Germany, the Netherlands, Switzerland, Belgium), established religion secularism (Denmark, Norway, Sweden), and "respect all, positive cooperation and principled distance secularism" (India, Senegal).[1] This important work on religion and state, led by the democratic theorist Alfred Stepan, has helped scholars move beyond the false presumption that a sharp separation is necessary for democracy. Within Stepan's framework, NU and Muhammadiyah's vision for governance is closest to the model of a "Nonsecular, But Friendly to Democracy" pattern of religious-state relations.[2]

That said, the language of secularism cannot adequately represent the vision of Indonesia's Islamic organizations, which are less interested varieties of

---

[1] Kuru (2007); Buckley (2013); Bhargava (1998); Stepan et al. (2011).
[2] Stepan (2000, 42).

secularism than they are varieties of religious governance. Their goal is to see belief in God, religious education, religious values, and religious organizations celebrated and incorporated into social and political life rather than merely tolerated by a secular state. Without the reconceptualization done in Chapters 4 and 6, the language of secularism, religion-state relations, and nation-states poorly captures their categories of analysis. More broadly, using the varieties of secularism literature as a starting point may mask the reasons that religious organizations support democracy. The same is true for the concept of "illiberal democracy,"[3] which as a negative category like 'nonsecular' tells us nothing about the positive values that sustain plural democracies, as well as denying agency to the actors whose values shape democractic practices in Indonesia and elsewhere. Likewise, the category of 'ethnic democracy' developed in studies of Israel is a poor fit for states that do not privilege a single religious group.[4] One step in the right direction is Veit Bader's *associative democracy*, which supports the legal, administrative, and political recognition of organized religions and actively embraces religious values and goals rather than merely tolerating them.[5] Here I want to build on Bader's abstract philosophical arguments for associative democracy by drawing on examples from consolidated democracies in order to demonstrate how godly nationalism and communal tolerance as positive ethical virtues have been integrated into the policies of democratic institutions.

Notice my contention is that godly nationalism and communal tolerance are already synthesized with democracy around the world. Michael D. P. Driessen makes a similar claim on the basis of a close reading of Italian history and a cross-national analysis, finding that positive endorsement of religion is not necessarily harmful to national levels of democracy, and may even be beneficial.[6] To arrive at this vantage point we have to take seriously, like Indonesia's godly nationalists, the argument that religious organizations' presence in the public sphere can be beneficial to the public good rather than starting with the secular-liberal presumption that religion in the public sphere is a threat to liberty and modernization.

Such a view is not unusual outside the American context. According to the World Values Survey, majorities in twenty-four countries say that belief in God is necessary for a person to have good values, and there are another twenty-nine countries where more than 40 percent of the population agrees. Likewise, majorities in eighteen countries say that politicians who do not believe in God are unfit for office, or that people with strong religious beliefs will make better politicians. And there are another twenty-three countries where more than 40 percent of the public agrees.[7] In Romania, a consolidated

---

[3] Hamid (2014).
[4] Peled (1992); Smooha (1990).
[5] Bader (2007).
[6] Driessen (2010).
[7] World Values Survey (2005–2009).

democracy, registered religious denominations are recognized as public utilities that benefit the entire population.[8] In Western Europe, the sociologist of religion Grace Davie argues that "Europeans, by and large, regard their churches as public utilities rather than competing firms."[9] These views have institutional effects; according to Jonathan Fox's dataset on state involvement in religion, forty-nine governments provide support to religious organizations through general grants, sixty-five provide funding for religious sites, and twenty-five provide funding for religious pilgrimage.[10] Such support suggests that rather than being exceptional, the Indonesian and Romanian governments' view of religion as a public utility is shared by many states.

I follow Robert A. Dahl and Stepan in defining democracy based on ten institutional conditions: (1) freedom to form and to join organizations; (2) freedom of expression; (3) the right to vote; (4) eligibility for public office; (5) the right of political leaders to compete for support and votes; (6) alternative sources of information; (7) free and fair elections; (8) institutions for making government policies that depend on voters and other expressions of preference; (9) a democratic constitution that respects fundamental liberties and offers considerable protections for minority rights; (10) a democratically elected government that rules within the confines of the constitution and is bound by law and a complex set of vertical and horizontal institutions that help to ensure accountability.[11] In the following section I pay closest attention to the aspects of godly nationalism and communal tolerance that may contravene democracy, then demonstrate how consolidated democracies have dealt with these problems in order to reconcile the promotion of religion with the guarantee of fundamental liberties for both individuals and groups.

Godly Nationalism and Communal Tolerance in Democratic Institutions

How does a political system of group rights, individual rights, and legal pluralism work in practice? This system is worth elaborating in terms of recognition, freedom of expression, education, political representation, and religious freedom.

Godly nationalism privileges recognized religions over unrecognized ones. No religious belief (or unbelief) disqualifies anyone from obtaining or keeping

---

[8] Stan and Lucian Turcescu (2011, 140).

[9] Davie (2002, 43–44).

[10] Data here and discussed below were developed by Jonathan Fox and were coded from the 2008 US Department of State's International Religious Freedom Reports and downloaded from the Association of Religion Data Archives. Democracy score is based on 2008 polity scores, which use a −10 to +10 scale to measure how authoritarian or democratic a state is, with 6–10 equal to democracy. The examples in this chapter are from consolidated democracies with 'Free' scores of 1 or 2 in Freedom House's 2014 *Freedom in the World* country rankings.

[11] Dahl (1971, 1–3); Stepan (2001, 38–39).

citizenship, but all citizens are incentivized through various means to belong to one of the recognized religions. In contemporary Indonesia, those individuals who follow unrecognized religions, such as the Sundanese *Sunda Wiwitan*, are denied funding for their schools, cannot list their religion on their ID cards, and are socially stigmatized. Article 2 of the elucidation section of the 1965 law states that beliefs in the recognized religions and a single God are superior to mystical or syncretic faiths.

In Indonesia, the current practice of outright discrimination against nonrecognized faiths is incompatible with the democratic protection of the freedom to form and join organizations, freedom of expression, equality, and minority protection. In a democracy, individuals cannot be persecuted on the grounds that their beliefs differ from those of the majority. Nor can organizations based on heterodox beliefs be subject to restrictions that are intended to impede their development. Individuals who follow nonrecognized faiths cannot be prevented from gaining access to the courts or police; similarly, they cannot be prevented from joining the military or other national political institutions or disallowed from holding political office.

Such outright discrimination could be alleviated without restructuring Indonesian nationalism. The Indonesian state could recognize other religions. Article 1 of the 1965 law explicitly states that other religions such as Judaism, Zoroastrianism, Shintoism, and Taoism cannot be banned in Indonesia. Creating a new category for Ahmadiyah would allow its members to regulate themselves and define their own version of orthodoxy. Likewise, other persecuted groups such as Shia Muslims and the *kepercayaan* would be able to organize and receive the benefits of recognition for religious education.[12]

Another practice that reconciles godly nationalism and democracy is to formalize the multi-tiered system of religious governance. As stated in Chapter 4, godly nationalism may be informally policed through providing financial support for some religious organizations and discouraging the advocacy of disbelief. Such practices are surprisingly common in democracies. Eleven democracies have multi-tiered registration systems with different rights and privileges attached to different tiers. Austria, for example, has three tiers of registration. The highest are religious societies, which have the authority to participate in mandatory church contributions programs, provide government-funded religious instruction in both public and private schools, and bring religious workers into the country. Religious societies must have the membership of 2 percent of the country's population and have been in existence for twenty years. Only five religions meet this requirement, but another nine have been recognized because they have been active internationally for at least 100 years and in country for ten. The second tier are confessional communities, which must have 300 members and a written version of their doctrine, must differ from

[12] This is the position of the Jesuit priest Franz Magnis Suseno (Personal observation, Petitioner's Strategy Meeting, Jakarta, February 9, 2010); court transcript, 140/puu-vii/2009, VI, 45–48.

other societies or confessional communities, and are subject to a determination by the Education Ministry as to whether their beliefs violate public order, security, health, moralism, and the rights and freedom of citizens. Religious groups that do not qualify for these tiers may become legal associations, which have juridical standing and can own real estate but receive no government funding. This tiered registration system is an example of an institutional mechanism for promoting religious values based on recognized beliefs without persecuting heterodox faiths.

A similar example is Romania, which also requires that all religious organizations gain official recognition. The State Secretariat recognizes eighteen religious denominations that enjoy the right to build houses of worship, the right to perform rites of baptism, marriage, or burial, a guarantee to state noninterference, and protection against public stereotypes and negative media campaigns. To qualify, denominations must demonstrate that they are legally established and have operated uninterrupted for twelve years and that their membership includes 1 percent of the country's population. Religious associations, which also get tax breaks, need only 300 members to register. Those 385 faiths, organizations, and foundations do not enjoy the financial advantages of recognition, but their nonrecognition does not lead to persecution or punishment.[13] Like the Austrian system, Romania's provides an example of how the state can recognize particular religious values without persecuting heterodox beliefs. In other words, Austria and Romania provide examples of how states can promote belief in God while protecting fundamental democratic liberties.

A multi-tiered registration system creates challenges, however, when it comes to splinter groups. The Austrian government gives recognized religions wide authority to regulate communal affairs, including denying a splinter group's recognition as a separate community. Bulgaria goes one step further; it demands that all religious groups register with the Sofia City Court in order to become legal persons and punishes any person carrying out religious activities in the name of a religion without representational authority. This puts splinter groups in an unjust position: an Ahmadi group in Blagoevgrad was denied registration as a religion in 2005 and 2007, and then its NGO was closed in 2008. The Sofia Court of Appeals has upheld these judgments on the grounds that the Ahmadis, as a heretical splinter sect, may cause dissent in the Muslim community. Similar restrictions have been leveled against splinter groups from the Bulgarian Orthodox Church and include large fines for those practicing publicly on behalf of an unregistered religious group.[14] By both denying splinter groups the right to register in any way and punishing Ahmadis for not registering, Bulgaria's law contravenes the democratic right to form organizations and participate in civil society. Democratic states such as Indonesia and Bulgaria that demand registration may allow recognized religions to regulate

[13] Stan and Turcescu (2007, 26–27; 2011, 141).
[14] Stan and Turcescu (2011, 25).

communal affairs and promote orthodox religious values through recognized privileges, but they must also allow splinter and heterodox groups to exist and to register at some level.

Allowing splinter groups to exist means democracies can punish expressions of blasphemy (defiling religions), but not acts of heresy (belief or opinion that runs counter to orthodox doctrines). In comparative perspective, Indonesia's blasphemy law is not unusual in forbidding instigation of religious hatred through speech, press, or disturbing religious rituals. The Greek constitutional blasphemy provision allows seizure of newspapers and other publications in cases of offense against Christians or other religions. Likewise, the Greek penal law regarding blasphemy attaches a penalty to blasphemy against God, divinity, or Greek Orthodox religion.[15] Forty-two countries have blasphemy laws or other restrictions on speech about religious matters of the majority, including the democratic countries India, Ireland, Romania, Greece, Finland, Italy, Denmark, Poland, and Lithuania. For example, in India, another consolidated democracy, chapter 15 of the Indian Penal Code prohibits blasphemy. Preaching against other religions in public is considered a violation of national security, and it is illegal to destroy, damage, or defile a place of worship with the intention of insulting others' religion, an offense punishable with imprisonment up to three years. It is also a crime to disturb a religious assembly, to encourage communal hatred, or to use gestures to insult religious feelings.[16]

India also provides a good example of how splinter groups can exist without being persecuted, but also not receive the same benefits as the recognized faiths. The Kerala High Court has ruled that Ahmadis cannot be declared apostates and denied the benefits of being Muslim despite doctrinal differences from orthodox Sunni doctrine. "Minor cults in every religion cannot be equated with major desertion of faith even if they may produce quakes in a section of the community."[17] India, like Greece, manages to punish acts of blasphemy that are intended to insult the religious views of others without punishing for heresy religious communities that hold beliefs that differ from those of the majority. The key to any limits on expression in a democracy is that there are neither double standards nor hypocrisy. Ensuring that limits on free expression are reciprocal and transparent will be difficult in practice and prone to abuse as has been the case in Indonesia, but it is in principle compatible with democracy.

In a democracy based on communal tolerance, each student will receive a religious education by a teacher of his or her faith, in order to develop religious values and communal ties. Indonesia's 1989 National Education Act on Religious Education and the 2003 education law require that in state schools,

---

[15] Temperman (2010, 240).
[16] Mahmood (2006, 754–755).
[17] Mahmood (2010, 61); Shihabuddin Imbichi Koya Thangal vs. K.P. Ahammed Koya, citation A.I.R. 1971 Ker 206.

the Ministry of Religious Affairs or the Ministry of Education develop curriculum for Muslim students and each student receive a mandatory two hours of instruction in religious subjects every week. This system is tolerant to the recognized religions, but infringes on the liberties of students whose faiths fall outside the six recognized by the state. Members of unrecognized faiths have kept their children out of schools rather than subject them to mandatory education in one of the recognized religions.[18] This practice contravenes the protection of minority rights that is required of democracies.

Such discrimination, however, is not inherent to the system of communal tolerance. Students who adhere to beliefs outside the recognized ones can be accommodated in a class on comparative religions or ethics. Indonesia is an outlier among democratic governments in not providing such an option. But Indonesia is not unusual in making religious education mandatory; thirty-eight states including fourteen democracies make religious education mandatory while including an option to study ethics or comparative religion. Greece has compulsory religious education in primary and secondary schools, at government expense, but students may be exempted upon request. The 1995 Romanian Law on Education makes religious classes mandatory in primary schools and optional in high school and vocational schools. With written parental consent, students can choose to study religion in a particular denomination or not to enroll at all.[19] In Austria, attendance in religious instruction is mandatory for all students unless they formally withdraw at the beginning of the school year, with parental permission for those under fourteen; some schools offer ethics classes. In some Swiss cantons religious education is mandatory although parents can submit a waiver, while in other cantons it is optional. In sum, democracies can mandate religious education in public schools as long as students have a choice in which religion they are incorporated in, including an option to study comparative religion or ethics.

Political representation is a known challenge in political systems based on group rights.[20] Lebanon's system of confessional consociationalism with reserved seats for members of recognized groups is one model for group representation in a democracy, but an unstable one in which patrimony, sectarianism, and political fragmentation are endemic. The degree to which educational, political, social, and economic institutions are organized along sectarian lines has prevented the emergence of a common national identity and has led to internally fragmented institutions. Once established, the allocation of seats for religious sects is difficult to change as demographics shift, which leads to both under- and overrepresentation of certain groups. Lebanon's instability cannot be solely attributed to its political institutions; the involvement of Syria, Israel, Saudi Arabia, Iran, Qatar, and France in Lebanese politics bears equal

---

[18] Court transcript, 140/puu-vii/2009, VI, 74–78.
[19] Stan and Turcescu (2007, 160).
[20] Spinner-Halev (2000).

responsibility for the polarization between religious sects. The problem is the scale of group rights, not their presence.

Like many other postcolonial states, Indonesia has struggled to resolve a colonial legacy of a legal regime focused on the individual and an administrative structure focused on the group. While most postcolonial states have since moved in the direction of liberal individualism, often with disastrous results, Indonesia, like India, has continued in both the group and individual direction.[21] This has been a productive move from the perspective of democratic transition and consolidation. By permitting group rights in a limited number of areas, but not in the military, allocation of electoral seats, or the civil service, Indonesia's system avoids the fragmentation that can accompany the institutionalization of group rights. NU and Muhammadyah's desire to deny Christians the right to hold office in overwhelmingly Muslim areas is acceptable as a social attitude, but cannot be incorporated into state law without injurious implications for democracy. Reserving some demographically configured areas for one religion and others for other religions creates incentives for all groups to engage in ethnic cleansing rather than the kind of intergroup cooperation that characterizes contemporary Indonesian politics. The inclusion and participation of Indonesia's Islamic political parties in elections has been a source of strength for the country, and their engagement has fostered considerable moderation; allowing that aspect of group rights into formal politics is consistent with democracy. But as the Lebanese case suggests, it is unwise for political representation to be exclusively based on communal identities. Instead, legal pluralism provides the best framework in Indonesia like in other democracies. Like democratic India and Greece, Indonesia has a long and rich history of legal pluralism with overlapping jurisdictions between Islamic law, secular law, and customary law.[22] This pluralism allows individuals the choice of cultural identity while the group maintains control over their institutionalized rules for membership. While this can lead to legal uncertainty and a lack of legal hierarchy, it also gives group boundaries a fluidity that increases the incentives for cooperation across group lines and for politicians to make out-group appeals.[23]

Religious freedom is arguably another difficult area for communal tolerance and democracy, owing to the primacy of religious belief among the Islamic organizations. It is no surprise that this is a locus for contemporary conflicts in Indonesia. In a democracy grounded in communal tolerance, the rule of thumb should be similar to laws regarding free expression: building a church, a mosque, or a temple requires community approval and that approval must

[21] I am grateful to Humeira Iqtidar for this point.
[22] Lev (1972); Bowen (2003).
[23] Election advertisements from the municipal level show that Indonesia's high rate of pluralism and plurality elections offer politicians incentives to make broad, out-group appeals (Fox and Menchik 2011).

be reciprocal and transparent. If Muslims are unable to build a mosque in Denpasar, Bali, because of community feelings, then Hindus cannot build a temple in Banda Aceh. The current law demands that sixty members of the surrounding community support the building of a new house of worship. While neither liberal nor secular, this is a communitarian way to regulate freedom of worship.

The counter-argument is that absolute religious freedom is necessary in a democracy, and anything less is capitulation to illiberal majority domination. Some activists argue that any individual, regardless of faith or nationality, should be able to manifest religious beliefs as they see fit including active proselytization.[24] But this is an unrealistic position with imperialist overtones. It is also not the position of many governments; forty-six countries around the globe put restrictions on missionaries and religious workers including twenty-four democracies. A total of thirty-four democracies put restrictions on proselytizing by foreign clergy or missionaries including Switzerland, Belgium, the United Kingdom, Denmark, Austria, Bolivia, and Costa Rica – all of which frequently deny visas to foreigners who wish to proselytize. Greece, a consolidated democracy, prohibits proselytism in Article 13 of the 2001 constitution, defined as a "direct or indirect attempt to intrude on the religious beliefs of a person of a different religious persuasion, with the aim of undermining those beliefs, either by any kind of inducement or promise of an inducement or moral support or material assistance, or by fraudulent means or by taking advantage of his inexperience, trust, need, low intellect or naivety."[25] India limits proselytizing to specific locations such as places of worship; laws protecting local people against foreign missionaries or other attempts to convert are common, and are found in at least eight states.[26] Switzerland, one of the world's longest-standing democracies, allows proselytizing only if missionaries can demonstrate knowledge of Swiss customs and culture, are conversant in at least one of the main national languages, and hold a degree in theology. There is nothing in democratic theory that demands unrestricted religious freedom. Instead, the goal of democratic theorists should be comprehensive toleration within the context of an ongoing political and legal order.[27]

Conclusion

The prominence of religious actors in democratic politics offers opportunities as well as cautions to scholars. While Western scholars usually focus on the impact of religious actors on women and religious minorities, and fear

---

[24] This is the position of activists for religious freedom including Farr (2008, 2011); Farr and Hoover (2009), and Grim and Finke (2010).

[25] Temperman (2010, 218).

[26] Mahmood (2006, 761–762).

[27] Murphy (1997, 619–620).

potential restrictions on freedom that may accompany religion in the public sphere, we might take their agency seriously by looking not just at the freedoms they may restrict but the values they may promote: hope, love, brotherhood, compassion, justice, charity, respect, community, harmony. Likewise, we might consider the impact of religious actors' opposition to the values of narcissism, greed, selfishness, arrogance, and willful social alienation that so often accompany modernity. Having done so, we might come to see different approaches to the most pressing concerns of our century. How might education in the value of compassion aid in the fight against poverty? How can the promotion of brotherhood reduce militarism? How might the virtues of respect and selflessness and the condemnation of greed advance the struggle against economic inequality?

The first generation of theory on religion in modernity posited that it would disappear. The second predicted that religion's resurgence would engender conflict along civilizational lines, that these conflicts would last longer than other wars, and that Islam in particular would bring new challenges to the dominance of Western modernity. This second generation has also engendered a productive rebuttal: religious conflicts are not inevitable but rather one of the many challenges of modern politics. In the third generation, I hope that we can move beyond mere conflict and coexistence to see the multiple manifestations of religion in public life both past and present. Situating religious agency and virtue at the center of politics rather than at the dying periphery suggests new ways of understanding social movements, political theory, and the world's multiple modernities.

Methodological Appendices

Appendix A: Survey Protocol

In March, July, and September 2010, I collected survey data from a random sample of branch (*cabang*) leaders from Persis, NU, and Muhammadiyah. The branch leaders are the managers of the organizations on the ground: they choose the central board, implement all programs, raise funds, shape relations with political parties, and govern interfaith and intrafaith relations at the local and national levels. The sample includes 1,000 observations (n), representing a total population (N) of 6,550 leaders; there are 2,300 Muhammadiyah branch leaders, 3,500 for NU, and 750 for Persis. The population also roughly maps onto the size of the organizations. NU is the largest with approximately 40–60 million members and makes up 53 percent of the survey population; Muhammadiyah is second with approximately 30 million members and 35 percent of the survey population. Persis is considerably smaller with only 500,000 members. The survey population, however, includes 11 percent from Persis in order to represent the broader population of Muslim leaders, a necessary move since Islamists are active in other important Islamic organizations such as Dewan Dakwah Islamiyah in addition to Persis. The sample includes 387 Muhammadiyah leaders, 379 from NU, and 234 from Persis. For statistics representing the opinions of all Islamic elites, their responses are weighted in order to reflect the survey population of branch leaders. In other words, NU leaders' responses are weighted up and Persis' weighted down in order to better reflect the population. The response rate is 96.6 percent using the American Association for Public Opinion Research definition of answering 80 percent or more of the questions. The sample is not completely random in that only leaders who attended the 2010 meetings of their respective institutions were surveyed. Inactive elites were thus not included in the sample. These meetings took place every five years and were attended by active elites from all over the country. The meetings took place within a six-month period from March to

September 2010, and the lag time between meetings should not have biased the results in any theoretically relevant way. At the meetings, exact respondents were selected randomly by approaching every third person walking through a central area of the meeting.

The primary goal in the survey was to describe the attitudes among elites in Islamic organizations. The questions were structured around these goals and based on other surveys measuring levels of tolerance, although specifying the target group rather than having respondents choose from a list. The major concern shaping the survey instrument was avoiding response bias based on social desirability, as well as avoiding redundancy.[1] Any survey that investigates levels of tolerance has to deal with potential response bias based on social desirability.[2] Respondents, particularly image-conscious elites, may want to make a good impression on the researcher by appearing sensible, free of prejudice, and rational.

For this study, there were three types of response bias: the first type was the desire to appear tolerant to the researcher. Maintaining the appearance of tolerance in Indonesia is a long-standing priority for the government and social elites. In order to minimize this type of social desirability bias, the survey used three techniques: assurances of anonymity and scientific importance, the use of self-administered forms with sealable envelopes that provided more privacy than phone or face-to-face interviews, and statements that sanctioned less desirable responses.[3] The assurance of anonymity and scientific importance were read to each interviewee and printed on a cover letter attached to a sealable envelope. To maximize privacy, the survey was self-administered and upon completion, it was sealed in an envelope. The statements that sanctioned less desirable responses were written above each set of questions.

The second concern is the pressure to conform to organizational policy. In all three organizations, the national executive board creates policy, and once finalized, all activists are supposed to conform to policy. To minimize social desirability bias in favor of institutional policy, non-Indonesian survey administrators were used. Especially at a conference of activists, Indonesian administrators were likely to be assumed to be a member of the organization and could trigger a response that 'sounds like our policy.' The administrators were professionally dressed in Western clothing. Such clothing and background characteristics were intended to invoke the authority of a scientific research study.[4]

The third concern was the pressure to not oppose government policy toward minority religions. The Indonesian state has historically controlled the activities of religious groups by completely banning certain groups, proscribing the tenets of organizations' ideology, and co-opting the leadership of organizations by enveloping elites into the state's patronage networks. In the author's

[1] Grice (1975).
[2] DeMaio (1984).
[3] de Vaus (1996, 110); Singleton and Straights (2005, 270–273).
[4] Cialdini (1984); Dillman (2000, 248).

in-depth interviews, Islamist elites have been particularly reluctant to oppose the state's policy allowing minority religious groups to build a house of worship anywhere with a significant minority community. As with the first type of bias, this was also addressed using statements sanctioning less desirable responses.

The final concern shaping the survey instrument was redundancy that can lead respondents to engage in satisficing. Since the survey used questions developed in previous research on tolerance and newly developed questions, respondents could perceive some questions to be repetitive. To address this concern, questions were ordered from the most general to the most specific with a break between sections.[5] Questions 1–6 were the most general, followed by a series of questions on identity and the activity of non-Muslim groups. Subsequent questions addressed political protest, education, representation, and other areas in which respondents might demonstrate more or less tolerance. All respondents were given a small incentive, a keychain carabineer from the University of Wisconsin–Madison, to encourage them to take the survey seriously.

Appendix B: Survey Questions in English

Survey Questions for Leaders and Members of _____ (NU, Muhammadiyah, or Persis)

This survey asks your opinion about religion in Indonesia. You are under no obligation to participate. If you do participate, you are asked to answer all questions honestly and to the best of your ability. Please do not write your name on the survey, as this is anonymous and your response will never be displayed in a way that would allow anyone to connect them to you.

Your answers will be used for a research project concerning religion in Indonesia, and for no other purpose. After collection, this research will be used as part of a doctoral dissertation.

If you have any questions about this survey, the research, or the data collection, please contact:

Please indicate whether you perform the following rituals very frequently, quite frequently, rarely, or never.

1. Five daily prayers
2. Recite Qur'an
3. Give charity (*sedekah zakat*) in the form of money or food

Some people believe that Christians in Indonesia should be kept apart from Muslims while other people think that the two groups should freely interact. What do you think? Please indicate whether you strongly agree, agree, disagree, strongly disagree, or have no opinion/do not know about the following statements.

---

[5] Tourangeau (1999, 113–115).

4. Christians should be prohibited from teaching in public schools.
5. Christians should be prohibited from teaching in Islamic schools.
6. Christians should be prohibited from holding government office.
7. Christians should be prohibited from holding public demonstrations.
8. I would not want a new Christian church to be built in my neighborhood.
9. I would not want to live next door to a Christian.

Which of the following best describes your identity?

10. My primary identity is as someone who is (pick only one) Muslim-Indonesian-Indigenous Ethnic-NU/Muh/Persis-No opinion or Do not know
11. My secondary identity is as someone who is (pick only one) Muslim-Indonesian-Indigenous Ethnic-NU/Muh/Persis-No opinion or Do not know
12. My third identity is as someone who is (pick only one) Muslim-Indonesian-Indigenous Ethnic-NU/Muh/Persis-No opinion or Do not know
13. My fourth identity is as someone who is (pick only one) Muslim-Indonesian-Indigenous Ethnic-NU/Muh/Persis-No opinion or Do not know

Please indicate whether you strongly agree, agree, disagree, strongly disagree, or have no opinion/do not know about the following statements.

14. The behavior of Christians threatens my way of life.
15. The behavior of Hindus threatens my way of life.
16. The behavior of members of Ahmadiyah Qadiani threatens my way of life.
17. The behavior of Communists threatens my way of life.

Some people believe that political protests should occur only on certain topics and in certain locations, while others feel that people should be free to demonstrate on any topic. What do you think?

18. Christians should be prohibited from demonstrating in Monas (Jakarta) about the price of gasoline.
19. Christians should be prohibited from demonstrating in Monas (Jakarta) in favor of interfaith marriage.
20. Christians should be prohibited from demonstrating in Monas (Jakarta) against the Shari'a bylaws in Aceh.

Some people believe that Christians and Muslims should live in different areas, while others feel that people from religious groups should mix freely. What do you think?

21. I would not want to live in the same city/village as a Christian.
22. I would not want to live in the same province as a Christian.

Some people feel that elected leaders should have the same religion as their constituency, while others feel that any individual can be a political representative. What do you think?

23. Christians should be prohibited from becoming the mayor in Manado, North Sulawesi.
24. Christians should be prohibited from becoming the mayor in Jakarta.
25. Christians should be prohibited from becoming the mayor in Banda Aceh.
26. Christians should be prohibited from becoming the president of Indonesia.
27. Hindus should be prohibited from becoming the mayor in Denpasar, Bali.
28. Hindus should be prohibited from becoming the mayor in Jakarta.
29. Members of Ahmadiyah Qadiani should be prohibited from becoming the mayor in Jakarta.
30. Communists should be prohibited from becoming the mayor of Jakarta.

Some people feel that teachers should have the same religion/faith as their students, while other people feel that any individual can teach anyone. What do you think?

31. Christians should be prohibited from teaching math at Islamic schools.
32. Christians should be prohibited from teaching math at public schools.
33. Hindus should be prohibited from teaching math at Islamic schools.
34. Members of Ahmadiyah Qadiani should be prohibited from teaching math at Islamic schools.

Some people feel that teachers can teach any subject, while other people feel that teachers should have the same religion that they teach about. What do you think?

35. Christians should be prohibited from teaching Qur'anic exegesis at public schools.
36. Hindus should be prohibited from teaching Qur'anic exegesis at public schools.
37. Members of Ahmadiyah Qadiani should be prohibited from teaching Qur'anic exegesis at public schools.

Some people feel that there is no need for new Christian churches, Hindu temples, or Ahmadiyah buildings in Indonesia, while other people feel that people should be permitted to build new houses of worship. What do you think?

38. New Christian churches should be prohibited in Manado, North Sulawesi.
39. New Christian churches should be prohibited in Jakarta.
40. New Christian churches should be prohibited in Banda Aceh.
41. New Hindu temples should be prohibited in Jakarta.
42. New Ahmadiyah Qadiani buildings should be prohibited in Jakarta.

Some people believe that Christians in Indonesia should be kept apart from Muslims while other people think that the two groups should interact freely. What do you think?

43. Muslims should be prohibited from teaching Christian theology in public schools.
44. Muslims should be prohibited from becoming the mayor in Manado, North Sulawesi.
45. Muslims should be prohibited from holding a demonstration in Monas against Christmas.
46. Muslims should not be allowed to build a mosque in a predominantly Christian neighborhood.

Please provide the following background information. Again, please do not write your name. This survey is anonymous.

47. Age:
48. Origin (Province):
49. Current Home: City/Village
50. Gender: Perempuan/Laki-laki
51. Ethnic Group (suku):
52. Committee membership within NU/Muhammadiyah/Persis:
53. Education (choose all that apply):
    - Pesantren/Madrasah NU
    - Pesantren/Madrasah Muhammadiyah
    - Pesantren/Madrasah Persis
    - Pesantren/Madrasah other
    - State elementary school
    - Public middle school
    - Public high school
    - Diploma (D3)
    - University graduate (S1)
    - Masters education (S2)
    - PhD (S3)
54. Monthly income (choose one):
    - Less than Rp. 300,000
    - Rp. 300,000–399,999
    - Rp. 600,000–1,999,999
    - Rp. 2,000,000–3,999,999
    - Rp. 4,000,000–9,999,999
    - Rp. 10,000,000 and above
55. How often do you interact with non-Muslims (circle only one):
    - Very often
    - Often
    - Sometimes

- Rarely
- Never

Finished!

Thank you for your participation in this survey. Please seal the questionnaire in the attached envelope and return it to the administrator.

Appendix C: Survey Questions in Indonesian

Pertanyaan Survei untuk Pimpinan dan Anggota _____ (Muhammadiyah, NU, atau Persis)

Survey ini menanyakan pendapat anda tentang kehidupan beragama di Indonesia. Anda tidak berkewajiban untuk berpartisipasi dalam survei ini. Tetapi jika anda berpartisipasi, silakan menjawab semua pertanyaan dengan jujur dan sebaik mungkin sesuai dengan kemampuan anda. Tolong jangan menulis nama anda di survei, karena survei ini adalah anonim (yang tidak diketahui namanya). Respons anda tidak akan ditampilkan dengan cara yang memungkinkan orang lain untuk menghubungkannya dengan diri anda.

Jawaban anda akan digunakan dalam suatu proyek penelitian tentang kehidupan beragama di Indonesia, dan tidak akan digunakan untuk tujuan yang lain. Hasil pengumpulan survei penelitian ini nantinya akan digunakan sebagai bagian dari sebuah disertasi doktoral (program S-3). Jika Anda memiliki pertanyaan mengenai survei, penelitian, atau pengumpulan data ini, silahkan hubungi saya. Terima kasih.

Tolong tunjukkan apakah anda pernah melakukan ritual-ritual berikut ini sangat sering/selalu, sering, kadang-kadang, jarang, atau tidak pernah.

1. Salat lima kali sehari
2. Membaca al-Qur'an
3. Memberikan sedekah zakat dalam bentuk uang atau makanan

Ada yang mengatakan bahwa orang Kristen di Indonesia seharusnya hidup terpisah dari orang Muslim tetapi ada juga yang mengatakan bahwa kedua kelompok seharusnya hidup berdampingan dan bercampur bebas. Bagaimana pendapat anda? Tolong tunjukkan sikap anda, apakah sangat setuju, setuju, tidak setuju, sangat tidak setuju, atau tidak ada pendapat/tidak tahu tentang pernyataan-pernyataan berikut ini.

4. Orang Kristen seharusnya tidak boleh mengajar di sekolah negri.
5. Orang Kristen seharusnya tidak boleh mengajar di pesantren.
6. Orang Kristen seharusnya tidak boleh menjadi penjabat pemerintah
7. Orang Kristen seharusnya tidak boleh mengadakan demonstrasi.
8. Saya tidak ingin dibangun gereja baru di lingkungan saya
9. Saya tidak ingin tinggal bertetangga yang bersama orang Kristen.

Yang terbaik berikut menggambarkan identitas anda?

10. Identitas utama saya adalah seorang (pilih salah satu):
    Muslim/Indonesia/Suku/Muhammadiyah-NU-Persis/Tidak ada pendapat
    atau Tidak tahu
11. Identitas kedua saya adalah seorang (pilih salah satu):
    Muslim/Indonesia/Suku/Muhammadiyah-NU-Persis/Tidak ada pendapat
    atau Tidak tahu
12. Identitas ketiga saya adalah seorang (pilih salah satu):
    Muslim/Indonesia/Suku/Muhammadiyah-NU-Persis/Tidak ada pendapat
    atau Tidak tahu
13. Identitas keempat saya adalah seorang (pilih salah satu):
    Muslim/Indonesia/Suku/Muhammadiyah-NU-Persis/Tidak ada pendapat
    atau Tidak tahu

Tolong tunjukkan sikap anda, apakah sangat setuju, setuju, tidak setuju, sangat
tidak setuju, atau tidak ada pendapat/tidak tahu tentang pernyataan-pernyataan
berikut ini.

14. Kegiatan orang Christian menggangu cara hidup saya.
15. Kegiatan orang Hindu menggangu cara hidup saya.
16. Kegiatan orang Ahmadiyah Qadiani menggangu cara hidup saya.
17. Kegiatan orang Komunis menggangu cara hidup saya.

Ada yang mengatakan bahwa demonstrasi politik seharusnya hanya untuk
topik-topik tertentu, tetapi ada juga yang merasa masyarakat seharusnya
bebas untuk menunjukkan sikap dan pendapat mereka tentang topik apa saja.
Bagaimana pendapat Anda?

18. Orang Kristen seharusnya tidak boleh berdemonstrasi di Monas
    (Jakarta) tentang harga bensin.
19. Orang Kristen seharusnya tidak boleh berdemonstrasi di Monas
    (Jakarta) untuk mendukung perkawinan antar-agama.
20. Orang Kristen seharusnya tidak boleh berdemonstrasi di Monas
    (Jakarta) untuk menentang undang-undang Syari'ah (Qanun Syari'ah)
    di Aceh.

Ada yang mengatakan bahwa orang Kristen dan Muslim seharusnya tinggal
di daerah yang berbeda, tetapi ada juga yang mengatakan bahwa orang-orang
dari kelompok agama yang berbeda seharusnya dapat hidup berdampingan
dan bercampur dengan bebas. Apa pendapat Anda?

21. Saya tidak ingin tinggal di desa yang bersama orang Kristen.
22. Saya tidak ingin tinggal di kota yang bersama orang Kristen.

Ada pendapat yang mengatakan bahwa pemimpin yang terpilih seharusnya
memiliki agama yang sama dengan konstituen mereka, sementara ada pendapat

lain yang merasa bahwa setiap individu dapat menjadi perwakilan politik. Apa pendapat Anda?

23. Orang Kristen seharusnya tidak boleh menjadi walikota di Manado, Sulawesi Utara.
24. Orang Kristen seharusnya tidak boleh menjadi walikota di Jakarta.
25. Orang Kristen seharusnya tidak boleh menjadi walikota di Banda Aceh.
26. Orang Kristen seharusnya tidak boleh menjadi Presiden Indonesia.
27. Orang Hindu seharusnya tidak boleh menjadi walikota di Denpasar, Bali.
28. Orang Hindu seharusnya tidak boleh menjadi walikota di Jakarta.
29. Orang Ahmadiyah Qadiani seharusnya tidak boleh menjadi walikota di Jakarta.
30. Orang Komunis seharusnya tidak boleh menjadi walikota di Jakarta.

Ada pendapat yang mengatakan bahwa seorang guru seharusnya memiliki agama/kĕpĕrcayaan yang sama dengan siswa mereka, ada yang mengatakan bahwa setiap individu dapat mengajar siapa saja tidak peduli mereka beragama apa. Apa pendapat Anda?

31. Orang Kristen seharusnya tidak boleh mengajar matematika di pesantren.
32. Orang Kristen seharusnya tidak boleh mengajar matematika di sekolah negeri.
33. Orang Hindu seharusnya tidak boleh mengajar matematika di pesantren.
34. Orang Ahmadiyah Qadiani seharusnya tidak boleh mengajar matematika di pesantren.

Beberapa orang berpikir bahwa guru dapat mengajar semua subjek, sementara orang lain berpikir bahwa guru seharusnya memiliki agama yang sama yang mereka ajarkan. Apa pendapat Anda?

35. Orang Kristen seharusnya tidak boleh mengajar pelajaran agama Islam di sekolah negeri.
36. Orang Hindu seharusnya tidak boleh mengajar pelajaran agama Islam di sekolah negeri.
37. Orang Ahmadiyah Qadiani seharusnya tidak boleh mengajar pelajaran agama Islam di sekolah negeri.

Ada yang mengatakan bahwa tidak ada kebutuhan untuk pembangunan Gereja-gereja Kristen baru, tempat ibadah Hindu, atau gedung Ahmadiyah Qadiani di Indonesia, tetapi ada juga yang mengatakan bahwa seharusnya setiap kelompok diizinkan untuk membangun rumah ibadah baru dimana saja. Apa pendapat Anda?

38. Gereja-gereja baru seharusnya tidak boleh dibangun di Manado, Sulawesi Utara.
39. Gereja-gereja baru seharusnya tidak boleh dibangun Jakarta.

40. Gereja-gereja baru seharusnya tidak boleh dibangun di Banda Aceh.
41. Tempat ibadah Hindu baru seharusnya tidak boleh dibangun di Jakarta.
42. Gedung Ahmadiyah Qadiani baru seharusnya tidak boleh dibangun di Jakarta.

Ada yang mengatakan bahwa orang Kristen di Indonesia seharusnya hidup ter-pisah dari orang Islam, tetapi ada juga yang mengatakan bahwa kedua kelom-pok seharusnya dapat hidup berdampingan dan bercampur dengan bebas. Apa pendapat Anda?

43. Orang Muslim seharusnya tidak boleh mengajar pelajaran agama Kristen di sekolah negri.
44. Orang Muslim seharusnya tidak boleh menjadi walikota di Manado, Sulawesi Utara.
45. Orang Muslim seharusnya tidak boleh mengadakan demonstrasi di Monas (Jakarta) menentang perayaan Hari Natal.
46. Orang Muslim seharusnya tidak diperbolehkan untuk membangun sebuah masjid di lingkungan yang didominasi oleh orang Kristen.

Tolong sediakan berikut mengenai latar belakang. Sekali lagi, tolong jangan menulis nama Anda karena survei itu anonim. Identitas dan nama yang tidak dikenal.

47. Umur:
48. Asli (provinci):
49. Asli perkotaan atau pedesaan (linkaran salah satu): Kota / Desa
50. Jenis Kelamin (lingkaran salah satu): Perempuan / Laki-laki
51. Suku bangsa:
52. Keanggotaan Di Dalam Muhammadiyah-NU-Persis (Majelis, Lembaga, Badan dll.):
53. Pendidikan (linkaran semua yang sesuai):
    - Pesantren/Madrasah NU
    - Pesantren/Madrasah MuhammadiyahPesantren/Madrasah Persis
    - Pesantren/Madrasah lain-lain
    - Sekolah Menengah Pertama (SMP) negeri
    - Sekolah Menengah Atas (SMA) negeri
    - Sekolah Menengah Kejuruan (SMK) negeri
    - Diploma (D3)
    - Sarjana (S1)
    - Sarjana (S2)
    - Sarjana (S3)
54. Pendapatan/penghasilan bulanan (linkaran salah satu):
    - Kurang dari Rp. 400,000
    - Rp. 400,001–1,000,000
    - Rp. 1,000,001–3,000,000
    - Rp. 3,000,001–lebih

55. Berapa sering anda interaksi dengan orang non-Muslim (linkaran salah satu):
    - Sangat sering
    - Sering
    - Kadang-kadang
    - Jarang
    - Tidak pernah

Selesai! Terima Kasih.

Terima kasih atas partisipasi anda dalam survei ini. Silakan masukkan ke dalam amplop yang terlampir dan segel. Tolong langsung kembalikan kepada administrator survey.

References

Abalahin, Andrew 2005. "A Sixth Religion? Confucianism and the Negotiation of Indonesian-Chinese Identity under the Pancasila State," in Willford, Andrew Clinton and George, Ken M. (eds.), *Spirited Politics: Religion and Public Life in Contemporary Southeast Asia*. Ithaca: Cornell Southeast Asia Program Publication, 119–142.

Abdurrahman, Asymuni and Moelyadi (ed.) 1992. *Tanya-Jawab Agama II*. Yogyakarta: Yayasan Penerbit Pers Suara Muhammadiyah.

Aboebakar, H. 1948. *Sedjarah al-Qur'an*. Jogjakarta: Kementrian Agama.

   1952. *Sedjarah al-Qur'an*. Djakarta: Sinar Pudjangga.

Agrama, Hussein 2010a. "Ethics, Tradition, Authority: Toward an Anthropology of the Fatwa," *American Ethnologist* 37:1, 2–18.

   2010b. "Secularism, Sovereignty, Indeterminacy: Is Egypt a Secular or a Religious State?" *Comparative Studies in Society and History* 52:3, 495–523.

Akkeren, Philip van 1969. *Sri and Christ: A Study of the Indigenous Church in East Java*. London: Lutterworth.

Alfian 1989. *Muhammadiyah: The Political Behavior of a Muslim Modernist Organization under Dutch Colonialism*. Yogyakarta: Gadjah Mada Press.

Alfitri 2008. "Religious Liberty in Indonesia and the Rights of 'Deviant' Sects," *Asian Journal of Comparative Law* 3:1, 1–27.

Ali, Abdullah Yusuf 1987. *The Qur'an: Text, Translation and Commentary*. Elmhurst, New York: Tahrike Tarsile Qur'an, Inc.

Ali, Moehammad 1925. *Pergerakan Ahmadiah itoe apakah? Pengertian-pengertian salah*. Djokjakarta: Persatoean Moehammadijah.

Ali-Fauzi, Ihsan, Panggabean, Samsu Rizal, Sumaktoyo, Nathanael Gratias, Anick, H. T., Mubarak, Husni, Testriono, and Siti Nurhayati 2011. "Disputed Churches in Jakarta." Melbourne: Asian Law Centre and Centre for Islamic Law and Society. Accessed from http://www.law.unimelb.edu.au/alc.

Amrullah, Hadji Abdul Malik Karim (Hamka) 1982. *Ajahku*. Jakarta: Widjaja.

Anderson, Benedict O. G. 1972. "The Idea of Power in Javanese Culture," in Holt, Claire (ed.), *Culture and Politics in Indonesia*. Ithaca, NY: Cornell University Press.

   1977. "Religion and Politics in Indonesia," in Anderson, Benedict O. G., Nakamura, Mitsuo, Slamet, Mohammad (ed.), *Religion and Social Ethos in Indonesia*. Monash: Monash University.

1999. "Indonesian Nationalism Today and in the Future," *Indonesia* 67 (April), 1–11.

2003. *Imagined Communities*, 2nd ed. London: Verso.

Anderson, Robert and Fetner, Tina 2008. "Economic Inequality and Intolerance: Attitudes toward Homosexuality in 35 Democracies," *American Journal of Political Science* 52:4, 942–958.

Arat, Yeşim 1998. "Feminists, Islamists, and Political Change in Turkey," *Political Psychology* 19:1, 117–131.

Arendt, Hanna 1958. *The Human Condition*. Chicago: University of Chicago.

Aritonang, Jan and Steenbrink, Karel 2008. *A History of Christianity in Indonesia*. Leiden: Koninklijke Brill.

Arjomand, Saïd Amir 2009. "The Constitution of Medina: A Sociolegal Interpretation of Muhammad's Acts of Foundation of the Umma," *International Journal of Middle East Studies* 41, 555–575.

Asad, Talal 1986. *The Idea of an Anthropology of Islam*. Washington, DC: Center for Contemporary Arab Studies, Georgetown University.

1993. *Genealogies of Religion: Discipline and Reasons of Power in Christianity and Islam*. Baltimore: John Hopkins University Press.

2003. *Formations of the Secular: Christianity, Islam, Modernity*. Stanford: Stanford University Press.

Ashour, Omar 2009. *The Deradicalization of Jihadists: Transforming Armed Islamist Movements*. London and New York: Routledge.

Aspinall, Edward 2007. "From Islamism to Nationalism in Aceh, Indonesia," *Nations and Nationalism* 13:2, 245–263.

Assyaukanie, Luthfi 2009. *Islam and the Secular State in Indonesia*. Singapore: ISEAS Publications.

Asyari, Suaidi 2009. *Nalar Politik NU & Muhammadiyah: Over Crossing Java Sentris*. Yogyakarta: LKiS Yogyakarta.

Bachtiar, Harsja W. 1973. "The Religion of Java: A Commentary," *Madjalah Ilmu-Ilmu Sastra Indonesia* 5:1, 85–118.

Bader, Veit 2007. *Secularism or Democracy? Associational Governance of Religious Diversity*. Amsterdam: Amsterdam University Press.

Bajpai, Rochana 2011. *Debating Difference: Group Rights and Liberal Democracy in India*. New Delhi: Oxford University Press.

Barkey, Karen 2005. "Islam and Toleration: Studying the Ottoman Imperial Model," *International Journal of Politics, Culture and Society* 19, 5–19.

2008. *Empire of Difference: The Ottomans in Comparative Perspective*. Cambridge: Cambridge University Press.

Barth, Fredrick 1969. *Ethnic Groups and Boundaries*. Boston: Little, Brown.

Barton, Greg 1996. "The Liberal Progressive Roots of Abdurraham Wahid's Thought," in Barton, Greg and Fealy, Greg (eds.), *Nahdlatul Ulama, Traditional Islam and Modernity in Indonesia*. Melbourne: Monash Asia Institute, Monash University, 190–226.

Barton, Greg and Fealy, Greg (eds.) 1996. *Nahdlatul Ulama, Traditional Islam and Modernity in Indonesia*. Melbourne: Monash Asia Institute, Monash University.

Bayat, Asef 2007. *Making Islam Democratic: Social Movements and the Post-Islamist Turn*. Stanford: Stanford University Press.

Beck, Herman 2005. "The Rupture between the Muhammadiyah and the Ahmadiyya," *Bijdragen tot de Taal-, Land-en Volkenkunde* 161:2, 1–33.

Bejczy, Istvan 1997. "Tolerantia: A Medieval Concept," *Journal of the History of Ideas* 58:3, 365–384.

Bellah, Robert 1975. *The Broken Covenant: American Civil Religion in a Time of Trial.* New York: Seabury Press.

Bellin, Eva 2008. "Faith in Politics: New Trends in the Study of Religion and Politics," *World Politics* 60:2, 315–347.

Benda, Harry 1958. *The Crescent and the Rising Sun: Indonesian Islam under the Japanese Occupation 1942–1945.* The Hague and Bandung: W. van Hoeve.

Benhabib, Seyla 2002. *The Claims of Culture: Equality and Diversity in the Global Era.* Princeton: Princeton University Press.

Bhargava, Rajeev (ed.) 1998. *Secularism and Its Critics.* New Delhi: Oxford University Press.

Binder, Leonard 1988. *Islamic Liberalism: A Critique of Development Ideologies.* Chicago: University of Chicago Press.

Boland, B. J. 1982. *The Struggle of Islam in Modern Indonesia.* The Hague: Martinus Nijhoff.

Bowen, John 2003. *Islam, Law and Equality in Indonesia: An Anthropology of Public Reasoning.* Cambridge: Cambridge University Press.

Braungart, Richard and Braungart, Margaret 1986. "Life-course and Generational Politics," *Annual Review of Sociology* 12, 205–231.

Brooks, Risa 2011. "Muslim 'Homegrown' Terrorism in the United States: How Serious Is the Threat?" *International Security* 36:2, 7–47.

Browers, Michaelle 2009. *Political Ideology in the Arab World: Accommodation and Transformation.* Cambridge: Cambridge University Press.

Brown, Nathan and Hamzawy, Amr 2010. *Between Religion and Politics.* Washington, DC: Carnegie Endowment for International Peace.

Brown, Wendy 2006. *Regulating Aversion: Tolerance in the Age of Identity and Empire.* Princeton: Princeton University Press.

Browning, Christopher R. 1998. *Ordinary Men: Reserve Police Battalion 101 and the Final Solution in Poland.* New York: HarperPerennial.

Brubaker, Rogers 2004. *Ethnicity without Groups.* Cambridge: Harvard University Press.

Bruinessen, Martin van 1995. "Muslims of the Dutch East Indies and the Caliphate Question," *Studia Islamika* 2:3, 115–140.

Brumberg, Daniel 2001. *Reinventing Khomeini: The Struggle for Reform in Iran.* Chicago: University of Chicago Press.

Buckley, David Timothy 2013. "Benevolent Secularism: The Emergence and Evolution of the Religious Politics of Democracy in Ireland, Senaral and the Philippines." PhD dissertation, Georgetown University.

Burhani, Ahmad Najib 2011. "Lakum dīnukum wa-liya dīnī: The Muhammadiyah's Stance towards Interfaith Relations," *Islam and Christian-Muslim Relations* 22:3, 329–342.

2014. "Hating the Ahmadiyya: The Place of 'Heretics' in Contemporary Indonesian Muslim Society," *Contemporary Islam* 8, 133–152.

Bush, Robin 2009. *Nahdlatul Ulama and the Struggle for Power within Islam and Politics in Indonesia.* Singapore: Institute of Southeast Asian Studies.

2014. "A Snapshot of Muhammadiyah Social Chance and Shifting Markers of Identity and Values," *Asia Research Institute Working Paper Series*, No. 221, May, www.ari.nus.edu.sg/pub/wps.htm.

Calhoun, Craig, Juergensmeyer, Mark and van Anteroen, Jonathan 2011. *Rethinking Pluralism*. Oxford: Oxford University Press.

Cameron, David 2012. "Prime Minister's King James Bible Speech," Number 10 Downing Street: The Official Site of the British Prime Minister's Office, http://www.number10.gov.uk (accessed June 26, 2012).

Cassanova, José 1994. *Public Religions in the Modern World*. Chicago: University of Chicago Press.

Center for Dialogue and Cooperation among Civilisations (2013). "Profile CDCC" http://www.cdccfoundation.org/index.php/2013-11-16-20-27-43/profile (accessed December 13, 2013).

Centraal Kantoor voor de Statistiek, 1931. *Statistische Jaaroverzicht van Nederlandsche-Indië over het Jaar 1930 [Annual Statistics for the Dutch East Indies in the Year 1930]*. Batavia: Landsdrukkerij.

Center for Dialogue and Cooperation among Civilisations 2013. "Profile CDCC" http://www.cdccfoundation.org/index.php/2013-11-16-20-27-43/profile (accessed December 13, 2013).

Chakrabarty, Dipesh 2008. *Provincializing Europe: Postcolonial Thought and Historical Difference*. Princeton: Princeton University Press.

Chatterjee, Partha 1999. "On Religious and Linguistic Nationalism: The Second Partition of Bengal," in van der Veer, Peter and Lehmann, Harmut (eds.), in *Nation and Religion: Perspectives on Europe and Asia*. Princeton: Princeton University Press, 112–128.

Cheah, Pheng 2003. *Spectral Nationality: Passages of Freedom from Kant to Postcolonial Literatures of Liberation*. New York: Columbia University Press.

Cialdini, Robert B. 1984. *Influence. How and Why People Agree to Things*. New York: William Morrow and Company.

Ciftci, Sabri 2010. "Modernization, Islam, or Social Capital: What Explains Attitudes toward Democracy in the Muslim World?" *Comparative Political Studies* 43:11, 1442–1470.

Collier, David and Levitsky, Steven 1997. "Democracy with Adjectives: Conceptual Innovation in Comparative Research," *World Politics* 49:3, 430–451.

Cox, Harvey 1965. *The Secular City: Secularization and Urbanization in Theological Perspective*. New York: The Macmillan Company.

Crick, Bernard 1971. "Toleration and Tolerance in Theory and Practice," *Government and Opposition* 6:2, 143–171.

Crouch, Melissa 2007. "Regulation on Places of Worship in Indonesia: Upholding the Right to Freedom of Religion for Religious Minorities?" *Singapore Journal of Legal Studies* July, 1–21.

2009. "Indonesia, Militant Islam and Ahmadiyah: Origins and Implications," Melbourne Law School Background Paper.

2011. "Ahmadiyah in Indonesia: A History of Religious Tolerance under Threat?" *Alternative Law Journal* 36:1, 56–57.

2012. "Law and Religion in Indonesia: The Constitutional Court and the Blasphemy Law," *Asian Journal of Comparative Law* 7:1, 1–46.

Dahl, Robert 1971. *Polyarchy: Participation and Opposition*. New Haven: Yale University Press.

Davie, Grace 2002. *Europe – The Exceptional Case: Parameters of Faith in the Modern World*. London: DLT, 2002

Deeb, Lara 2006. *An Enchanted Modern: Gender and Public Piety in Shi'i Lebanon.* Princeton: Princeton University Press.

DeMaio, Theresa 1984. "Social Desirability and Survey Measurement: A Review," in Turner, Charles F. and Martin, Elizabeth (eds.), *Surveying Subjective Phenomena,* vol. 2. New York: Russell Sage Foundation, 257–282.

De Soysa, Indra and Nordås, Ragnhild 2007. "Islam's Bloody Innards? Religion and Political Terror, 1980–2000," *International Studies Quarterly* 51:4, 927–943.

de Vaus, D. A. 1996. *Surveys in Social Research,* 4th ed. Sydney: Allen & Unwin and London: University College of London Press.

Diamond, Larry 2002. "Elections without Democracy: Thinking about Hybrid Regimes," *Journal of Democracy* 13:2, 21–35.

Dillman, Don 2000. *Mail and Internet Surveys: The Tailored Design Method.* New York: J. Wiley.

Dionne Jr., E. J., Bethke Elshtain, Jean and Drogosz, Kayla 2004. *One Electorate under God? A Dialogue on Religion & American Politics.* Washington, D.C.: The Pew Forum on Religion and Public Life.

Djakababa, Yosef 2009. "The Construction of History under Indonesia's New Order: The Making of the Lubang Buaya Official Narrative," Ph.D. thesis, University of Wisconsin–Madison.

Doorn-Harder, Pieternella van 2006. *Women Shaping Islam: Reading the Qur'an in Indonesia.* Champaign: University of Illinois Press.

Driessen, Michael D. P. 2010. "Religion, State and Democracy: Analyzing two dimensions of church-state arrangements," *Politics and Religion* 3:1, 55–80.

Duffy Toft, Monica 2007. "Getting Religion? The Puzzling Case of Islam and Civil War," *International Security* 31:4, 97–131.

Duffy Toft, Monica, Philpott, Daniel and Shah, Timothy 2011. *God's Century: Resurgent Religion and Global Politics.* New York: W. W. Norton & Company, Inc.

Dumitru, Diana and Johnson, Carter 2011. "Constructing Interethnic Conflict and Cooperation: Why Some People Harmed Jews and Others Helped Them during the Holocaust in Romania," *World Politics* 63:1, 1–42.

Durkheim, Émile 2001 [1915]. *The Elemental Forms of Religious Life.* Oxford and New York: Oxford University Press.

Echols, John M. and Shadily, Hassan 2002. *An English Indonesian Dictionary.* Ithaca: Cornell University Press and Jakarta: Penerbit PT Gramedia.

Eisenstadt, Shmuel 2000. "Multiple Modernities," *Daedalus* 129:1, 1–29.

Elson, Robert 2009a. "Another Look at the Jakarta Charter Controversy of 1945," *Indonesia* 88, 105–130.

    2009b. "Disunity, Distance, Disregard: The Political Failure of Islamism in Late Colonial Indonesia," *Studia Islamika* 16:1, 1–60.

    2010. "Nationalism, Islam, 'Secularism' and the State in Contemporary Indonesia," *Australian Journal of International Affairs* 64:3, 328–343.

Esposito, John and Mogahed, Dalia 2007. *Who Speaks for Islam? What a Billion Muslims Really Think.* New York: Gallup Press.

Euben, Roxannen 1999. *Enemy in the Mirror: Islamic Fundamentalism and the Limits of Modern Rationalism: A Work of Comparative Political Theory.* Princeton: Princeton University Press.

Farr, Thomas 2008. *World of Faith and Freedom: Why International Religious Liberty Is Vital to American National Security.* New York: Oxford University Press.

Farr, Thomas F. and Hoover, and Dennis R. 2009. *The Future of U.S. International Religious Freedom Policy: Recommendations for the Obama Administration.* Washington, DC: Berkley Center for Religion, Peace, and World Affairs and Center on Faith & International Affairs, 2009. http://repository.berkleycenter.georgetown.edu/IRFPolicyReport.pdf (accessed November 7, 2014).

Farr, Thomas F. 2011. "The Trouble With American Foreign Policy And Islam," *The Review of Faith & International Affairs* 9:2, 65–73.

Fealy, Greg 1998. "Ulama and Politics in Indonesia: A History of Nahdlatul Ulama, 1952–1967," Ph.D. dissertation, Monash University.

    2005. "The Masyumi Legacy: Between Islamic Idealism and Political Exigency," *Studia Islamika* 12:1, 73–100.

Fealy, Greg and Hooker, Virginia 2006. *Voices of Islam in Southeast Asia: A Contemporary Sourcebook.* Singapore: Institute of Southeast Asian Studies.

Fearon, James and Laitin, David 2003. "Ethnicity, Insurgency, and Civil War," *American Political Science Review* 97:1, 75–90.

Federspiel, Howard 1970. *Persatuan Islam: Islamic Reform in Twentieth Century Indonesia.* Ithaca: Cornell University Press.

    1977. "Islam and Nationalism," *Indonesia* 24, 39–85.

    1995. *A Dictionary of Indonesian Islam.* Athens: Ohio University Press.

    2001. *Islam and Ideology in the Emerging Indonesian State: The Persatuan Islam (Persis), 1923–1957.* 2nd ed. Brill: Leiden.

Feener, Michael R. 2007. *Muslim Legal Thought in Modern Indonesia.* Cambridge: Cambridge University Press.

Feillard, Andrée 1999. *NU vis-à-vis Negara: Pencarian Isi, Bentuk dan Makna.* Yogyakarto: LKIS, The Asia Foundation.

Feith, Herbert 1978 [1962]. *The Decline of Constitutional Democracy in Indonesia.* Ithaca: Cornell University Press.

Fish, M. Steven 2002. "Islam and Authoritarianism," *World Politics* 55:1, 4–37.

    2011. *Are Muslims Distinctive? A Look at the Evidence.* Oxford: Oxford University Press.

Fish, M. Steven, Jensenius, Francesca and Michel, Katherine 2010. "Islam and Large-Scale Political Violence: Is There a Connection?" *Comparative Political Studies* 43:11, 1327–1362.

Fogg, Kevin 2012. "The Fate of Muslim Nationalism in Independent Indonesia," Ph.D. thesis, Yale University.

Formichi, Chiara 2010. "Pan-Islam and Religious Nationalism: The Case of Kartosuwiryo and Negara Islam Indonesia," *Indonesia* 90, 125–146.

    2012. *Islam and the Making of the Nation: Kartosuwiryo and Political Islam in 20th Century Indonesia.* Leiden: KITLV; Manoa: University of Hawaii Press.

Fox, Jonathan 2001. "Two Civilizations and Ethnic Conflict: Islam and the West," *Journal of Peace Research* 38:4, 459–472.

    2005. "Paradigm Lost: Huntington's Unfulfilled Clash of Civilizations Prediction into the 21st Century," *International Politics* 42, 428–457.

    2006. "World Separation of Religion and State into the 21st Century," *Comparative Political Studies* 39:5, 537–569.

Fox, Colm and Menchik, Jeremy 2011. "The Politics of Identity in Indonesia: Results from Campaign Advertisements," APSA 2011 Annual Meeting Paper.

Friedmann, Yohanan 1989. *Prophecy Continuous: Aspects of Arophe Religious Thought and Its Medieval Background.* Berkeley: University of California Press.

2003. *Tolerance and Coercion in Islam: Interfaith Relations in the Muslim Tradition.* Cambridge: Cambridge University Press.

Furnivall, J. S. 1944. *Netherlands India: A Study of Plural Economy.* Cambridge: Cambridge University Press.

Geertz, Clifford 1968. *Islam Observed: Religious Development in Morocco and Indonesia.* Chicago: University of Chicago Press.

1973. *The Interpretation of Cultures.* New York: Basic Books.

1976. *The Religion of Java.* Chicago: University of Chicago Press.

Gellner, Ernest 1983. *Nations and Nationalism.* Oxford: Blackwell.

George, Alexander and Bennett, Andrew 2005. *Case Studies and Theory Development in the Social Sciences.* Cambridge: The MIT Press.

Gerring, John 2007. *Case Study Research: Principles and Practices.* Cambridge: Cambridge University Press.

Gibson, James 1992a. "Alternative Measures of Political Tolerance: Must Tolerance Be 'Least-Liked'?" *American Journal of Political Science* 36:2, 560–577.

1992b. "The Political Consequences of Intolerance: Cultural Conformity and Political Freedom," *The American Political Science Review* 86:2, 338–356.

2005. "On the Nature of Tolerance: Dichotomous or Continuous?" *Political Behavior* 27:4, 313–323.

Gibson, James and Gouws, Amanda 2001. "Making Tolerance Judgments: The Effects of Context, Local and National," *The Journal of Politic* 63:4, 1067–1090.

Gill, Anthony 1998. *Rendering unto Caesar: The Catholic Church and the State in Latin America.* Chicago: University of Chicago Press.

2001. "Religion and Comparative Politics," *Annual Review of Comparative Politics* 4, 117–138.

Goertz, Gary 2006. *Social Science Concepts: A User's Guide.* Princeton: Princeton University Press.

Goldberg, J. J. 1996. *Jewish Power: Inside the American Jewish Establishment.* Reading: Addison-Wesley Publishing Co.

Grice, Paul H. 1975. "Logic and Conversation." in Peter Cole and Jerry L. Morgan (eds.), *Syntax and Semantics 3,* New York: Academic Press, 41–58.

Grim, Brian and Finke, Roger 2010. *The Price of Freedom Denied: Religious Persecution and Conflict in the Twenty-First Century.* Cambridge: Cambridge University Press.

Grzymala-Busse, Anna 2012. "Why Comparative Politics Should Take Religion (More) Seriously," *Annual Review of Political Science* 15, 421–442.

Hadler, Jeffrey 2008. *Muslims and Matriarchs: Cultural Resilience in Indonesia through Jihad and Colonialism.* Ithaca: Cornell University Press.

Hall, Peter A. 1993. "Policy Paradigms, Social Learning, and the State: The Case of Economic Policymaking in Britain," *Comparative Politics* 25:3, 275–296.

Hall, Rodney Bruce 1997. "Moral Authority as a Power Resource," *International Organization* 51:4, 591–622.

Hallaq, Wael 2005. *The Origins and Evolution of Islamic Law.* Cambridge: Cambridge University Press.

Hallencreutz, Carl 1966. *Kramer towards Tambaram.* Upsalla: Almquist and Wiksclis.

Hamid, Shadi 2014. *Temptations of Power: Islamists and Illiberal Democracy in a New Middle East*. Oxford: Oxford University Press.

Harsono, Andreas 2012. "No Model for Muslim Democracy," *New York Times*, May 22, http://www.nytimes.com/2012/05/22/opinion/no-model-for-muslim-democracy. html (accessed February 19, 2013).

Harun, Lukman 1991. "Endeavors to Create Religious Harmony Among Believers of Different Religions in Indonesia," Conference paper, Monash University, February 2–5.

Harvey, Clare 2011. *Muslim Intellectualism in Indonesia: The Liberal Islam Network Controversy*. Lambert Academic Publishing.

Hassan, A., Ma'sum, Moh and Aziz, H. Mahmud 2007. *Soal-Jawab Tentang Berbagai Masalah Agama*. Bandung: CV Penerbit Diponegoro.

Hasyim, Syafiq 2011. "The Council of Indonesian Ulama (Majelis Ulama Indonesia, MUI) and Religious Freedom," *Irasec's Discussion Papers*, No. 12.

Hefner, Robert 2000. *Civil Islam: Muslims and Democratization in Indonesia*. Princeton: Princeton University Press.

Herrera, Yoshiko 2005. *Imagined Economies: The Sources of Russian Regionalism*. Cambridge: Cambridge University Press.

Hirschkind, Charles 2001. "Civic Virtue and Religious Reason: An Islamic Counterpublic," *Cultural Anthropology* 16:1, 3–34.

Hisanori, Kato 2002. *Agama dan Peradaban: Islam dan Terciptanya Masyarakat Demokratis yang Beradab di Indonesia*. Jakarta: Dian Rakyat.

Hodgson, Marshall 1974. *The Venture of Islam: Conscience and History in a World Civilization*. Chicago: University of Chicago Press.

Hooker, M. B. 2003. *Indonesian Islam: Social Change through Contemporary Fatāwā*. Australia: Allen & Unwin.

Hopf, Ted 1998. "The Promise of Constructivism in International Relations Theory," *International Security* 23:1, 171–200.

Howell, Julia 2005. "Muslims, the New Age and Marginal Religions in Indonesia: Changing Meanings of Religious Pluralism," *Social Compass* 52:4, 473–493.

Human Rights First 2011. "Blasphemy Laws Exposed: The Consequences of Criminalizing 'Defamation of Religions'," http://www.humanrightsfirst.org/wp-content/uploads/Blasphemy_Cases.pdf (accessed June 23, 2015).

Human Rights Watch 2013. "In Religion's Name: Abuses against Religious Minorities in Indonesia," http://www.hrw.org/sites/default/files/reports/indonesia0213_ForUpload_0.pdf(accessed June 23, 2015).

Huntington, Samuel 1993. "The Clash of Civilizations," *Foreign Affairs* 72:3, 22–49.
  1996. *The Clash of Civilizations and the Remaking of the Modern World*. New York: Simon & Schuster Inc.

Hurgronje, Christiaan Snouck 1959. *Ambtelijke Adviezen van C. Snouck Hurgronje, 1889–1936* [Official Advisories of C. Snouck Hurgronje, 1889–1936] Gravenhage: Nijhoff.

Hurgronje, Christiaan Snouck and Wilkinson, Richard James 1906. *The Achehnese V1 (1906)*. Whitefish: Kessinger Publishing.

Ichwan, Moch Nur 2001. "Differing Responses to an Ahmadi Translation and Exegesis: The Holy Qur'ân in Egypt and Indonesia," *Archipel* 62, 143–161.
  2013. "Towards a Puritanical Moderate Islam: The Majelis Ulama Indonesia and the Politics of Religious Orthodoxy," in van Bruinessen (ed.), *Contemporary*

Developments in Indonesian Islam: Explaining the "Conservative Turn." Singapore: Institute of South East Asian Studies, 60–104.

Inglehart, Ronald 1990. *Culture Shift in Advanced Industrial Society.* Princeton: Princeton University Press.

1997. *Modernization and Postmodernization: Cultural, Economic, and Political Change in 43 Societies.* Princeton: Princeton University Press.

International Crisis Group 2008. "Indonesia: Implications of the Ahmadiyah Decree," *Asia Briefing*, no. 78.

2012. "Indonesia: From Vigilantism to Terrorism in Cirebon," *Asia Briefing*, no. 132.

Iqbal, Muhammad 1974. *Islam and Ahmadism.* Lucknow: Islamic Research and Publications Academy.

Iqtidar, Humeira 2012. "State Management of Religion in Pakistan and Dilemmas of Citizenship," *Citizenship Studies* 16:8, 1013–1028.

Johansen, Baber 2003. "Apostasy as Objective and Depersonalized Fact: Two Recent Egyptian Court Judgments," *Social Research* 70:3, 687–710.

Jones, Jeffrey M. 2012. "Atheists, Muslims See Most Bias as Presidential Candidates," http://www.gallup.com/poll/155285/atheists-muslims-bias-presidential-candidates.aspx (accessed April 2, 2014).

Jones, Sidney 1980. "'It Can't Happen Here': A Post-Khomeini Look at Indonesian Islam," *Asian Survey* 20:3, 311–323.

Juergensmeyer, Mark 1995. "The New Religious State," *Comparative Politics* 27:4, 379–391.

Kalyvas, Stathis 1996. *The Rise of Christian Democracy in Europe.* Ithaca: Cornell University Press.

2000. "Commitment Problems in Emerging Democracies: The Case of Religious Parties," *Comparative Politics* 32:4, 379–398.

Kang, Alice 2009. "Studying Oil, Islam, and Women as if Political Institutions Mattered," *Politics & Gender* 5:4, 560–568.

Karl, Terry 1995. "The Hybrid Regimes of Central America," *Journal of Democracy* 6:3, 72–86.

Katznelson, Ira and Stedman Jones, Gareth (eds.) 2010. *Religion and the Political Imagination.* New York: Cambridge University Press.

Kendhammer, Brandon 2013. "The *Sharia* Controversy in Northern Nigeria and the Politics of Islamic Law in New and Uncertain Democracies," *Comparative Politics* 45:3, 281–311.

Kersten, Carool 2011. *Cosmopolitans and Heretics: New Muslim Intellectuals and the Study of Islam.* New York: Columbia University Press.

Kopstein, Jeffrey and Wittenberg, Jason 2011. "Deadly Communities: Local Political Milieus and the Persecution of Jews in Occupied Poland," *Comparative Political Studies* 44:3, 259–283.

Kratochwil, Friedrich and Ruggie, John Gerard 1986. "International Organization: A State of the Art on an Art of the State," *International Organization* 40:4, 753–775.

Kunkler, Mirjam 2013. "How Pluralist Democracy Became the Consensual Discourse among Secular and Nonsecular Muslims in Indonesia," in Kunkler, Mirjam and Stepan, Alfred (eds.), *Democracy and Islam in Indonesia.* New York: Columbia University Press.

Kuru, Ahmet T. 2007. "Passive and Assertive Secularism: Historical Conditions, Ideological Struggles, and State Policies toward Religion," *World Politics* 59:4, 568–594.

Kurzman, Charles 1998. *Liberal Islam: A Sourcebook*. Oxford: Oxford University Press.

Kymlicka, Will 1989. *Liberalism, Community and Culture*. Oxford: Oxford University Press.

1992. "Two Models of Pluralism and Tolerance," *Analyse & Kritik* 13, S, 33–56.

1995. *Multicultural Citizenship: A Liberal Theory of Minority Rights*. Oxford: Oxford University Press.

Laffan, Michael 2003. *Islamic Nationhood and Colonial Indonesia: The Umma below the Winds*. London and New York: RoutledgeCurzon.

2011. *The Makings of Indonesian Islam*. Princeton: Princeton University Press.

Lev, Daniel 1966. "Indonesia 1965: The Year of the Coup," *Asian Survey* 6:2, 103–110.

1972. *Islamic Courts in Indonesia: A Study in the Political Bases of Legal Institutions*. Berkeley: University of California Press.

LeVine, Robert and Campbell, Donald 1972. *Ethnocentrism: Theories of Conflict, Ethnic Attitudes, and Group Behavior*. New York: John Wiley & Sons.

Levitsky, Steven and Way, Lucan 2002. "The Rise of Competitive Authoritarianism," *Journal of Democracy* 13:3, 51–65.

Lewis, Bernard 1984. *The Jews of Islam*. Princeton: Princeton University Press.

1990. "The Roots of Muslim Rage: Why So Many Muslims Deeply Resent the West, and Why Their Bitterness Will Not Easily Be Mollified," *The Atlantic*, September.

1991 [1988]. *The Political Language of Islam*. Chicago: University of Chicago Press.

Liddle, R. William 1996. "The Islamic Turn in Indonesia: A Political Explanation," *Journal of Asian Studies* 55:3, 613–634.

Lieberman, Robert 2002. "Ideas, Institutions, and Political Order: Explaining Political Change," *American Political Science Review* 96:4, 697–712.

Lijphart, Arend 2004. "Constitutional Design for Divided Societies," *Journal of Democracy* 15:2, 96–109.

Lipset, Seymour and Rokkan, Stein 1967. "Cleavage Structures, Party Systems, and Voter Alignments: An Introduction," in Lipset, Seymour and Rokkan, Stein (eds.), *Party Systems and Voter Alignments*. New York: Free Press, 1–64.

Liu, Amy H. and Baird, Vanessa A. 2012. "Linguistic Recognition as a Source of Confidence in the Justice System," *Comparative Political Studies* 45:10, 1203–1229.

Locke, John 1983 [1689]. *A Letter Concerning Toleration*. Indianapolis: Hackett Publishing Company, Inc.

Lublin, David 2012. "Dispersing Authority or Deepening Divisions? Decentralization and Ethnoregional Party Success," *The Journal of Politics* 74:4, 1079–1093.

Mahmood, Tahir 2010. "Religious Communities and the State in Modern India," in Ferrari, Silvio and Cristofori, Rinaldo (eds.), *Law and Religion in the 21st Century: Relations between States and Religious Communities*. Surrey: Ashgate Publishing Company, 53–66.

Mahmood, Saba 2005. *Politics of Piety: The Islamic Revival and the Feminist Subject*. Princeton: Princeton University Press.

2006. "Secularism, Hermeneutics, and Empire: The Politics of Islamic Reformation," *Public Culture* 18:2, 323–347.

2012. "Religious Freedom, the Minority Question, and Geopolitics in the Middle East," *Comparative Studies in Society and History* 54:2, 418–446.

Mamdani, Mahmood. 2002. "Good Muslim, Bad Muslim: A Political Perspective on Culture and Terrorism," *American Anthropologist* 104: 3, 766–775.

March, Andrew F. 2009. *Islam and Liberal Citizenship: The Search for an Overlapping Consensus.* Oxford: Oxford University Press.

Marquart-Pyatt, Sandra and Paxton, Pamela 2007. "In Principle and in Practice: Learning Political Tolerance in Eastern and Western Europe," *Political Behavior* 29:1, 89–113.

Marx, Anthony 2003. *Faith in Nation: Exclusionary Origins of Nationalism.* New York: Oxford University Press.

Marx, Karl and Engels, Frederick 1999 [1848]. *The Communist Manifesto.* New York: International Publishers Co., Inc.

Masroori, Cyrus 2010. "An Islamic Language of Toleration: Rumi's Critique of Religious Persecution," *Political Research Quarterly* 63:2, 243–256.

Mecham, R. Q. 2004. "From the Ashes of Virtue, and Promise of Light: The Transformation of Political Islam in Turkey," *Third World Quarterly* 25:2, 339–358.

Menchik, Jeremy 2007. "Illiberal but Not Intolerant: Understanding the Indonesian Council of Ulamas," *Inside Indonesia* http://www.insideindonesia.org/illiberal-but-not-intolerant (accessed June 23, 2015).

2011. "Tolerance without Liberalism: Islamic Institutions and Political Violence in Twentieth Century Indonesia," Ph.D. thesis, University of Wisconsin–Madison.

2014. "Productive Intolerance: Godly Nationalism in Indonesia," *Comparative Studies in Society and History* 56:3, 591–621.

2014. "The Coevolution of Secular and Sacred: Islamic Law and Family Planning in Indonesia," *South East Asia Research* 22:3, 359–378.

Mietzner, Marcus 2009. *Military Politics, Islam, and the State in Indonesia: From Turbulent Transition to Democratic Consolidation.* Singapore: Institute of Southeast Asian Studies.

Mill, John Stuart 1843. *A System of Logic, Ratiocinative and Inductive, Being a Connected View of the Principles of Evidence, and the Methods of Scientific Investigation.* London: Parker, Son and Bourn.

Mitchell, Timothy 1991. *Colonising Egypt.* Berkeley: University of California Press.

Moaddel, Mansoor 2005. *Islamic Modernism, Nationalism, and Fundamentalism: Episode and Discourse.* Chicago: University of Chicago Press.

Monnig Atkinson, Jane 1983. "Religions in Dialogue: The Construction of an Indonesian Minority Religion," *American Ethnologist* 10:4, 684–696.

Mortimer, Rex 1972. *The Indonesian Communist Party and Land Reform, 1959–1965.* Clayton: Centre for Southeast Asian Studies.

Moustafa, Tamir 2000. "Conflict and Cooperation between the State and Religious Institutions in Contemporary Egypt," *International Journal of Middle East Studies* 32, 3–22.

Mueller, John and Stewart, Mark G. 2012. "The Terrorism Delusion: America's Overwrought Response to September 11," *International Security* 37:1, 81–110.

Muhammadiyah, Hoofdcomite Congres 1929. *Kitab Iman dan Sembahjang Poetoesan Madjlis Tardjih Muhammadiyah Disambung Dengan Beberapa Masalah* [Book of Faith and Prayer by the Council for Renewal for Muhammadiyah with Miscellaneous Matters]. Djokjakarta: Hoofdcomite Congres Muhammadiyah.

Muhammadiyah, Majelis Tarjih dan Pengembangan Pemikiran Islam 2000. *Tafsiran Tematik Al-Qur'an tentang Hubungan Sosial Antarumat Beragama.* Yogyakarta: Pustaka Suara Muhammadiyah.

Muhammadiyah, Majelis Tabligh dan Dakwah Khusus Pimpinan Pusat 2010. *1 abad Muhammadiyah: Istiqomah Membendung Kristenisasi & Liberalisasi* [100 years of Muhammadiyah: Its Mission to Prevent Christianization and Liberalization]. Yogyakarta: MTDK-PPM.

Muhammadiyah, Pimpinan Besar 1929. *Pemandangan: Agama Islam dan Kaoem Moeslimin* [Viewpoint: Islam and the Muslims]. Yogyakarta: Bahagian Taman Pustaka.

Muhammadiyah, Pimpinan Pusat Majlis Tarjih 1974. *Himpunan Putusan Majlis Tarjih* [Decisions of the Islamic Law Council]. Yogyakarta: PP Muhammadiyah.

Mujani, Saiful 2003. "Religious Democrats: Democratic Culture and Muslim Political Participation in Post-Suharto Indonesia," Ph.D. dissertation, Ohio State University.

Mujani, Saiful and Liddle, R. William 2004. "Politics, Islam, and Public Opinion," *Journal of Democracy* 15:1, 109–123.

2009. "Muslim Indonesia's Secular Democracy," *Asian Survey* 49:4, 575–590.

Mulder, Niels 1978. *Mysticism and Everyday Life in Contemporary Java*. Singapore: Singapore University Press.

Murphy, Andrew P. 1997. "Tolerance, Toleration, and the Liberal Tradition," *Polity* 29:4, 593–623.

1998. "Rawls and a Shrinking Liberty of Conscience," *The Review of Politics* 60:2, 247–276.

Mu'ti, Abdul and Riza ul Haq, Fajar 2009. *Kristen Muhammadiyah: Konvergensi Muslim dan Kristen Dalam Pendidikan* [Christian Muhammadiyah: The Convergence of Muslims and Christians in Education]. Jakarta: Al-Wasat.

Muskens, M. P. M. 1979. *Partner in National Building: The Catholic Church in Indonesia*. Aachen: Missio Aktuell Verlag.

Nahdlatul Ulama 2007. *Ahkam al-Fuqaha' fi Muqarrarat Mu'tamarat Nahdlati al-'Ulama: Solusi Problematika Aktual Hukum Islam Keputusan Muktamar (1926–1999)* [Legal Decisions from the Jurists of the Nahdlatal Ulama: Solutions to Problems of Islamic Law from the Decrees, Congresses, and National Conference of NU (1926–1999)]. Surabaya: Lajnah Ta'lif Wan Nasyer Jawa Timur and "Khalista" Surabaya.

Nahdlatul Ulama, Sekretariat Jenderal PBNU 2004. *Hasil-Hasil Muktamar XXXI Nahdlatul Ulama* [Results of the XXXI Nahdlatul Ulama Congress]. Jakarta: Sekretariat Jenderal PBNU.

2008. "NU Calls on Nahdliyin Not to Engage in Polemics on Ahmadiyah Issue," June 7, 2008, http://www.nu.or.id (accessed June 25, 2015).

National Family Planning Coordinating Board 1993. *The Muslim Ummah and Family Planning Movement in Indonesia*. Jakarta: National Family Planning Coordinating Board and Department of Religious Affairs.

Natsir, Mohammad 1954. "Islamic Tolerance," in Feith, Herbert and Castles, Lance (eds.), *Indonesian Political Thinking 1945–1965* (1970; repr., Jakarta: Equinox, 2007).

1969. *Islam dan Kristen di Indonesia* [Islam and Christianity in Indonesia]. Bandung: Pelajar dan Bulan Sabit.

Nederman, Cary J. 1994. "Tolerance and Community: A Medieval Communal Functionalist Argument for Religious Toleration," *The Journal of Politics* 56:4, 901–918.

Niel, R van 1960. *The Emergence of the Modern Indonesian Elite*. The Hague: Williem van Hoeve.

Noeh, Munawar Fuad and Mastuki, H. S. (eds.) 2002. *Menghidupkan Ruh Pemikiran K. H. Achmad Siddiq*. Jakarta: Gramedia Pustaka Utama.

Noer, Deliar 1978. *The Modernist Muslim Movement in Indonesia 1900–1942*. Singapore: Oxford University Press.

Norris, Pippa 2008. *Driving Democracy: Do Power-Sharing Institutions Work?* New York: Cambridge University Press.

Norris, Pippa and Inglehart, Ronald 2004. *Sacred and Secular: Religion and Politics Worldwide*. Cambridge: Cambridge University Press.

"NU Calls On Nahdliyin Not to Engage in Polemics on Ahmadiyah Issue," June 7, 2008, http://www.nu.or.id/a,public-m,dinamic-s,detail-ids,15-id,29172-lang,en-c,news-t, NU+calls+on+Nahdliyin+not+to+engage+in+polemics+on+Ahmadiyah+issue-.phpx (accessed June 13, 2015).

O'Brian, F. William 1963. "Church and State in Switzerland: A Comparative Study," *Virginia Law Review* 49, 904–924.

Office for the Research and Development of Religion 1993. *Organization of the Department of Religion*. Jakarta: Department of Religion.

Parsons, Craig 2002. "Showing Ideas as Causes: The Origins of the European Union," *International Organization* 56:1, 47–84.

Peled, Yoav 1992. "Ethnic Democracy and the Legal Construction of Citizenship: Arab Citizens of the Jewish State," *American Political Science Review* 86:2, 432–443.

Pepinsky, Tom, Liddle, Bill and Mujani, Saiful 2010. "Indonesian Democracy and the Transformation of Political Islam" (unpublished manuscript). http://www.lsi.or.id/riset/385/Indonesian%20Democracy (accessed June 13, 2015).

Petkoff, Peter 2005. "Church-State Relations under the Bulgarian Denominations Act 2002: Religious Pluralism and Established Church and the Impact of Other Models of Law on Religion," *Religion, State & Society* 33:4, 315–337.

Pew Research Center 2014. "Worldwide, Many See Belief in God as Essential to Morality," March, www.pewresearch.org.

Philpott, Daniel 2000. "The Religious Roots of Modern International Relations," *World Politics* 52, 206–245.

2007. "Explaining the Political Ambivalence of Religion," *American Political Science Review* 101:3, 505–525.

2009. "Has the Study of Global Politics Found Religion," *Annual Review of Political Science* 12, 183–202.

2012. *Just and Unjust Peace: An Ethic of Political Reconciliation*. Oxford: Oxford University Press.

Picard, Michel 1997. "Cultural Tourism, Nation Building and Regional Culture: The Making of a Balinese Identity," in Picard, Michel and Wood, R. E. (eds.), *Tourism, Ethnicity and the State in Asian and Pacific Societies*. Honolulu: University of Hawai'i Press, 181–214.

1999. "The Discourse of Kebalian: Transcultural Constructions of Balinese Identity," in Rubinstein, Raechelle and Conner, Linda H. (eds.), *Staying Local in the Global Village: Bali in the Twentieth Century*. Honolulu: University of Hawai'i Press, 15–49.

2004. "What's in a Name? *Agama Hindu Bali* in the Making," in Ramstedt, Martin (ed.), *Hinduism in Modern Indonesia: A Minority Religion between Local, National, and Global Interests*. London and New York: RoutledgeCurzon, 56–75.

2011. "Balinese Religion in Search of Recognition: From *Agama Hindu Bali* to *Agama Hindu* (1945–1965)," *Bijdragen tot de Taal-, Land- en Volkenkunde* 167:4, 482–510.

Pierson, Paul 2004. *Politics in Time: History, Institutions, and Social Analysis*. Princeton: Princeton University Press.

Pijper, G. F. 1992. *Empat Penelitian Tentang Agama Islam di Indonesia Antara 1930–1950* [Four Studies of Islam in Indonesia Between 1930–1950]. trans. Tudijamah. Jakarta: Penerbit Universitas Indonesia.

Pringle, Robert 2010. *Understanding Islam in Indonesia: Politics and Diversity*. Honolulu: University of Hawaii Press.

Putnam, Robert 1993. *Making Democracy Work: Civic Traditions in Modern Italy*. Princeton: Princeton University Press.

2000. *Bowling Alone*. New York: Simon & Schuster Inc.

Rabinow, Paul and Sullivan, William M. 1987. *Interpretive Social Science: A Second Look*. Berkeley: University of California Press.

Ramage, Douglas 1995. *Politics in Indonesia: Democracy, Islam and the Ideology of Tolerance*. London and New York: Routledge.

Ramage, Douglas E., Barton, Greg and Fealy, Greg 1996. "Democratisation, Religious Tolerance and Pancesila: The Political Thought of Abdurrahman Wahid," in *Nahdlatul Ulama, Traditional Islam and Modernity in Indonesia*. Clayton: Monash Asia Institute.

Rawls, John 1993. *Political Liberalism*. New York: Columbia University Press

1996. *Political Liberalism*. New York: Columbia University Press.

Remer, Gary 1992. "Humanism, Liberalism & the Skeptical Case for Religious Toleration," *Polity* 25:1, 21–43.

Reynolds, Andrew 2010. *Designing Democracy in a Dangerous World*. Oxford University Press.

Ricklefs, M. C. 2001. *A History of Modern Indonesia since c. 1200*. Stanford: Stanford University Press.

Ricklefs, Merle 2006. *Mystic Synthesis in Java: A History of Islamization from the Fourteenth to the Early Nineteenth Centuries*. Norwalk: Eastbridge.

2007. *Polarizing Javanese Society: Islamic and Other Visions (c. 1983–1930)*. Singapore: National University of Singapore Press.

2008. *A History of Modern Indonesia since c. 1200*. 4th ed. Stanford: Stanford University Press.

Rogers, Benedict 2012. "Indonesia's Rising Religious Intolerance," *New York Times*, May 21, http://www.nytimes.com/2012/05/22/opinion/indonesias-rising-religious -intolerance.html (accessed June 23, 2015).

Roosa, John 2006. *Pretext for Mass Murder: The September 30th Movement and Suharto's Coup d'État in Indonesia*. Madison: University of Wisconsin Press.

Ropi, Ismatu 1999. "Depicting the Other Faith: A Bibliographical Survey of Indonesian Muslim Polemics on Christianity," *Studia Islamika* 6:1, 77–111.

Rosefsky Wickham, Carrie 2004. "The Path to Moderation: Strategy and Learning in the Formation of Egypt's Wasat Party," *Comparative Politics* 36:2, 205–228.

2013. *The Muslim Brotherhood: Evolution of an Islamist Movement*. Princeton: Princeton University Press.

Ross, Michael L. 2008. "Oil, Islam, and Women," *American Political Science Review* 102:1, 107–123.

Sadiki, Larbi 2007. "Tunisia," in Archer, Toby and Huuhtanen, Heidi (eds.), *Islamist Opposition Parties and the Potential for EU Engagement*. Helsinki: The Finnish Institute of International Affairs, 93–110. www.upi-fiia.fi (accessed January 18, 2011).

Said, Edward 2003 [1978]. *Orientalism*. 25th anniversary ed. New York: Vintage Books.

Salim, Arskal 2008. *Challenging the Secular State: The Islamization of Law in Modern Indonesia*. Honolulu: University of Hawaii Press.

Samson, Allan A. 1968. "Islam in Indonesian Politics," *Asian Survey* 8:12, 1001–1017.

Sartori, Giovanni 1970. "Concept Misinformation in Comparative Politics," *The American Political Science Review* 64:4, 1033–1053.

Schatz, Edward (ed.) 2009. *Political Ethnography: What Immersion Contributes to the Study of Power*. Chicago: University of Chicago Press.

Schiller, Anne 1996. "An 'Old' Religion in 'New Order' Indonesia: Notes on Ethnicity and Religious Affiliation," *Sociology of Religion* 57:4, 409–417.

Schmidt, Vivian 2008. "Discursive Institutionalism: The Explanatory Power of Ideas and Discourse," *Annual Review of Political Science* 11, 303–326.

Schwedler, Jillian 2006. *Faith in Moderation: Islamist Parties in Jordan and Yemen*. New York: Cambridge University Press.

2011. "Can Islamists Become Moderates? Rethinking the Inclusion-Moderation Hypothesis," *World Politics* 63:2, 347–376.

Scott, Rachel M. 2007. "Contextual Citizenship in Modern Islamic Thought," *Islam and Christian-Muslim Relations* 18:1, 1–18.

Selway, Joel and Templeman, Kharis 2010. "The Myth of Consociationalism? Conflict Reduction in Divided Societies," *Comparative Political Studies* 45, 542–1571.

Setara Institute for Democracy and Peace 2009. "Siding and Acting Intolerantly: Intolerance by Society and Restriction by the State in Freedom of Religion/Belief in Indonesia," http://www.setara-institute.org/en/content/report-freedom-religion-and-belief-2008 (accessed February 28, 2013). Jakarta: SETARA Institute.

2011. "Report on Freedom of Religion and Belief in 2011," http://www. setara-institute.org/en/content/report-freedom-religion-and-belief-2011 (accessed February 28, 2013). Jakarta: SETARA Institute.

Setara Institute for Democracy and Peace 2012. "Report on Freedom of Religion and Belief in 2012," http://www.setara-institute.org/en/content/ report-freedom-religion-and-belief-2012 (accessed February 28, 2013). Jakarta: SETARA Institute.

Shachar, Ayelet 2000. "On Citizenship and Multicultural Vulnerability," *Political Theory* 28:1, 64–89.

2001. *Multicultural Jurisdictions: Cultural Differences and Women's Rights*. Cambridge: Cambridge University Press.

Shakman Hurd, Elizabeth 2007. *The Politics of Secularism in International Relations*. Princeton: Princeton University Press.

Shihab, Alwi 1995. "The Muhammadiyah Movement and Its Controversy with Christian Mission in Indonesia," Ph.D. dissertation, Temple University.

Shiraishi, Takashi 1990. *An Age in Motion: Popular Radicalism in Java, 1912–1926*. Ithaca: Cornell University Press.

Siddiq, Achmad K. H. 2006 [1979]. *Khittah Nahdliyyah* [Goals of the Members of Nahdlatul Ulama]. Surabaya: Lajnah Ta'lif Wan Nasyer Jawa Timur and "Khalista" Surabaya.

Siegel, James 1998. *A New Criminal Type in Jakarta: Counter-Revolution Today*. Durham: Duke University Press.

Singleton Jr, Royce A. and Straits, Bruce C. 2005. *Approaches to Social Research*. New York: Oxford University Press.

Slater, Dan 2005. "Ordering Power: Contentious Politics, State-Building, and Authoritarian Durability in Southeast Asia," Ph.D. dissertation, Emory University.

Slater, Dan and Ziblatt, Daniel 2013. "The Enduring Indispensability of the Controlled Comparison," *Comparative Political Studies* 46:10, 1301–1327.

Smith, Anthony 2003. *Chosen Peoples: Sacred Sources of National Identity*. Oxford: Oxford University Press.

2008. *The Cultural Foundations of Nations: Hierarchy, Covenant and Republic*. Malden, MA: Blackwell.

Smooha, Sammy 1990. "Minority Status in an Ethnic Democracy: The Status of the Arab Minority in Israel," *Ethnic and Racial Studies* 13:3, 389–413.

Spinner-Halev, Jeff 2000. "Land, Culture and Justice: A Framework for Group Rights and Recognition," *The Journal of Political Philosophy* 8:3, 319–342.

2005. "Hinduism, Christianity, and Liberal Religious Toleration," *Political Theory* 33:1, 28–57.

Stan, Lavinia and Turcescu, Lucian 2007. *Religion and Politics in Post-Communist Romania*. Oxford: Oxford University Press.

2011. *Church, State and Democracy in an Expanding Europe*. Oxford: Oxford University Press.

Steenbrink, Karel 1993. *Dutch Colonialism and Indonesian Islam: Contacts and Conflicts 1596–1950*. Amsterdam: Rodopi.

2007. *Catholics in Indonesia, 1808–1942: A Documented History. Volume 2: The Spectacular Growth of a Self-Confident Minority, 1903–1942*. Leiden: Brill.

Stepan, Alfred 2000. "Democracy, the World's Religion and the Problems of the 'Twin Tolerations'," *Journal of Democracy* 11:4, 37–57.

Stepan, Alfred and Kunkler, Mirjam 2007. "An Interview with Amien Rais," *Journal of International Affairs* 61:1, 205–218.

Stepan, Alfred, Linz, Juan and Yadav, Yogendra 2011. *Crafting State-Nations: India and Other Multinational Democracies*. Baltimore: Johns Hopkins University Press.

Straus, Scott 2006. *The Order of Genocide: Race, Power, and War in Rwanda*. Ithaca: Cornell University Press.

Streeck, Wolfgang and Thelen, Kathleen 2005. *Beyond Continuity: Institutional Change in Advanced Political Economies*. Oxford: Oxford University Press.

Sullivan, Winnifred 1994. *Paying the Words Extra: Religious Discourse in the Supreme Court of the United States*. Cambridge, MA: Harvard University Press.

2005. *The Impossibility of Religious Freedom*. Princeton: Princeton University Press.

Sullivan, John, Pierson, James and Marcus, George 1982. *Political Tolerance and American Democracy*. Chicago: University of Chicago Press.

Sumartana, T. 1993. *Mission at the Crossroads: Indigenous Churches, European Missionaries, Islamic Associations and Socio-religious Change in Java 1812–1936*. Jakarta: BPK Gunung Mulia.

Sya'roni, Mizan 1998. "The Majlisul Islamil a'la Indonesia (MIAI): Its Socio-Religious and Political Activities (1937–1943)," MA thesis, McGill University.

Tambar, Kabir 2010. "The Aesthetics of Public Visibility: Alevi *Semah* and the Paradoxes of Pluralism in Turkey," *Comparative Studies in Society and History* 53:3, 652–679.

Taylor, Charles 1989. *Sources of the Self: The Making of Modern Identity*. Cambridge, MA: Harvard University Press.

Temperman, Jeroen 2010. *State-Religion Relationships and Human Rights Law*. Leiden: Martinus Nijhoff Publishers.

The Jakarta Post, "NU Opposes Blasphemy Law Review," February 1, 2010, http://www.thejakartapost.com/news/2010/02/01/nu-opposes-blasphemy-law-review.html (accessed June 23, 2015).

Tessler, Mark 1978. "The Identity of Religious Minorities in Non-secular States: Jews in Tunisia and Morocco and Arabs in Israel," *Comparative Studies in Society and History* 20:3, 359–373.

2002. "Islam and Democracy in the Middle East: The Impact of Religious Orientations on Attitudes toward Democracy in Four Arab Countries," *Comparative Politics* 34:3, 337–354.

Tezcür, Güneş M. 2010. "The Moderation Theory Revisited: The Case of Islamic Political Actors," *Party Politics* 16:1, 69–88.

Tourangeau, Roger 1999. "Context Effects on Answers to Attitude Questions," in M. G. Sirken, D.J. Herrmann, S. Schechter, N. Schwarz, J. Tanur, and R. Tourangeau (eds.), *Congnition and Survey Research*. New York: John Wiley and Sons, 111–131.

Tully, James 1983. "Introduction," in *A Letter Concerning Toleration*. Indianapolis, IN: Hackett Publishing Company.

1995. "Cultural Demands for Constitutional Recognition," *The Journal of Political Philosophy* 3:2, 111–132.

Van der Eng, Pierre 2006. "Accounting for Indonesia's Economic Growth: Recent Past and Near Future," Paper presented at the Seminar on World Economic Performance: Past, Present and Future, Long-Term Performance and Prospects of Australia and Major Asian Economies. Brisbane: University of Queensland.

Van der Veer, Peter 1994. *Religious Nationalism: Hindus and Muslims in India*. Berkeley: University of California Press.

Van der Veer, Peter and Lehmann, Hartmut (eds.) 1999. *Nation and Religion: Perspectives on Europe and Asia*. Princeton: Princeton University Press.

Varshney, Ashutosh, Panggabean, Rizal and Tadjoeddin, Mohammad Zulfan 2004. "Patterns of Collective Violence in Indonesia (1990–2003)," United Nations Support Facility for Indonesian Recovery (UNSFIR) Working Paper, www.unsfir.or.id (accessed October 10, 2009).

Vickers, Adrian 1987. "Hinduism and Islam in Indonesia: Bali and the Pasisir World." *Indonesia* 44, 30–58.

Villalón, Leonardo A. 2010. "From Argument to Negotiation: Constructing Democracy in African Muslim Contexts," *Comparative Politics* 42:4, 375–393.

Wahid, Abdurrahman (ed.) 2009. *The Illusion of an Islamic State: The Expansion of Transnational Islamist Movements to Indonesia*. Jakarta: LibForAll Foundation.

Wahid Institute 2008. *Monthly Report on Religious Issues*. Jakarta: The Wahid Institute, June.

Wald, Kenneth D. and Wilcox, Clyde 2006. "Getting Religion: Has Political Science Rediscovered the Faith Factor," *American Political Science Review* 100:4, 523–529.

Walzer, Michael 1997. *On Toleration*. New Haven: Yale University Press.

Warner, Carolyn M. 2000. *Confessions of an Interest Group: The Catholic Church and Political Parties in Europe*. Princeton: Princeton University Press.

Warren, David H. and Gilmore, Christine 2013. "One Nation under God? Yusuf al-Qaradawi's Changing Fiqh of Citizenship in the Light of the Islamic Legal Tradition," *Contemporary Islam: Dynamics of Muslim Life* 8:3, 217–237.

Weber, Max 1918. "Wissenschaft als Beruf" [Science as a Vocation], in Gerth, H. H. and Mills, Wright C. (trans. and ed.), *Max Weber: Essays in Sociology*. New York: Oxford University Press, 1946, 129–156.

Wedeen, Lisa 1999. *Ambiguities of Domination: Politics, Rhetoric and Symbols in Contemporary Syria*. Chicago: University of Chicago Press.

2002. "Conceptualizing Culture: Possibilities for Political Science," *American Political Science Review* 96:4, 713–728.

2008. *Peripheral Visions: Publics, Power and Performance in Yemen*. Chicago: University of Chicago Press.

Weldon, Steven 2006. "The Institutional Context of Tolerance for Ethnic Minorities: A Comparative, Multilevel Analysis of Western Europe," *American Journal of Political Science* 50:2, 331–349.

Wendt, Alexander 1987. "The Agent-Structure Problem in International Relations Theory," *International Organizations* 41:3, 335–370.

White, Jenny Barbara 2002. *Islamist Mobilization in Turkey: A Study in Vernacular Politics*. Seattle: University of Washington Press.

Wiktorowicz, Quinton 2001. *The Management of Islamic Activism: Salafis, the Muslim Brotherhood, and State Power in Jordan*. Albany, NY: State University of New York Press.

Wilcox, Clyde, Wald, Kenneth D. and Jelen, Ted G. 2008. "Religious Preferences and Social Science: A Second Look," *The Journal of Politics* 70:3, 874–879.

Wildan, Dadan 1995. *Sejarah Perjuangan Persis 1923–1983* [History of Persis's Struggle 1923–1983]. Bandung: Gema Syahida.

Wildavsky, Aaron 1989. "Choosing Preferences by Constructing Institutions: A Cultural Theory of Preference Formation," in Berger, A. A. (ed.), *Political Culture and Public Opinion*. New Brunswick, NJ: Transaction, 21–46.

Wilkinson, Steven Ian 2000. "India, Consociational Theory, and Ethnic Violence," *Asian Survey* 40:5, 767–791.

Wilson, C. J. 1952. *Apostle to Islam: A Biography of Samuel M. Zwemer*. Grand Rapids, MI: Baker House Books.

Wilson, Thomas 1996. "Cohort and Prejudice: Whites' Attitudes toward Blacks, Hispanics, Jews, and Asians," *The Public Opinion Quarterly* 60:2, 253–274.

Wittenberg, Jason 2006. *Crucibles of Political Loyalty: Church Institutions and Electoral Continuity in Hungary*. Cambridge: Cambridge University Press.

Wolff, Steven 2007. "Conflict Resolution between Power Sharing and Power Dividing, or Beyond?" *Political Studies Review* 5, 363–379.

Woodberry, Robert D. 2012. "The Missionary Roots of Liberal Democracy," *American Political Science Review* 106:2, 244–274.

Woodward, Mark 1989. *Islam in Java: Normative Piety and Mysticism in the Sultanate of Yogyakarta*. Tucson: University of Arizona Press.

World Values Survey Wave 5 2005-2009. OFFICIAL AGGREGATE v.20140429. World Values Survey Association (www.worldvaluessurvey.org). Aggregate File Producer: Asep/JDS, Madrid SPAIN.

Würgler, Andreas 2008. "'The League of Discordant Members' or How the Old Swiss Confederation Operated and How it Managed to Survive for so Long," in *The Republican Alternative: The Netherlands and Switzerland Compared* by André Holenstein, Thomas Maissen, Maarten Prak, eds. Amsterdam: Amsterdam University Press, 29-50.

Yamin, Muhammad 1959. *Naskah Persiapan Undang-Undang Dasar 1945* [Drafting the 1945 Constitution] vol 1. Djakarta: Jajasan Prapatja.

Young, Iris Marion 1990. *Justice and the Politics of Difference*. Princeton: Princeton University Press.
   2000. *Inclusion and Democracy*. Oxford: Oxford University Press.
   2005. "Justice and the Politics of Difference," in Fainstein, Susan S. and Servon, Lisa J. (eds.), *Gender and Planning: A Reader*. Rutgers, NJ: Rutgers University Press.
Zameret, Zvi and Tlamim, Moshe 1999. "Judaism in Israel: Ben Gurion's Private Beliefs and Public Policy," *Israel Studies* 4:2, 64–89. Quoting Ben Gurion Diaries, The Ben-Gurion Heritage Archives, March 14, 1959.

Index

The letter f following a page number denotes a figure, and the letter t denotes a table.